# Insurance Law in Montenegro

# Insurance Law in Montenegro

Nikola Dožić

This book was originally published as a monograph in the International Encyclopaedia of Laws/Insurance Law.

Founding Editor: Roger Blanpain
General Editor: Frank Hendrickx
Volume Editor: Herman Cousy

Wolters Kluwer

*Published by:*
Kluwer Law International B.V.
PO Box 316
2400 AH Alphen aan den Rijn
The Netherlands
E-mail: lrs-sales@wolterskluwer.com
Website: www.wolterskluwer.com/en/solutions/kluwerlawinternational

*Sold and distributed by:*
Wolters Kluwer Legal & Regulatory U.S.
920 Links Avenue
Landisville, PA 17538
United States of America
E-mail: customer.service@wolterskluwer.com



ISBN 978-94-035-3978-2

e-Book: ISBN 978-94-035-3988-1
web-PDF: ISBN 978-94-035-3998-0

# The Author

Dr Nikola Dožić was born on 19 December 1980 in Kolasin, Montenegro.

He graduated in 2003 from the Faculty of Law in Podgorica. He was a scholarship holder of the 'Konrad Adenauer' German Foundation for postgraduate studies in the country and the Government of Montenegro for postgraduate studies. In 2014, he finished his PhD studies at the Law School of Union University in Belgrade with a doctoral dissertation on the topic 'Insurance Fraud'.

From 2007 to 2009, he worked at the Securities Commission of the Republic of Montenegro. From 2008 to 2014, he worked as a teaching assistant at the Law Faculty of Mediterranean University in Podgorica.

Since February 2014, he has been working as a teaching assistant at the University of Montenegro at civil law chair. In November 2016, he was elected Secretary General of the Centre of Young Scientists at the Montenegrin Academy of Sciences and Arts.

In January and February of 2017, he conducted academic research at the Europa-Institut – Saarland University (Germany) within the SEE | EU Cluster of Excellence in European and International Law.

From 2020 on, he has held the title of Assistant Professor, specialising in civil and commercial law.

## The Author

# Table of Contents

**Table of Contents**

Table of Contents

# List of Abbreviations

| | |
|---|---|
| EU | European Union |
| GDP | Gross Domestic Product |
| ISA | Insurance Supervision Agency |
| LCMSI | Law on Contributions for the Mandatory Social Insurance |
| LI | Law on Insurance |
| LMIN | Law on Maritime and Inland Navigation |
| LMIT | Law on Mandatory Insurance in Traffic |
| LO | Law on Obligations |
| LOBORAT | Law on Obligations and Basic Ownership Relations in Air Transport |
| LOLBIC | Law on Liquidation and Bankruptcy of the Insurance Companies |
| LVPF | Law on Voluntary Pension Funds |
| MTOM | Maximum Take-Off Mass |
| OECD | Organization for Economic Cooperation and Development |
| OJM | Official Journal of Montenegro |
| OJFRY | Official Journal of the Federal Republic of Yugoslavia |
| OJRM | Official Journal of the Republic of Montenegro |
| OJSAM | Official Journal of Serbia and Montenegro |
| PDIA | Pension and Disability Insurance Act |
| SDR | Special Drawing Rights |

## List of Abbreviations

# Preface

This monograph is part of the Cluver International Law series on insurance law.

The text was prepared during 2022 and the beginning of 2023 and encompasses all the relevant legal sources on insurance in Montenegro.

In some parts of the monograph, the previous rules were presented, followed by the most recent changes that happened in 2022.

# General Introduction

## §1. General Background Information

*1.* Montenegro is a country on the Balkan Peninsula, located on the coast of the Adriatic Sea. Montenegro covers an area of 13,812 km$^2$ and has a population of 620,739 inhabitants, according to the projections of the National Bureau of Statistics for 1 January 2021. The capital (and largest) city in Montenegro is Podgorica. Montenegro regained its full independence in 2006 after a referendum in favour of independence from the former state union of Serbia and Montenegro. The current constitution of Montenegro was adopted by the Parliament in 2007.

*2.* Since 2010, Montenegro has been a European Union (EU) candidate country, and in 2012, accession negotiations were opened with the EU. In 2017, Montenegro became a member of the North Atlantic Treaty Organisation (NATO).

*3.* By the end of June 2020, Montenegro will have opened all thirty-three negotiation chapters and provisionally closed three out of them

*4.* In May 2021, the Council agreed on the application of the revised enlargement methodology to the accession negotiations.

### I. Political System

*5.* Montenegro is a parliamentary republic, defined as a civil, democratic and ecological state, a state of social justice based on the rule of law.[1] In line with the principle of the separation of powers, Montenegro is governed by executive, legislative and judicial branches.

*6.* The Parliament of Montenegro is unicameral, has eighty-one deputies, passes all laws in Montenegro, adopts international agreements, elects the prime minister, ministers, and judges, adopts the budget, and performs other duties prescribed by the constitution. The Parliament may pass a vote of no confidence in the government by a simple majority.

1. *See*: Article 1, Constitution of Montenegro, OJM, Nos 1/07 & 38/13.

*7.* The President of Montenegro is elected on the basis of general and equal electoral rights through a direct and secret ballot for a period of five years. As head of state, he proposes the prime minister-designate upon the constitution of the parliament after the general elections.

*8.* The government consists of the prime minister, who represents the government and manages its work, one or more deputy prime ministers, and the ministers.[2] The prime minister-designate presents to the Parliament their programme and proposes the composition of the government.[3] The resignation of the prime minister is considered the resignation of the government. The prime minister may propose to the Parliament to impeach a member of the government.[4] The government can pass regulations within its competence and other general legal acts in order to implement the laws adopted by the Parliament of Montenegro.[5]

*9.* The Montenegrin courts are autonomous and independent, and their judicial function is permanent.[6] They adjudicate on the basis of the Constitution, laws, ratified and published international treaties, and other general acts adopted by the legislative or executive branches. The courts apply the law, but in the case of statutory lacuna, there is a possibility for the courts to create rules that are binding only for the parties in a particular civil law case.

## II. Commerce and Industry

*10.* Montenegro is an open economy, vulnerable to external shocks, due to its high debt-to-Gross domestic product (GDP) ratio. There is no distinction between domestic and foreign companies regarding the percentage of ownership, and profits and dividends may be repatriated without limitations or restrictions. Privatisation of the formerly state-owned enterprises is almost complete.

*11.* The Montenegrin economy relies heavily on tourism, which accounts for 25% of its GDP. Besides tourism, the energy sector is one of the more developed industries with new investments in green energy projects, such as wind, solar and hydroelectric power plants. Montenegro has issued its first licence for oil and gas exploration in the Adriatic Sea, but this type of industry is in its early stages.

*12.* The main products exported are tobacco, salt, steel, aluminium, beer, wine and energy. More than 70% of the labour force is employed by the tertiary sector (services). The World Bank has measured the growth rate of GDP at 124% in 2021.

2. *See*: Article 102, Constitution of Montenegro.
3. *See*: Article 103, Constitution of Montenegro.
4. *See*: Article 105, Constitution of Montenegro.
5. Petar Šturanović, *Zakonodavna nadležnost skupštine u savremenom parlamentarnom sistemu*, JU Službeni list Crne Gore, Podgorica, 2017, p. 34.
6. *See*: Article 118, Constitution of Montenegro.

## III. Financial Institutions

*13.* The regulatory framework of the financial market in Montenegro is not centralised. Three regulators – the Central Bank of Montenegro, the Insurance Supervision Agency (ISA) and the Capital Market Authority – oversee the financial market. Still, the financial system in Montenegro is bank-oriented, since more than 90% of financial intermediation goes through the banks. The insurance sector has roughly a 5% share of the total sector assets.

*14.* The Central Bank of Montenegro is an independent institution responsible for monetary policy, the establishment and maintenance of a sound banking system, and an efficient payment system in Montenegro.[7] Although it is independent within the powers set forth in the law, the Central Bank of Montenegro does not have an issuing function, but this is reserved as an exclusive right of the Central Bank of Montenegro in the event that Montenegro decides to introduce a national currency.[8] The Central Bank has the authority to: oversee the preservation of the stability of the financial system as a whole and to pass pertinent regulations and measures; regulate the operations of credit institutions; issue licences and approvals to credit institutions; and supervise credit institutions in accordance with the law; etc. Without standard monetary policy, Montenegro has only fiscal and structural policies as its macroeconomic toolkit.

*15.* Although the Central Bank of Montenegro is the oldest regulator in the financial market in Montenegro, the state has opted to promote the system of three separate regulators, which consequently means that the Central Bank of Montenegro does not exercise supervision over insurance companies in Montenegro.

*16.* The ISA is the one that exercises supervision in accordance with the Law on Insurance (LI) and Core Principles for Efficient Insurance Supervision over the operations of insurance companies, branches of foreign insurance companies, insurance brokerage companies, insurance agency companies, insurance agents-entrepreneurs, and ancillary insurance service providers.[9] The ISA performs continuous supervision of insurance companies' business operations, primarily to verify whether the insurance companies have an adequately established management system and whether they comply with risk management rules and other requirements in accordance with the LI and to verify the compliance of business operations with other regulations governing the business operations of insurance companies.[10]

*17.* The Capital Market Authority oversees the financial market in the area of the capital market as an autonomous and independent regulatory body, accountable to

7. *See*: Article 4, Law on the Central Bank of Montenegro, OJM, Nos 40/10, 46/10, 6/14 & 111/22.
8. *See*: Article 5, para. 1, Law on the Central Bank of Montenegro.
9. *See*: Article 115, para. 1, LI. OJRM, Nos 78/06 & 019/07, and OJM, Nos 53/09, 73/10, 40/11, 45/12, 06/13, 55/16 & 146/21.
10. *See*: Article 117, LI.

the Parliament of Montenegro. This authority encourages, organises and undertakes measures for the effective functioning of financial markets and supervises the implementation of the Law on the Capital Market,[11] the Law on Investment Funds,[12] the Law on the Acquisition of Joint Stock Companies[13] and the Law on Private Pension Funds.[14]

## IV. Currency Legislation and Monetary Regulations

*18.* The euro is used as a means of payment in Montenegro as of 1 January 2002, although Montenegro is not part of the euro zone. Montenegro has unilaterally adopted the euro as its currency, as was the case earlier with the German mark.

*19.* The European Commission acknowledged the use of the euro in Montenegro in its staff working document, the Montenegro 2019 Report, accompanying the document 'Communication from the Commission to the European Parliament, the Council, the European Economic and Social Committee and the Committee of the Regions'. In this report, the use of the euro was decided under exceptional circumstances, which is distinct from membership in the euro zone.[15]

*20.* The Central Bank of Montenegro uses other instruments in monetary policy regulation, such as reserve requirements for credit institutions, granting loans to credit institutions, and other operations of the Central Bank on the open market.

## V. Insurance Business, General Organisation and Special Features

*21.* In 2022, nine insurance companies operated in the Montenegrin insurance market, of which five companies dealt with non-life insurance, while life insurance was dealt with by four insurance companies. This means that companies in Montenegro have to choose if they want to be life or non-life insurance companies, and they have to abide by both the Law on Business Organisations and the LI in terms of the statutory requirements. The Law on Business Organisations is subsidiarily applicable if there are no rules in the LI.

*22.* Almost all insurance companies are foreign subsidiaries, which hold more than 93% of the total capital, which also accounts for most of the total premiums.

*23.* In 2021, the share of premiums out of the GDP of Montenegro was 2.01%. Although the total amount has shown an increase, the percentage is actually decreasing in comparison to 2020 due to the significant GDP growth in 2021. When

11. OJM, No. 1/18.
12. OJM, Nos 54/11 & 3/18.
13. OJM, Nos 18/11 & 52/16.
14. OJRM, Nos 78/06 & 14/07 and OJM, Nos 73/10, 40/11 & 13/18.
15. *See*: page 75 of the report.

we compare the penetration in the sectors of insurance, it is clear that the penetration of non-life insurance, in the amount of 1.60%, is much higher than the penetration of life insurance, which was 0.41% in 2021.

*24.* Almost 80% of all premiums are in the non-life insurance sector, and as is usual in developing countries, the majority of these premiums are for compulsory insurance.

## §2. Historical Background of Insurance and Insurance Legislation

### I. The First Insurance Companies on the Territory of Montenegro

*25.* The Statute of Budva, a Montenegrin town on the Adriatic Coast, mentions insurance for the first time in the fifteenth century. Prior to that, a so-called maritime risk-sharing fraternity was present in Montenegro in 1353.[16] Actually, the Statute of Budva deals with insurance only to a certain extent, or rather, it provides protection for citizens of Budva who have been robbed by creating the obligation of the municipality to recover damages incurred by citizens.[17] This document can be construed as the first official document in Montenegrin history to mention insurance, although at that time, the Boka Kotorska (Kotor Bay) was not part of Montenegrin territory.

*26.* The first attempt at creating a marine insurance organisation in Boka Kotorska dates back to 1805, but in 1849, the 'Society of Fraternal Maritime Security' was formed in Dobrota Municipality, which was replaced by 'National Insurance' in the period from 1858 to 1874.[18] This insurance company was established as a joint-stock company with thirty-two shareholders.[19] In that period, Boka Kotorska was part of the Austro-Hungarian Empire, which had one of the strongest fleets in the world.[20] This insurance company was engaged in marine insurance and operated for nine years before undergoing voluntary liquidation in July of 1858.

*27.* The same year, in February, also in Dobrota, the 'Fraternal Society' was formed. In the literature, it is stated that the 'Society of Fraternal Maritime Security' merged with the 'Fraternal Society' since some of the management members held the same positions in both companies. This new company defined its activities

16. V. Kašćelan & M. Nović, *The Development of the Insurance Market in Montenegro, Monograph 'Achieved Results and Prospects of Insurance Market Development in the Modern World'*, Chapter 8, Faculty of Economics, University of Belgrade, Centar za izdavačku delatnost Ekonomskog fakulteta u Beogradu (CID), 2012, pp. 139–154.
17. Zdravko Petrović, Vladimir Čolović & Duško Knežević, *History of Insurance in Serbia, Montenegro and Yugoslavia until 1941*, Dosije studio, Belgrade, 2013, p. 99.
18. V. Kašćelan & M. Nović, *supra,* pp. 139–154.
19. History of Insurance, *Bankar*, available at: https://www.bankar.me/2013/12/23/istorija-osiguranja, accessed: 1 Sep. 2022.
20. V. Kašćelan & M. Nović, *Osiguranje i akturaska matematika*, I. izdanje, Univerzitet Crne Gore, Podgorica, 2009, p. 206.

as underwriting the marine and riverine insurance of vessels and monetary funds that would be transported by these vessels, but it was also envisaged to assume other risks with the consent of the authorities.[21] This company had an authorised representative in Trieste, so it can be concluded that the company intended to operate not only in local markets.

*28.* The policy of the 'Fraternal Society' covered ordinary risks, including shipwreck, fire, piracy (if total loss had occurred) and ship stranding that had caused the ship to be unseaworthy. Partial loss was covered only in cases where the losses reached 75% of the ship's value. The insurance premium was related to the value of the insured item: actually, it was set at 5% of the insured value.[22] After a few good years in business, a period of insecurity followed, caused by a number of major accidents that occurred and stronger competition in the market from mutual insurance companies. The opening of a new affiliate in Sulina did not help much. In August of 1875, this company suspended its operations.

## II. The First Insurance Legislation in the Principality of Montenegro

*29.* The General Property Code for Montenegro from 1888 contained only the principal provisions governing insurance contracts. The Insurance Companies Law of the Principality of Montenegro was enacted in 1904 and later amended in 1909.[23] This law regulated not only the statutory requirements for the insurance companies but also the rights and obligations of the insured.

*30.* Under the provisions of this law in the Principality of Montenegro, the activities of anonymous, mutual, auxiliary and other societies of any kind are granted insurance against the risks of fire, lightning, hail, accidents at sea or on land, life insurance in the event of death, etc.[24] The Montenegrin Ministry of Finance was the licensing authority. This law presented one major requirement in the licensing process. The company applying for the licence could originate only from the counties enumerated in the law: the Austro-Hungarian Monarchy, Germany, Italy, France, the United Kingdom, the United States of America and Russia. The insurance company had to present the annual financial report and the rules of the company (general terms and conditions), certified by a consul of the country where the company's head office was located. The insurance company had to appoint its representative in Montenegro. The dispute settlement in insurance cases was reserved for the Montenegrin courts. The amount of capital that had to be invested in Montenegro was prescribed, not as a fixed amount but rather as a percentage of the total invested insurance sums and profit that would be generated through the business activities. This capital could be invested in government securities by providing a guarantee from one of the permitted countries of origin. If this company did not

21. Zdravko Petrović, Vladimir Čolović & Duško Knežević, *supra*, p. 102.
22. *Ibid.*, p. 105.
23. *Ibid.*, p. 100.
24. *See*: Article 1, Law on Insurance Companies of the Principality of Montenegro.

invest in the manner described, it had to deposit in the State Treasury an amount equal to one-fifth of the insurance premiums paid by the insured in Montenegro. Additionally, a fixed amount (caution) was asked from the company, depending on the type of insurance that the company was dealing with. These provisions were meant to ensure the proper stipulation of the insurance companies' obligations. A peculiarity of this law was that, apart from the obligation of the insurance company to present the financial report every year, it had to provide to the Ministry of Finance a list of all insurance contracts, together with the names of the insured, for all ongoing and terminated contracts. This document was confidential and could be accessed only by the authorised persons and their heirs.[25] We must bear in mind that in this period of Montenegrin development, most of the population was illiterate and undereducated, so the state opted to protect its citizens in this manner.

*31.* Although this law regulated the operations of insurance companies, it had one article devoted to the rights of the insured and one dedicated to the obligations of the insured. The article granting the right to the insured envisaged the situation of an insurance company's failure to fulfil its obligation under the insurance contract as determined by the court decision. In this case, the insured could present their claim to the Montenegrin Ministry of Finance, which would pay out the claim from the caution funds of the company. The payment of the claim by the Ministry of Finance created a new obligation for the insurance company – to supplement the caution funds over a one-month period. The only obligation of the insured established by this law was to notify the Ministry of Finance of the conclusion of an insurance contract and present the data on the insurance company, the date of the contract conclusion, and the amount of the insured sum. Failure to fulfil this obligation by the insured consequently deprived the insured of their rights towards the caution funds in the Ministry of Finance.[26] So, again, the legislator established a system designed to protect the insured, with appropriate sanction, in the event that the insured failed to carry out their obligations. This sanction was not intended to deprive the insured of their rights under the insurance contract but to form the rights under this special protection mechanism established by this law.

*32.* Several insurance companies were acting in the insurance sector in Montenegro under the provisions of this law: 'Mutual' from Trieste, 'Victoria' from Berlin, and 'Rosija'.[27]

## III. Legislation Between Two World Wars (The Kingdom of Serbs, Croats and Slovenes and the Kingdom of Yugoslavia)

*33.* Between the two World Wars, Montenegro was a part of the Kingdom of Serbs, Croats and Slovenes, founded after the First World War. The complexity of the insurance regulation existed due to the fact that in different parts of the country,

25. Zdravko Petrović, Vladimir Čolović & Duško Knežević, *supra,* pp. 109–112.
26. *Ibid.,* p. 113.
27. *Ibid.*

different legal sources were applicable to insurance. A multiplicity of the legal system was in force in this newly formed state. On the territory of Montenegro, the General Property Code for Montenegro from 1888 applied to insurance contracts, along with the rules of the Law on Insurance Companies from 1904. On other territories, such as Serbia, the Serbian Civil Code from 1844 and the Serbian Commercial Act from 1860 were applicable in Serbia and one part of Macedonia, and the Bulgarian Civil Code from 1898 was applicable in another part of Macedonia. In Vojvodina, the Hungarian Civil Code from 1875 was in place. In one part of Croatia, the Croatian-Hungarian Commercial Act from 1875 was applied, and in Dalmatia and Slovenia, the Austrian Contract Insurance Act from 1917 was applicable.

*34.* Although, in this period, efforts to unify the civil law were unsuccessful, there was a partial unification of the rules in the Law on Transport since a new Law on Air Transport was introduced and the Convention on Motor Traffic was ratified and published. Also, some partial regulation was introduced in the area of insurance of crops and fruits and in the area of supervision of insurance corporations.

*35.* Since more than three-quarters of the country's population was employed in agriculture, it was to be expected that major legal efforts would be taken in this area. The first Law on Insurance of Crops and Fruit from 1923 created the basic form of protection against risk: the money of the insured and help provided by the ministry and municipal authorities. The next law cleared the way for the compulsory insurance of crops against hail in 1931, but the implementation of this law was very difficult since the farmers were in a difficult economic position.

*36.* The rules on public transportation created the obligation to provide mandatory insurance for passengers and cargo transporters. Also, public storage facilities were obligated to conclude mandatory insurance of all goods against the risk of fire to their full value.[28] The rules on supervision of insurance companies were enacted in 1937 as a reaction to the bankruptcy of one of the largest insurance companies of that time, the Austrian company Fenix.

## IV. Developments after the Second World War (Yugoslavia)

*37.* After the Second World War, discontinuity with the previous legal system was declared by the socialist government by the Law on the Nullity of Regulations enacted before 6 April 1944 and during enemy occupation.[29] Under the provisions of this law, all previous legislation would not be enforced, and the courts could not base a decision on implementing previous legislation. The courts could use the legal rules of pre-war laws under the following conditions: that there is a statutory lacuna,

28. *Ibid.*, pp. 137–141.
29. This law was enacted in 1946.

that the laws do not contradict the constitution and other valid regulations, and that they do not contradict the principles of the constitutional order of the new state.[30]

*38.* In regard to the insurance companies, one of the major changes was caused by the decision of the government on the confiscation of all enemy property, which consequently meant that the property of all enemies was confiscated, including the property of German and Italian insurance companies. The DOZ[31] was created, which used all the property of enemy countries' insurance companies as well as the property of enemy-owned domestic insurance companies. The DOZ had a monopoly on the insurance of all state property and was a highly centralised company run by the Ministry of Finance. After a while, it was the only insurance company in Yugoslavia, since the new rules in the area of insurance practically incapacitated the work of privately owned insurance companies. As a monopoly, it imposed strict rules on losing the rights to insurance contracts and enacted very high premiums. New forms of insurance and new risks were not taken into consideration by the DOZ, although there was a demand for those types of insurance. Consequently, this system had to be dismissed because of all of its weaknesses.[32]

*39.* Since there was no legal regulation of insurance contracts during this period, the relevant sources were autonomous. We must point out that the state had enacted several ordinances and decrees that provided the rules on mandatory insurance, by which mandatory insurance could be established automatically (statutorily) or by a contract. Insurance of travellers and goods in public transport (railway, marine and road traffic) was of a statutory kind, while insurance of a company's assets, import or export goods, and of all other property of a socially owned property governed by state bodies, organisations and other socially owned companies was contractual.[33]

*40.* Reform of insurance companies began with the adoption of the new Law on Insurance Institutions and Insurance Communities in 1961. This reform brought the long-awaited decentralisation of insurance, since insurance institutions were organisations acting on a defined territory, which was the territory of a municipality, since they were formed by a municipal people's board. This change brought the opportunity to cover specified risks and new risks previously uncovered by the DOZ, but again, this institution would have a monopoly on insurance activities in its territory. Every municipal institution was affiliated with the Republic Insurance Association, and all these associations were part of the Yugoslav Insurance Association. The dispersion of the risks was vertical, so every municipal institute was reinsured by the Republic Insurance Association, which was reinsured by the Yugoslav Insurance Association. All insurance was based on the unified terms of insurance established by the Yugoslav Insurance Association with the confirmation of the Federal Assembly. Tariffs were also set in the same way, so there was no competition. All the losses of individual institutions were covered automatically through the designed system

30. Zoran Rašović, *Uvod u građansko pravo*, Pravni fakultet u Podgorici, 2009, p. 39.
31. Državni osiguravajući zavod – abbreviation in Montenegrin for the State Institution for Insurance.
32. Predrag Šulejić, *supra*, p. 36.
33. *Ibid.*, p. 40.

of reinsurance, so there were no incentives for good business decisions. The system of mandatory insurances established with ordinances was replaced by the Law on Mandatory Transport Insurance and the Law on Mandatory Insurance of Property and Persons from 1965, but there were no changes in the number of mandatory insurances.

*41.* The next reform followed in 1967 with the adoption of the Principal Law on Insurance and Insurance Organisations, which was aimed at eliminating territorial monopolies, mandatory affiliations of the insurance organisations to associations, mandatory reinsurance, and unified rules and tariffs. Insurance organisations were organised as insurance or reinsurance institutions, granting them the same status as other legal entities, but with some special rules, since insurance activity was recognised as an activity of special interest to the state. The new law recognised the possibility of organising mutual insurance organisations, companies that carry out intermediation, agency, loss assessment, or other activities in insurance.[34] One interesting fact is that this law, clearly a LI organisations, contains the basic rules on insurance contracts, since, at this time, there were no rules regulating the area of insurance contracts. But this reform was not long-lived and was criticised because of the alienation of insurance assets from its creators, so the next reform was instituted on the back of constitutional changes in 1974.[35] Some authors at that time pointed out that the basic principles of insurance adopted by capitalist states must be followed by insurance in socialist states, at least a basic issuing of the business techniques of capitalist insurance companies,[36] but a new experiment in the insurance area had begun.

*42.* A new era in insurance development in Yugoslavia followed the constitutional changes in 1974 that introduced the foundations of associated labour. The new economic developments were reflected in the insurance sector, since organisations of associated labour, self-management communities of interest, sociopolitical communities of interest, and other socially owned entities could accumulate their assets with other entities in establishing insurance organisations.[37] According to the constitution, insurance associations are the only form of insurance company. The system of insurance companies was regulated in detail by the following federal laws: the Law on the Principles of the Insurance System of Property and Persons; and the Law on Practising Business Abroad, both from 1976. Since the first law gave the republics and provinces the opportunity to additionally regulate insurance operations, Montenegro, like all the other republics, adopted the Law on the System of Insurance of Property and Persons in 1977.[38]

*43.* Contractual relations were finally regulated in 1978 by the federal law, the Law on Obligations (LO). This law did not follow the major trend in Yugoslav law

34. *Ibid.*, p. 37.
35. *Ibid.*, p. 41.
36. Branko Jakša, *Pravo osiguranja (Insurance Law)*, Informator, Zagreb, 1972, p. 11.
37. Predrag Šulejić, *supra*, p. 38.
38. *Ibid.*, p. 41.

at the time, the trend of socialist economic principles, but was built on the principles of the market economy and was in accordance with similar texts in the field. The previously created statutory lacuna in the field of contractual relations in insurance was finally filled with modern text that contained almost seventy articles on insurance contracts. However, this text did not apply to three areas: marine insurance, credit insurance, and reinsurance. So, these relations were regulated by the Law on Maritime and Internal Navigation and the Law on Obligations and Material and Legal Relations in Air Transport, both enacted a year earlier, in 1977.

*44.* Again, constitutional amendments from 1988 were the trigger for the next evolution of the insurance law in Yugoslavia. The Law on the Principles of the Insurance System of Property and Persons from 1990, as a federal law, created new rules in the insurance sector. This law contained rules on insurance companies and mandatory insurance.[39] New forms of insurance companies were allowed by this law, so, at the time, limited liability, mutual, public and mixed insurance companies were acknowledged, as well as companies for other insurance activities, insurance and reinsurance pools, and the Yugoslav Bureau for Insurance. This was a time of change, so all legal texts regulating certain aspects of the insurance companies changed significantly: the Law on Companies (1988), the Law on Securities (1989), the Law on Foreign Trade Business (1989), and the Law on Foreign Investments (1988).

*45.* This was indeed a time of change, not only for the insurance regulations but for the state of Yugoslavia as well. Slovenia, Croatia, Bosnia and Herzegovina, and Macedonia became sovereign states, and Serbia and Montenegro formed a federation, the Federal Republic of Yugoslavia, in 1992. In 1996, the new Law on the Insurance of Property and Persons was introduced, which limited insurance companies to joint-stock companies, mutual insurance companies and agencies providing additional services in insurance.[40] Under the provisions of this law, novelties were introduced in the area of the establishment of insurance companies in regard to a higher level of initial capital for their establishment and the procedures for the licensing of insurance companies by the competent authorities.

*46.* In this period, the LO from 1978 was the only source for general rules on insurance contracts, and the Law on Maritime and Internal Navigation and the Law on Obligations and Material and Legal Relations in Air Transport, both from 1977, in their respective fields were in force as the rules created by the federal government in the area of insurance.

*47.* Again, it was constitutional changes that brought about changes in insurance regulations. The Federal Republic of Yugoslavia transformed again in 2003 into the State Union of Serbia and Montenegro, with the Constitutional Charter as a founding document.[41] According to the wording of the Constitutional Charter, all civil

39. *Ibid.*, p. 42.
40. OJFRY, Nos 30/96, 57/98, 53/99 & 55/99.
41. OJSAM, Nos 01/03 & 26/05.

matters, including insurance, were under the jurisdiction of the founding republics. The laws of the previous Federal Republic of Yugoslavia were used as the laws of Montenegro until the enactment of new laws by the Parliament of Montenegro.[42] This State Union of Serbia and Montenegro set a time limit in regard to Montenegro's intent to declare independence, since its constitution provided for the procedure of leaving the State Union that could be initiated three years after the signing of the Constitutional Charter. The possibility of dissolution of the State Union was possible from 2006.

*48.* In 2006, Montenegro organised a referendum on independence and left the State Union of Serbia and Montenegro. Since 2006, Montenegro has been a sovereign state with full formal legislative sovereignty over its territory, so this is the most recent period in the development of the insurance law in Montenegrin history.

### V. Developments after Montenegrin Independence

*49.* After Montenegro regained its independence in 2006, the Constitution of Montenegro was adopted in October 2007. Even before the constitution was adopted, the Constitutional Assembly of the Republic of Montenegro, at the fifth session of the second regular session in 2006, after the declaration of Montenegrin independence, adopted as one of the first laws of the LI in December 2006.[43]

*50.* This LI is still in force, but it has been amended several times[44] in order to harmonise its provisions with EU legislation in the process of harmonising the Montenegrin legal system. Until 2008, contractual relations in insurance were regulated by the Federal Law on Obligations from 1978. The Montenegrin Law on Obligations was adopted in 2008, which represents the innovative text of the former LO, and this text is still in force.[45]

## §3. Sources of Insurance Law

### I. Legislation

*51.* The legal sources of insurance law in Montenegro can be divided into those sources regulating the status of insurance companies and those sources related to the regulation of contractual relations in insurance. The former sources regulate the position and status of insurance organisations, while the latter relate to the legal relationship established by insurance contracts.[46] The main sources in both areas are

42. This was the possibility set by Art. 64, para. 2 of the Constitutional Charter of Serbia and Montenegro.
43. OJRM, No. 78/06.
44. LI, OJRM, Nos 78/06 & 19/07 and OJM, Nos 53/09, 73/10, 40/11, 45/12, 6/13, 55/16 & 146/21.
45. OJM, Nos 47/08, 4/11 & 22/17.
46. Predrag Šulejić, *supra,* p. 44.

laws that are very often accompanied by a significant number of norms set by delegated legislative acts. Jurisprudence is not the formal source of insurance law in Montenegro. Since the majority of the laws in the insurance sector are dated after 2006, there are not so many court cases regarding insurance.

*52.* The most important statutory source for insurance, as a *lex specialis,* is the LI, which regulates all issues related to the establishment, the types of subjects in insurance, their management, financial activities, business, changes in their status, and termination of insurance companies. This text was influenced by insurance regulations in the Balkan region, mainly the former Yugoslav republics' regulation of insurance operations. Although many of them have changed their legislation significantly in recent years, the Montenegrin Law on Insurance stands on the same grounds, even though it has been amended nine times.[47] The manner of initiating, opening, and conducting liquidation and bankruptcy proceedings, as well as the rights and obligations of participants in liquidation and bankruptcy proceedings of insurance companies and branches of foreign insurance companies, is regulated by the Law on Liquidation and Bankruptcy of Insurance Companies.[48]

*53.* The legal status of insurance companies is also regulated by the Law on Commercial Companies,[49] which is a *lex generalis* in Montenegro regarding the establishment of legal entities. This law regulates the establishment, registration, management, restructuring, termination and other issues of importance for the work of legal entities, entrepreneurs and parts of foreign companies. The manner of initiating, opening and conducting liquidation and bankruptcy proceedings of all legal entities is regulated by the Law on Bankruptcy,[50] as a *lex generalis*. This method of separately regulating insurance liquidation and bankruptcy proceedings is a question of tradition since, in the past, liquidation and bankruptcy of insurance companies and banks were always regulated by separate laws from the general law on the liquidation and bankruptcy of other legal entities.

*54.* Many other laws have some relevance in the statutory domain of the regulation of insurance companies, such as: the Law on the Capital Market,[51] the Law on Privatisation,[52] the Law on Foreign Investments,[53] the Law on Accounting,[54] the Law on Auditing,[55] the Law on Current and Capital Transactions with Foreign Countries,[56] and the Law on Deposit Protection.[57]

47. One of the other characteristics is that there is an almost complete absence of jurisprudence in the LI. Besides one case of a company that failed to meet the criteria of this law, that initiated several proceedings against the decisions of the Montenegrin ISA, there is almost no other jurisprudence.
48. OJM, No. 42/15.
49. OJM, No. 65/20.
50. OJM, Nos 1/11, 53/16, 32/18, 62/18 & 1/22.
51. OJM, No. 1/18.
52. OJRM, Nos 23/96, 6/99, 59/00 & 42/04.
53. OJM, Nos 18/11, 45/14 & 73/19.
54. OJM, No. 145/21.
55. OJM, No. 1/17.
56. OJM, Nos 45/05, 62/08, 40/11, 62/13 & 70/17.
57. OJM, No. 72/19.

*55.* The most important source of insurance law in the area of contractual obligations of the parties is the LO,[58] which has sixty-nine articles dedicated to insurance contracts, but still, this law does not cover the entire area of insurance. By the very provisions of this law, as in the case of the Federal Law on Obligations from 1978, the areas of marine insurance, claims insurance, and reinsurance are excluded by clearly stating that the provisions of this law in Chapter XXXII will not apply to these areas.[59] The new LO presents some changes to the original text from 1978, but not in the area of insurance. The old text of the Law of Obligations was prepared by the university professor, Mihailo Konstantinovic, and took him nine years. In 1969, he published the Draft Law on Obligations and Contracts, which provoked wide discussion in the academic and professional communities. The text was formulated in the draft of the LO and was adopted in 1978, with all ideological admixtures of the socialist regime removed from the text afterwards. The draft and, subsequently, the LO were developed for a market economy according to modern models,[60] among which we can single out Switzerland's Law on Obligations.

*56.* Traffic insurance is regulated by a special law containing special provisions regarding contractual relations in traffic insurance, although there is no mention of the exclusion of the application of the Law of Obligations in traffic insurance. All mandatory insurances are regulated by special laws. Again, this type of regulation of mandatory insurance in traffic is traditional, since this division in insurance regulation was inherited from the former Yugoslavia.

*57.* The Air Traffic Insurance Contract is regulated by the Law on Obligations and Property Relations in Air Transport.[61] This type of separate regulation of air traffic insurance is a question of tradition, since, in the former Yugoslavia, air transport was regulated by a separate law.

*58.* The Law on Mandatory Traffic Insurance[62] codifies the rules on compulsory traffic insurance. The types of compulsory insurance in traffic regulated by this law are: accident insurance of passengers in public transport; insurance of a vehicle's owner against liability for damage caused to third parties; insurance of an aircraft's owner against liability for damage caused to third parties and passengers; and insurance of boat owners against liability for damage caused to third parties.[63] Subsequent application of the LO is envisaged by the Law on Mandatory Traffic Insurance in all the cases otherwise not specified by this law.

58. OJM, Nos 47/08, 4/11 & 22/17.
59. *See*: Article 996, LO.
60. *See*: Jakov Radišić, *Obligaciono pravo*, deveto izmijenjeno i dopunjeno izdanje, Centar za publikacije Pravnog fakulteta u Nišu, 2014, p. 16.
61. OJM, Nos 18/11, 46/14 & 43/18.
62. OJM, Nos 44/12 & 146/21.
63. *See*: Article 2, Law on Compulsory Traffic Insurance.

## II. Governmental Regulations

*59.* By virtue of the constitutional division of powers, the Government of Montenegro can pass bylaws in all domains, including insurance. In the insurance sector, there are some regulations regarding the minimum amount of professional liability insurance in the field of building construction and regulations on the conditions, procedures and criteria for group exemption from the prohibition of agreements in the insurance sector.

## III. Regulation by Governmental Agencies

*60.* The ISA is the regulatory authority in Montenegro which carries out supervision of the implementation of the LI and insurance operations. The Governing Council of the ISA is, among other things, competent to pass bylaws and guidelines and instructions concerning the application of good business practices in the insurance operations and the composition of individual insurance companies' business policies.[64]

*61.* More than twenty different rules have been passed so far by the Governing Council pertaining to the financial operations of insurance companies, requirements for licensing insurance business activities, the manner of calculating the mathematical reserves and solvency margin, the criteria and manner of calculating unearned premiums, the criteria for determining the amount of contributions to the Guarantee Fund, the criteria and manner of calculating technical reserve outstanding claims, the contents of the authorised actuary's opinion, and so on.

*62.* The Governing Council of the ISA passed three decisions on the method of valuation of financial investments and receivables for insurance companies, the amount of regular contribution to the Guarantee Fund, and the fees of the ISA.

## IV. Private International Law

*63.* Private international law in Montenegro is regulated by the Private International Law Act.[65] Some of the rules regarding insurance are set in this law, some in the Law on Maritime and Inland Navigation (LMIN) and the Law on Obligations and Basic Ownership Relations in Air Transport (LOBORAT), but the others relate to the regime of the international conventions signed and ratified by the Montenegrin government.

*64.* Montenegro has been a Member State of the Hague Conference on Private International Law retroactively since 1 March 2007 and succeeded to the conventions previously ratified by the Socialist Federal Republic of Yugoslavia (SFRY) as

64. *See*: Article 185, LI.
65. OJM, Nos 1/14, 6/14, 11/14, 14/14 & 47/15.

of 3 June 2006.[66] One of the conventions binding on Montenegro is of special importance to the insurance contracts since it relates to traffic accidents – the Convention of 4 May 1971 on the Law Applicable to Traffic Accidents.

*65.* The Private International Law Act does not contain any special rules regarding the applicable law to insurance contracts, so the general rules stipulated for all contracts apply. If the parties do not agree on the applicable law, the governing law for the insurance contract will be the law of the habitual residence of the insurer, since this is the contracting party required to affect the characteristic performance of the insurance contract.[67] The application of the closest connection principle is possible if it is clear from all the circumstances of the case that the contract is obviously more closely related to another country than to the country of the habitual residence of the insurer or if the applicable law cannot be determined based on the described rules, then the contract is governed by the law of the country with which it has the closest relationship.[68]

*66.* The Private International Law Act also contains provisions on the rights of the injured person to take direct action against the insurer of the person liable to provide compensation if the law applicable to the non-contractual obligation or the insurance contract so provided.[69]

*67.* By the provision of the LMIN, the parties are free to choose the applicable law, unless all interested parties in the contract are Montenegrin nationals with their residence in Montenegro or legal persons having their head office in Montenegro, and unless the insurance concerns property which is exposed to insured risks exclusively within the territory of Montenegro.[70] The LOBORAT has almost the same provisions as Article 179.[71]

## V. Jurisdiction

*68.* The jurisdiction of the Montenegrin judiciary is regulated by the Private International Law Act for all matters with a foreign element. The place of domicile of the defendant is the usual rule, with exceptions in the case of the exclusive jurisdiction of the domestic judiciary or when the parties have selected the court to adjudicate their dispute.[72]

---

66. *See* Maja Kostić-Mandić, *Private International Law in Montenegro* (Walters Kluwer 2022), p. 29, para. 45.
67. *See*: Article 39, para. 2, Private International Law Act.
68. *See*: Maja Kostić-Mandić, *Private International Law in Montenegro*, (Walters Kluwer 2022), p. 101, para. 295, and Art. 39, paras 3 and 4, Private International Law Act.
69. *See*: Article 66, Private International Law Act.
70. *See*: Article 1047, para. 1, item 1, and para. 2, LMIN.
71. *See* more: Maja Kostić-Mandić, *Private International Law in Montenegro*, (Walters Kluwer 2022), p. 101, para. 298, Maja Kostić-Mandić, Međunarodno privatno pravo (Private International Law), Pravni fakultet Univerziteta Crne Gore, Podgorica, 2017, p. 132.
72. *See* Maja Kostić-Mandić, *supra*, p. 196, para. 613.

*69.* The jurisdiction of the Montenegrin courts exists if the defendant, a natural person, has a place of residence or, in the case of a legal person, has its head office in Montenegro. In the event that the defendant does not have a domicile in Montenegro or another country, the jurisdiction of the courts of Montenegro exists if the defendant has a residence in Montenegro.[73] The general jurisdiction of domestic courts can be extended in the case of the existence of material co-defendants, and in the case of non-litigious matters, if certain requirements are met.[74]

*70.* Since the exclusive jurisdiction in the cases of aircraft and ships is usually established when the register in which the aircraft or ship is registered is kept in Montenegro, we must emphasise that this jurisdiction does exist in Montenegro, but only for disputes about property rights on aircraft and ships, as well as in disputes regarding the lease of aircraft and ships.[75] For the insurance contract, there is no exclusive jurisdiction of the Montenegrin courts.

*71.* For contracts, including insurance contracts, the general rule is that the Montenegrin courts are competent for disputes arising from contractual relations even when the subject of the dispute is an obligation that has been performed or that should be performed in Montenegro. The place of performance is stipulated by the law in the event that the parties have not agreed otherwise.[76]

*72.* Since the insurance contract may be a consumer contract, when the contracting party is a consumer, the rules regarding consumer contracts are especially important. By the rules of the Private International Law Act, the jurisdiction of the court of Montenegro exists for a lawsuit filed by a consumer against a trader if the consumer has a residence in Montenegro. If the trader is the one filing the lawsuit, they may initiate proceedings against a consumer residing in Montenegro exclusively before the courts in Montenegro. These provisions on consumer contracts can be deviated from only on the basis of an agreement on jurisdiction, which: was concluded after the dispute arose; enables the consumer to initiate proceedings before another court that would have jurisdiction based on criteria that were not specified in this article; or is concluded between the consumer and the trader if, at the time of the conclusion of the contract, both parties have residence or habitual residence in the same country, and which entrusts jurisdiction to the courts of that country, if such an agreement is not contrary to the laws of that country. The agreement on jurisdiction also depends on several other conditions, one of which is important for insurance contracts. This agreement will be valid in a case in which the contract is concluded with a person who carries out commercial or professional activity in Montenegro or who by any means directs such activity to Montenegro or to several countries, including Montenegro, and the contract falls within the scope of such activity.[77]

---

73. *See*: Article 99, Private International Law Act.
74. *See*: Maja Kostić-Mandić, *supra*, p. 196, para. 615.
75. *See*: Article 121, Private International Law Act.
76. *See*: Article 123, para. 2, Private International Law Act.
77. *See*: Article 124, Private International Law Act.

*73.* One other rule stipulated by the Private International Law Act is important in the context of jurisdiction in insurance contracts: the general rule on jurisdiction in non-contractual relations. By this rule, in disputes about non-contractual liability for damage, the court of Montenegro is competent even when a harmful event has occurred or may occur on the territory of Montenegro. This rule is relevant because it also applies in disputes against the insurance company for compensation of damages to third parties based on the regulations on the direct liability of the insurance company, as well as in disputes about recourse claims based on compensation of damages against recourse debtors.[78]

## §4. Dispute Settlement and Arbitration

*74.* Dispute settlement in Montenegro may be achieved through court proceedings or in an alternative manner. Court settlement is by far the most common way of settling disputes in insurance matters.

*75.* The courts in Montenegro are independent in their work, and their activity is confined by the Constitution, laws, ratified and published international treaties, and other general acts in accordance with the laws. Since jurisprudence is not the formal source of insurance law and the majority of the laws in the insurance sector are dated after 2006, there are not so many court cases regarding insurance.

*76.* The organisation of the court system in Montenegro is regulated by the Law on the Courts.[79] In civil law matters, there is a differentiation between civil and commercial courts, whereby civil courts are regarded as courts of general jurisdiction. Although there is a differentiation of jurisdiction in civil matters, the Law on Civil Procedure is the law primarily governing procedural matters. A commercial court is one that has jurisdiction in all matters arising from the commercial activities of natural and legal persons engaged in commercial activities as an economic operator and in all cases concerning the commercial aspects of intellectual property. In cases where only one contracting party is the economic operator, the civil court has competence. The exception to the previous rule is the case of bankruptcy proceedings, where the commercial courts have exclusive competence for all disputes.

*77.* The alternative dispute mechanisms are regulated by the Law on Alternative Dispute Resolution,[80] the Law on Consumer Protection[81] and the Law on Arbitration.[82] The alternative dispute mechanisms are regulated by the Law on Alternative Dispute Resolution. By the provisions of this law, alternative dispute mechanisms

78. *See*: Article 126, Private International Law Act.
79. Law on the Courts, OJM, Nos 011/15 & 076/20.
80. OJM, No. 77/20.
81. OJM, Nos 2/14, 6/14, 43/15, 70/17 & 67/19.
82. OJM, No. 47/15.

represent the resolution of disputes with the participation of a neutral third party who helps the parties resolve the dispute before or after the initiation of court or other proceedings.

*78.* The Law on Alternative Dispute Resolution has enumerated three cases in which mediation is mandatory. The first is the case of disputes in the compensation of damages on the grounds of an insurance contract if one of the parties is an insurance company; the second is the case of small-value disputes, and the third encompasses all other cases of mandatory mediation set by other laws. So, in Montenegrin law, it is the obligation of the contracting party to contact the Centre for Alternative Dispute Resolution before filing a lawsuit with the court in order to try to resolve the dispute through mediation in cases of compensation of damages on the grounds of an insurance contract if one of the parties is an insurance company. In cases where the parties to the dispute are both insurance companies, by the right of recourse in cases where the responsible party was also insured, the mediation procedure is not mandatory, and the parties are free to present their case to the courts. Since this law uses the wording 'compensation of damages', it clearly relates to cases of non-life insurance contracts, which are based on the principle of compensation, unlike life insurance contracts, where the obligation of the insurance company is to pay the insurance sum, which is not based on the compensatory principle. During the mediation procedure, both parties are obliged to attend the first meeting with the mediator. A mediator is appointed by the parties or by the Centre for Alternative Dispute Resolution if the parties have not previously appointed a mediator.[83]

*79.* The Law on Consumer Protection presents additional methods of out-of-court settlement by introducing the Committee for Out-of-Court Resolution of Consumer Disputes within the Chamber of Commerce of Montenegro, which is a functionally independent body. This committee consists of representatives of business entities and consumers, which are represented by an equal number of members, and was designed to provide an alternative, efficient and inexpensive way of resolving consumer disputes in all areas of commerce, with some exceptions.[84] Proceedings before the Committee may be initiated only by a consumer.

*80.* Although arbitration in insurance matters is possible under Montenegrin law, there are almost no cases settled by arbitration in commercial practice in Montenegro. The general rules of arbitration are applied to insurance cases before the arbitration, so the general precondition of a valid arbitration clause or arbitration contract is a prerequisite both for ad hoc and institutional arbitration. In ad hoc arbitration, the rules of the Law on Arbitration apply and, in the case of institutional arbitration, the rules of the Arbitral Court attached to the Montenegrin Chamber of Commerce applies.[85] This is the only permanent arbitration in Montenegro. The

83. *See*: Article 12, Law on Alternative Dispute Resolution, OJM, No. 77/20.
84. *See*: Article 137, Law on Consumer Protection.
85. Arbitral rules of the Arbitral Court attached to the Montenegrin Chamber of Commerce, 11 Nov. 2015.

rules of this arbitration must comply with the mandatory rules of the Law on Arbitration and may be supplemented with the rules agreed upon by the arbitrators as appropriate. An arbitral tribunal may decide on a dispute under the principle *amiable compositeur* or *ex aequo et bono* based on the express consent of the parties.

## §5. Consumer Protection (In General, and with Regard to Insurance)

*81.* Consumer protection is a term that originated in more recent Montenegrin legislation, although some rules regarding the protection of weaker parties in contracts originated even before the opening of the accession negotiations. The serious efforts and results in developing Montenegrin consumer legislation relate to the opening of negotiations with the EU.

*82.* The first law in this field was the Law on Consumer Protection of 2002, followed by the Law on Consumer Protection of 2007. The current Law on Consumer Protection was introduced in 2014 as an umbrella piece of legislation in the area of consumer protection.[86] Although this law was intended to harmonise Montenegrin law with the EU acquis, it was not fully harmonised with the Directive on Consumer Rights of 2011, and all amendments to this law up until 2019 were related to practical problems of its implementation. This law contains provisions relating to: the duty to inform the customer before the conclusion of contracts; unfair and aggressive business practices; the conclusion of distance contracts; unfair contract terms; out-of-court settlement of consumer disputes; and the procedure for the prohibition of unfair contract terms and unfair business practices.

*83.* Work on a new Law on Consumer Protection is underway and is expected to be passed by the end of 2023. Since the expected changes are so numerous, many legislators have opted for the approach of introducing the new text of the Law on Consumer Protection, which should encompass all the necessary changes in the alignment of the Montenegrin legislation with the *acquis*. Also, the new Law on Collective Redress is in the process of being adopted, and it should be passed by the end of 2023; it will introduce new rules on collective compensation for breaches of consumer rights, which should improve consumer protection. The new law, like the previous version, was developed in cooperation with legal practitioners and academics. The main inspiration for the majority of institutes and their regulation was found in the legal texts of the former Yugoslav constituting republics, which are now members of the EU; since there are large similarities and a joint legal tradition, this is understandable.

*84.* There are a number of special legal texts in the field of consumer protection that are intended to further strengthen consumer protection, such as the Law on

86. OJM, Nos 02/14, 06/14, 43/15, 70/17, 67/19 & 146/21.

Consumer Credits[87] and the Law on Consumer Protection – Users of Financial Services.[88] Although the name of the second law suggests that it encompasses the entire area of financial services, this law actually only covers the financial services provided by banks and providers of financial leasing. These two laws contain some provisions regarding the contracts related to loan contracts and some special rules regarding the right of withdrawal in accordance with the EU rules in this area. Since the Law on Consumer Protection – Users of Financial Services was enacted at the proposal of members of Parliament and was prepared without consultation with practitioners or academics, it had major shortcomings that created problems in its implementation and the implementation of the Law on Consumer Credits. These two laws have some conflicting provisions, since both regulate the same area of financial services and implement the same directive of the EU with different degrees of protection. This was a lone example of a politically inspired law that created more problems than it sought to solve.

*85.* Although there are no special laws on consumer protection in the area of insurance, the laws that govern the area of insurance – the LI and the LO – contain some provisions regarding the protection of the interests of the insurance contractor, policyholder, beneficiary or third-party claimant. In the LI, there are special provisions on the performance of intermediation and representation in insurance and on the provision of information for the purpose of consumer protection, on the collection of information by the commission, information provided to the insurance contractor by an intermediary, that is, an insurance agent, information provided to the contractor by the insurance company, the method of resolving complaints in insurance companies, and on marketing activities and information.

*86.* Although the LO contains yielding (dispositive) norms, the provisions on insurance contracts are mandatory. Deviation from the provisions of Chapter XXXII on insurance contracts is allowed only if such a deviation is expressly permitted, as well as from those provisions that provide the contracting parties with the opportunity to act according to their wishes. So, there is a specific norm, underscoring the imperative character of the norms on insurance contracts. This is one of the guarantees to the insured that it will be protected from the insurer since the insurer is the one who usually drafts the terms of the contract. Additionally, the general rules on contract interpretation contain the provision that, in cases where the contract was concluded according to pre-printed content or when the contract was otherwise prepared and proposed by one contracting party, unclear provisions will be interpreted in favour of the other party. Since the insurance contractor or the insured is usually unable to change anything in the insurance contract, this rule goes in their favour, since they are the party that did not have the option to adjust the contractual terms to their needs. By these phrasings of the rules on insurance contracts and the general rules on contract interpretation, it is clear that the legislator was driven by the need for additional protection of the insured as an economically weaker contracting party, often unable to influence the terms of the contract.

87. OJM, Nos 35/13, 73/17, 72/19 & 08/21.
88. OJM, No. 43/15.

*87.* One of the characteristics of the norms of this law in insurance contracts is that this text introduces so-called semi-mandatory norms. Deviation from any other provisions, if not prohibited by the LO or any other law, is allowed only if the deviation is in the undoubted interest of the insured.[89] So, deviations from these types of norms are allowed only in the undoubted interest of the insured. But, as we mentioned earlier, since the insurer is the one pre-printing the content of the contract on the basis of the general or special terms and conditions, the changes are subjected to the will of the insurer, so it is questionable whether the insurer will be the one changing the terms and conditions or the text of the contract to the special needs or the wishes of the consumer. This is one of the reasons why the legislator has opted to protect the insurance contractor by establishing the previously described system.

*88.* The LO contains the rules regarding the general terms and conditions and their supervision and implementation, which are again formulated in the interest of protecting the weaker contracting party.[90] In order to further protect the weaker contracting party in insurance contracts, the LO contains rules on the special obligations of the insurer, which declare that the insurer is obliged to warn the insurance contractor that the general and special insurance conditions are an integral part of the contract and to provide the contractor with the insurer's text if these conditions are not printed on the policy itself.[91] The systematic approach of the legislator to the protection of the one contracting party in the insurance contract the insurance contractor is evident throughout the Law of Obligations.

## §6. Compulsory Insurance

*89.* Insurance in Montenegro is generally based on voluntary insurance, a reflection of the principle of party autonomy in general contract law that is also applicable in insurance law contracts. The LI, as an umbrella law in the field of insurance, guarantees the principle of party autonomy in insurance contracts, with the exception of cases in which the conclusion of the insurance contract is mandatory by the provisions of the law.[92]

*90.* Looking from the point of view of frequency, the most commonly concluded cases of compulsory insurance in Montenegro are cases of compulsory insurance of the owners of motor vehicles against liability for damages caused to third parties, followed by compulsory accident insurance of passengers on public transport. These types of mandatory insurance were present in the earlier legislative history of Montenegro. There are now many other types of compulsory insurance in

89. *See*: Article 997, LO.
90. *See*: Article 138, LO.
91. *See*: Article 999, LO.
92. *See*: Article 5, LI.

the Montenegrin legal system.[93] These new types of mandatory insurances are regulated by special laws regulating particular fields of business.

*91.* Compulsory insurance is concluded as any other contract, but failure to conclude such a contract represents a breach of law. The necessity of compulsory insurance in these cases in Montenegro is justified by the need to protect the public interest. The limitations to party autonomy exist not only because these types of contracts have to be concluded but also because there is a limitation to the content of the contracts. The party has the option to choose the insurance company with which it will sign the contract, which is the only part of party autonomy that remains.

*92.* But we must remember that party autonomy is also limited at the other end, and the insurer must also conclude a contract with any subject that presents an offer to the insurance company which fulfils the conditions under which that insurance company provides its services. In some cases, legal relations in insurance can exist even without an insurance contract, under the very provisions of the law, if certain facts are established.[94] The addition of the *bonus-malus* system to mandatory traffic insurance has somewhat improved the position of the insurer, since the insurer's autonomy in the conclusion of these types of contracts is limited.

*93.* In cases where a public transporter has not concluded a contract on accident insurance for passengers on public transport, the injured party has the right to present its claim to the association of insurance companies. Also, in cases where a motor vehicle owner has not concluded insurance against the liability for damages caused to third parties, the injured party has the right to present its claim to the association of insurance companies. The same right is granted to a party that has sustained an injury or damage by an unknown vehicle. In these cases, it is the association of insurance companies that will pay out the damages to the injured parties, but it also acquires the right of recourse to the uninsured vehicle owner or to

---

93. These types of insurance are mandatory under the provisions of the Law on Mandatory Traffic Insurance, OJM, Nos 44/12 & 146/21. According to the provisions of the same law, insurance for aircraft owners against liability for damage caused to third parties and passengers and insurance for boat owners against liability for damage caused to third parties are also mandatory. Notaries in Montenegro are obliged to conclude mandatory insurance against liability for damage caused during their work, as well as on insurance of premises and objects received on deposit in case of damage, destruction or loss (Art. 18, Law on Notaries, Nos 68/05, 49/08, 55/16 & 84/18). Authorised appraisers under the Law on Accounting are obliged to conclude mandatory insurance against liability for damage caused during their work. The auditing company and auditors are obliged to conclude mandatory insurance against liability for damage caused during their work (Law on Auditing, OJM, No. 1/17). The insurance of intermediary companies is obliged to include liability insurance for damages that may arise from the performance of activities in the amount of at least EUR 200,000 for each damage or EUR 250,000 in aggregate for one year (LI, Art. 58a). The operator of activities that pose a risk to human health and/or the environment must be insured against liability for damage and immediate danger of damage to the environment or provide another instrument of financial security. In this case, however, there is a possibility of providing another instrument of financial security, so this is not strictly the case with compulsory insurance. (*See*: Law on Liability for Environmental Damage, OJM, Nos 27/14 & 55/16, Art. 34).
94. Predrag Šulejić, *supra*, p. 72.

the insurer of the previously unknown vehicle if it was later identified and was insured.[95] By the decision of the Supreme Court of Montenegro, a claim can be made only against the owner of an uninsured vehicle and not against the driver of an uninsured vehicle because it is not proven that the driver was the 'user' of the vehicle, which by a later decision of the Supreme Court, Rev. No. 171/17, means 'registered user'.[96]

*94.* Also, in the event that the insurer is under insolvency proceedings or the insurer's licence is suspended or terminated, the injured may present their claim to the association of insurance companies and the Guarantee Fund,[97] which will acquire the right of recourse only if the insurer is under insolvency proceedings.[98] The right to compensation for damage from the funds of the Guarantee Fund is not conditioned by the date of occurrence of the damage but by the existence of outstanding damage and open insolvency proceedings against the insurance company with which the liable party had concluded a compulsory insurance contract.[99] The damage caused by the use of an uninsured vehicle with foreign registration plates is compensated by the association of insurance companies from the Guarantee Fund, with the right of recourse to the paid amount of damage, interest and costs from the competent organisation of the country where the vehicle is registered.[100] The system is designed in this way because of the specific need to protect certain categories of persons, especially those outside of the compulsory insurance contract relationship, that will suffer in the case of the failure of the person who has to conclude the compulsory insurance contract, to carry out this obligation. For the same reason, some rights are also guaranteed to persons outside of the insurance contract, even if a compulsory insurance contract is concluded. This is the reason why specific instruments are implemented so that the injured can present the claim directly to the insurer.[101]

95. *See*: Article 12, Law on Compulsory Insurance in Traffic.
96. *See*: Supreme Court of Montenegro, Rev. No. 20/20. In that regard *see also*: Supreme Court of Montenegro, Rev. No. 855/19 – the owner, i.e., the user of the vehicle, who has not concluded a contract on compulsory insurance is obliged to compensate the insurance company for the recourse claim.
97. *See*: Article 54, Law on Compulsory Insurance in Traffic.
98. *See*: Article 58, Law on Compulsory Insurance in Traffic.
99. *See*: Supreme Court of Montenegro, Rev. No. 573/12.
100. *See*: Article 40, Law on Compulsory Insurance in Traffic. In the case of the insolvency of the insurer, there is no recourse rights of the Guarantee Fund towards the insured, since in this case the motor vehicle owner had concluded an insurance contract, which was his obligation under the law. This was reiterated by the Supreme Court of Montenegro, Rev. No. 1404/09, stating that a recourse claim after payment of damages is foreseen only for the vehicle owner who has not concluded a contract on compulsory insurance.
101. Predrag Šulejić, *supra*, p. 73.

# Part I. The Insurance Company

## Chapter 1. The Insurance Company: Its Form

*95.* Insurance companies in Montenegro consist of insurance operations, co-insurance operations, reinsurance operations and services directly related to insurance operations.

*96.* Insurance operations are the conclusion of insurance contracts, the implementation of insurance contracts and obligations, and the undertaking of measures aimed at the prevention and control of the risks jeopardising the insured property or persons. Co-insurance operations are: the conclusion and implementation of insurance contracts with several insurance companies that have agreed upon joint coverage and risk sharing. Reinsurance operations are the conclusion and implementation of contracts on the reinsurance of the insured surplus risks exceeding the self-insured retention amount of an insurance company with a reinsurance undertaking.

*97.* Activities directly related to insurance business operations are defined in the LI. These activities are: insurance brokerage (intermediation) and agency; processing and assessment of risks and damages; brokerage in sales; sales of salvaged insured damaged property; and rendering other intellectual and technical services relating to insurance operations.[102] With this definition, Montenegrin legislators have created confusion since, in foreign legal texts, activities that are related to insurance are not insurance activities but rather activities that are performed by the insurance companies in order to more successfully perform the function of insuring (the repair and sale of damaged vehicles, publishing jobs, real-estate investments, etc.).[103] This confusion was common in older legal texts in the region, as was the case in Serbia's older version of the LI, which was clearly the model that was followed by the Montenegrin legislator.[104]

102. *See*: Article 13, LI, OJRM, Nos 78/06 & 19/07 and OJM, Nos 53/09, 73/10, 40/11, 45/12, 6/13, 55/16 & 146/21.
103. *See*: Jasna Pak, *supra*, p. 144–145.
104. *See*: Serbian Law on Insurance, OJRS, Nos 55/04, 70/04, 61/05, 61/05, 85/05, 101/07, 63/09 & 107/09.

*98.* The right to carry out insurance business is reserved only for companies that have been licensed by the regulatory authority in accordance with the Montenegrin Law on Insurance for specific types of insurance activities.

*99.* Insurance, co-insurance and reinsurance may be carried out by companies established in Montenegro or by a subsidiary of a foreign company licensed by the Montenegrin authority. Activities of intermediation may be carried out by an insurance intermediation company founded in Montenegro and licensed by the Montenegrin authority. The business of agency may be conducted either by insurance agency companies or by a natural person with a head office or permanent residence in Montenegro, which has been licensed by the regulatory authority to carry out insurance agency operations. Ancillary insurance services may be provided by an agency for the provision of ancillary insurance services or by a subsidiary of a foreign company with a head office in Montenegro that was licensed by the regulatory authority to carry out ancillary insurance services.[105]

## §1. Mutual Insurance, Premium Insurance, and Others

*100.* The Montenegrin Law on Insurance recognises only premium insurance companies as insurance operators in Montenegro and prescribes only one set of rules regarding the formation and registration of an insurance company. There are no rules regarding mutual insurance companies, so the rules on the operation of insurance businesses in the Montenegrin Law on Insurance start with the norms on the insurance premium as the basic income of the insurance company.[106]

*101.* An insurance company may be established by legal and natural persons if they meet the conditions prescribed by the LI. The provisions of the LI restrict the freedom of establishment of an insurance company by making the formation of a joint-stock company mandatory.[107] The designation of that fact must be contained in the official name of the company. Any change of status, name of the company or head office of an insurance company is subject to the mandatory approval of the regulatory authority.

*102.* There are not so many differences between joint-stock companies regulated by the General Law on Commercial Companies and joint-stock companies formed in accordance with the LI, since the Law on Commercial Companies applies in all those aspects not regulated by the LI. The question of the legal status of joint-stock companies is regulated by the Law on Commercial Companies.[108]

105. *See*: Article 4, LI, OJRM, Nos 78/06 & 19/07 and OJM, Nos 53/09, 73/10, 40/11, 45/12, 6/13, 55/16 & 146/21.
106. *See*: Article 82, LI.
107. *See*: Article 18, LI.
108. *See*: Vladimir Savković, *Komentar zakona o privrednim društvima*, Pravni ekspert, Podgorica, 2022, pp. 275–282.

*103.* Since the formation of an insurance company may be achieved with a contract or with a decision on the formation of the joint-stock company, there are two options for the formation of the insurance company: a single-member or a multi-member joint-stock company.[109] This is the general rule in the Law on Commercial Companies as well, but it is stipulated again in the LI because this is the rule that can be a matter of different legislative regulations.

*104.* One of the differences is in the system of foundation, which in the case of insurance companies is the system of permits, and in the case of regular joint-stock companies is the system of registration (application). The system of permits requires a permit from the competent state authority for the establishment of the company, and in some cases, this competent authority may assess the purposefulness of the establishment of the company. The system of permits is also applicable in the banking and capital market sectors, so it is not exclusively applicable in the insurance sector.[110] However, in the system of application, which is the most liberal system of company establishment, the competent authority may only inquire if the applicant has presented all the documents required by the law for its establishment, and it may not examine the validity of documents or the accuracy of data.[111]

*105.* The second difference is in the minimum amount of capital of the insurance company, which is significantly higher than the capital of regular joint-stock companies. The differences in the minimum amount of initial capital differentiate further according to the type of insurance operation that the company wishes to carry out.

*106.* The next specificities are in the rules on shareholder categories for mutual and qualified participation. Cross-ownership of capital or voting rights in insurance companies, reinsurance companies, insurance brokerage companies, and insurance agency companies is prohibited by the LI.[112] The acquisition or increase of the qualified holding in an insurance company is subject to prior approval. Also, the disposal of the shares is subject to the prior approval of the regulatory authority. Actually, any change in qualifying holdings in the capital of the company creates the obligation for the insurance company to notify the regulatory authority of that change.[113] The procedures for obtaining the consent for the qualified holding consent are set forth in the LI, as are the consequences of failure to obtain the consent for the voting rights of the owner in this case.[114] The participation of the insurance company in the capital of the insurance representation company, where there is no

109. *See*: Article 30, para. 2, LI.
110. *See*: Dragan Radonjić, *Pravo privrednih društava*, Pobjeda, Podgorica, 2008, p. 19.
111. *Ibid.*, p. 20.
112. *See*: Article 22, LI.
113. *See*: Article 23, LI.
114. *See*: Articles 25 to 29a, LI.

simultaneous participation of the representation company in the capital of the insurance company, is not considered prohibited according to the provisions of the Insurance Law.[115]

*107.* Also, the rules on the members of the organs of the insurance companies, with the special requirements set in the law and appropriate procedures for obtaining the approval of the ISA, are the next specificity of the establishment of an insurance company compared to the establishment of a regular joint-stock company. The procedure for obtaining the approval of the management members of the insurance company is also conducted in parallel with the establishment and granting of a permit for the establishment of the company. After the establishment of the insurance company, if changes in management are needed, they are conditional upon the consent of the competent authority.

*108.* Additional restrictions are set out in the LI regarding the types of insurance activities that insurance companies may carry out. One of these restrictions is that insurance companies may only engage in insurance or reinsurance activities, provided that they obtain a licence from the Montenegrin ISA. The second restriction is that the insurance company may engage in either life insurance or non-life insurance. Whichever area of insurance they choose, the companies may perform services directly related to insurance activities in accordance with the LI.[116] If the company's activity is in the area of life insurance, it may also perform activities related to associated accident insurance and voluntary health insurance with respect to healthcare expenses, provided that these classes of insurance refer to the person who concluded the life insurance contract.[117]

*109.* An insurance company may also perform voluntary pension insurance activities in accordance with a special law – the Law on Voluntary Pension Funds (LVPF),[118] but the rules on conducting voluntary pension insurance will be presented in the part of this monograph especially dedicated to private and voluntary pension insurance.

*110.* Termination of the insurance company is also an area in which the many specificities of the insurance company require differentiation from the general rules on termination of the companies set by the Law on Companies and the Law on Insolvency and Liquidation, which are the general laws in this area. The Law on the

115. *See*: Opinion of the Montenegrin Supervision Authority of 21 Jan. 2014. In this opinion it was clarified that cross-ownership would imply such a relationship where one company has a share in the capital or voting rights in another company, and the other company also has a share in the capital or voting rights in the first company. Therefore, the prohibition of cross-ownership in the capital or the right to vote refers to a relationship that has the characteristics of reciprocity in the manner described.
116. *See*: Article 19, LI.
117. *See*: Article 20, LI.
118. Law on Voluntary Pension Funds, OJRM, Nos 78/06 & 14/07 and OJM, Nos 73/10, 40/11 & 13/18.

Liquidation and Bankruptcy of Insurance Companies is a special law for the termination of insurance companies,[119] in which the application of other laws is regulated in detail.

*111.* Mutual insurance companies are discussed in the theory of insurance law in Montenegro and are part of the course curricula in insurance law, but they are not a regulated form of insurance company in Montenegro in the laws on insurance.

## §2. Public or Private Nature

*112.* The rules on insurance companies in Montenegro set by the LI are for privately owned companies. In cases where there is an expectation that private insurance companies are not able to meet the interests of the insured parties, the State of Montenegro takes on the role of the insurer. This is the case in the area of regulating the social security of citizens, so retirement and health care fall under the domain of public insurance and will be presented in the chapter especially dedicated to social security. We must emphasise that, besides the obligatory healthcare and retirement insurance, both private retirement and healthcare insurance products are options for citizens as additional protection, providing more security for retirement or more options in regard to healthcare.

*113.* In the area of bank deposits, insurance of the banking monetary deposit is realised via a special government fund, a non-profit and independent legal entity.

## §3. Factual Data

*114.* The collection of official data on insurance is done by the ISA during the course of its work on supervision of insurance companies operating in Montenegro. The official data are presented to the Montenegrin Parliament once a year in the Report on the State of the Insurance Market, which is prepared based on the analysis of statistical, financial and supervisory reports submitted to the ISA by insurance companies, insurance agency companies, insurance intermediation companies, entrepreneurs/representatives in insurance, banks that perform insurance representation, agencies for providing other services in insurance and reports of the Association, the National Bureau of Insurers of Montenegro, and other information relevant to the insurance sector.

*115.* Nine insurance companies operated in the Montenegrin insurance market in 2022, of which five companies dealt with non-life insurance, while life insurance was dealt with by four insurance companies. The total gross invoiced premium exceeded the previous results of the insurance sector and amounted to EUR 98.8 million, which represents a growth of 5.5% compared to 2020. Total penetration is

119. OJM, No. 42/15.

lower compared to 2020 and amounted to 2.01%, while the insurance density was EUR 160 and growth of 6% was recorded compared to 2020.[120]

*116.* In 2021, the insurance sector continued its profitable operations, and all nine insurance companies achieved a net profit in the total amount of EUR 8.8 million, which represents a drop of 18.3% compared to 2020. The value of assets of insurance companies at the aggregate level, as of 31 December 2021, amounted to EUR 258.2 million, which represents growth of 3.5% compared to the aggregate value of assets at the end of 2020.[121]

*117.* In 2021, a total of 860 people were (in various ways) engaged in the work of insurance companies, which represents a decrease of 3.3% compared to 2020.

*118.* The structure of the total premium by type of insurance in 2021 was the following:

Non-life insurance – 79.7%:
- Compulsory insurance of motor vehicle owners – 38.5%.
- Accident insurance – 11.2%.
- Motor vehicle (Casco) insurance – 5.9%.
- Other property insurance – 9.6%.
- Property insurance against fire and other hazards – 3.9%.
- Health insurance – 3.2%.
- General liability insurance for damage – 2.4%.
- Loan insurance – 1.5%.

Life insurance – 20.3%.[122]

120. Report on the state of the insurance market in Montenegro for 2021, p. 7.
121. *Ibid.*
122. *Ibid.*, p. 16.

## Chapter 2. Access to Business

*119.* The establishment of companies conducting insurance business, insurance companies, co-insurance companies, reinsurance companies, insurance intermediation companies, insurance agencies, or agencies providing other insurance services is subject to the fulfilment of adequate requirements prescribed by the LI. Some of the conditions are the same for all types of companies in the insurance sector, but there are some special requirements that some companies have to meet that are particular to their operations, so the LI uses the technique of referring to certain legal provisions that give certain exemptions in cases where the application of the same rule would not be pertinent or possible, or the nature of the company demands a different criterion for the licensing.

*120.* Due to the use of the system of permits in the establishment of insurance companies, the ISA has a special role in the formation of insurance companies and assesses if the formation of a particular insurance company is justifiable. There is also a list of requirements that all insurance operators have to meet in order to receive permission to conduct insurance activities.

*121.* One of the greater requirements that was mentioned in the section on insurance companies is the share capital of an insurance company. The capital of a non-life insurance company that conducts all types of insurance, a life insurance company or a reinsurance company, may not be below EUR 3 million. Only the capital of a non-life insurance company that does not operate in the areas of motor vehicle liability insurance, aircraft liability insurance, vessel liability insurance, general liability insurance, credit insurance or suretyship insurance may be EUR 2 million.[123] This amount of capital is significantly higher than the amount of capital for the foundation of any other joint-stock company in accordance with the Law on Commercial Entities due to the specificity and importance of the activity undertaken by these companies.

*122.* Cross-ownership of capital and/or voting rights in insurance companies is prohibited. The other general limitation for all types of insurance companies is the rules on mutual and qualifying participation in the capital. These rules are set in order to prevent the same person from being a member of multiple insurance companies, which would give him the opportunity to influence the management or policies of the company. The rules set the limit on the acquisition of shares to 10% of capital or voting rights and specify the terms for increasing the qualified capital or voting rights percentage. A special procedure is set for the increase of the qualified holding that would reach 20%, 33% and 50%, and additional requirements are set if the increase exceeds 30% of capital or voting rights, whereby additional documentation has to be submitted to the ISA. Also, there is a special procedure for prior

123. The amount of the share capital in all these cases is adjusted annually with changes of the European consumer prices index published by EUROSTAT, according to the provision of the LI. *See* Art. 21, paras 4 and 5, LI.

notification of intent to acquire qualifying holdings in a foreign financial institution and cooperation with the regulatory authorities of EU Member States.[124]

*123.* The qualified holding permission also forms part of the establishment checks of the ISA in the process of licensing the company. Acquisition of the qualifying holding in an insurance company without the consent of the regulatory authority is sanctioned with more than one sanction. First and most effective is the loss of voting rights in the management of the insurance company, but only for the shares that were obtained without the prior approval of the ISA. All the decisions of the corporate bodies of the insurance company, with the participation of the votes of the qualifying holders, without consent for acquisition or after consent was withdrawn, are null and void.[125] The second sanction also pertains to shares that were obtained without the prior approval of the regulator, so the investor is obliged to divest them within thirty days of the day of acquisition.[126] If the deadline is breached, none of the property and non-property-based rights may be realised by their owner until their divestment day,[127] which consequently means that the owner of these shares cannot influence the decisions of the company, nor may the owner gain any monetary compensation for ownership of shares in that insurance company.

## §1. Application for Obtaining a Licence for the Pursuit of Insurance and Reinsurance Business

*124.* Founders of the insurance or reinsurance company, or persons authorised by the founders, must present an application to the ISA to obtain a licence for the pursuit of insurance business. The list of accompanying documents is the same in insurance and reinsurance operations, with one exception regarding the content of the business plan of the reinsurance organisation.

*125.* The founders must present documentation that can be divided into four categories: common documents for all companies, documents on future insurance activities of the company, documents on the ownership structure of the company and qualified holders, and documents on the management members and organisational capabilities of the company.

*The first category* is documents that are necessary for the establishment of all joint-stock companies. These documents are a contract or memorandum of association, proposed articles of association, and an act of the Capital Market Authority that will be evidence that monetary assets equal to the minimum share capital referred to before and funds for covering foundation and other start-up expenses have been provided.

*The second category* would be documents on the business operations of the insurance company: the business plan of the insurance company for a three-year period,

124. *See*: Articles 23–26b, LI.
125. *See*: Article 29, LI.
126. *See*: Article 27, LI.
127. *See*: Article 29a, LI.

with the opinion of an authorised actuary, the proposed system for managing the insurance company, and insurance terms and conditions and premium tariffs.

*The third category* is documents on shareholders, qualified holders and persons related to the founders or qualified holders, which could indicate possible prohibited holdings to the competent authorities. The list of shareholders contains the first name, surname and permanent residence of natural persons, or the name and head office of legal entities, the number of and total nominal value of the shares, and percentages of holdings in the share capital of the insurance company. In case a person intends to acquire a qualified holding, the founders must present data about that person, accompanied by evidence of that person's general and business reputation and financial standing, especially with respect to the types of business operations performed by the insurance company. Also, the founders must present proof of the purpose of the acquisition of that qualifying holding, planned changes in the organisation and business activities of the company, and the relationship of that company with the related parties, especially for companies that will be a part of the group of related legal entities. All these documents are required in order to assess the possibility that the qualified holding would affect the ability of the insurance company to permanently fulfil the requirements under this law. The founders must present data about persons related to the founders or the qualifying holders, along with a statement about the nature of such relations.

*The fourth category* would be documentation on members of the management and on the organisational, personnel and technical capacity of the company. The founders must present documents about the professional qualifications, knowledge, experience, good reputation and integrity of the proposed members of the Board of Directors and Executive Director of the company. Also, they must present proof that management members have not been convicted of criminal offences, which would make them unworthy to discharge the function for which they are being nominated. Since all insurance companies must have an authorised auditor, the founders must present the contract or precontract on rendering actuarial services concluded with the company for performing actuarial duties, including the evidence of liability insurance against the damage that the authorised actuary could cause by a given opinion.[128]

*126.* The ISA may, in the process of deliberation, request other evidence and data of importance for deciding about the application and may invite the person nominated to be the Executive Director of the company to present the programme for managing the company's business operations. In the deliberation process on the eligibility, competences and references of the qualifying holders and nominated members of the governing and management bodies of the insurance company, the Insurance Supervisory Agency may consult and request information from the competent supervisory body in the state of the insurance company, a credit institution or the head office of an investment company, which is the parent company or has control of the insurance company in the process of licensing.

128. *See*: Article 30, LI.

*127.* The ISA has the authority to specify the detailed requirements, documents and data that will be considered proof of fulfilment of the requirements, as well as detailed criteria for assessing the eligibility of future qualifying holders, members of the Board of Directors, and the Executive Director.[129] This does not give the ISA the right to create new rules in the licensing procedure or to prescribe new conditions, but only to clarify, where clarification is needed, the documents that will be considered proof of meeting the criteria prescribed by the law.

*128.* As in the case of the requirements, the procedure for the licensing of the insurance and reinsurance organisations is set in the same way. There is only one provision pertaining to the procedure for licensing the reinsurance companies, and that refers to the corresponding application of the rules pertaining to the licensing of the insurance company.[130] The decision on the application for the licence for an insurance company will be made in a decision granting or denying the licence within ninety days of the day of submission. This decision on licensing must list all the classes of insurance in which an insurance company is licensed and may be challenged in an administrative dispute.[131] This means that the decision of the ISA is final and may not be appealed, and the administrative procedure is finished in one step. The option is to challenge this decision before the Administrative Court in Montenegro by presenting a lawsuit against the decision of the ISA.

*129.* The rejection of applications is also regulated in detail. Article 36 of the LI states that the licence will not be granted in several cases:

- failure to submit evidence on fulfilling the conditions prescribed above;
- if the founder (qualifying holder) fails to meet the requirements for obtaining consent for the acquisition of qualifying holdings;
- if the provisions of the memorandum of association, articles of association, and business act of the insurance company contravene the provisions of the law;
- if members of the managing bodies of the insurance company fail to submit the necessary evidence for their eligibility to carry out the functions of members of the managing bodies or if nominated persons fail to meet the prescribed conditions;
- if, on the basis of the articles of association of the insurance company and other acts and submitted documents and data, it may be concluded that the insurance company does not have the organisational, staffing and technical capacities to carry out insurance operations in the scope envisaged in its business plan; and
- if the insurance company fails to meet other conditions stipulated by law.

129. Based on this provision the ISA has adopted the Rulebook on Detailed Requirements for Licensing Insurance Business Activities and Criteria for Assessing the Eligibility of Future Qualifying Holders and Members of the Management Bodies No. 58/22 from June 2022.
130. *See*: Article 38, LI.
131. *See*: Article 33, LI.

*130.* After the licence is granted, the founders of the insurance company have sixty days to present the registration application to the Central Registry of the Commercial Court, which will be accompanied by the licensing decision. After the registration is made, the decision on registration must be submitted to the ISA within seven days of receiving the decision on registration. The LI uses the name of the register, which was changed in the later laws in Montenegro. Not only that, but the name of the register has also changed to the Central Register of Business Entities, but this register is now under the direct control of the Revenue and Customs Administration of Montenegro. This change was brought about in order to improve and alleviate the process of company registration since, before this, the founders had to present a similar set of documents first to the Central Registry of the Commercial Court and then to the Revenue and Customs Administration of Montenegro in order to gain access to business. This was perceived as a major business concern. This change has significantly expedited the procedure for registering companies, but in the case of insurance companies, the most complex part of company establishment is the procedure before the Capital Market Authority and Insurance Supervision Authority.

*131.* During the course of business, the insurance company must present to the licensing authority all the changes that might be relevant to the licensing. In that regard, if the insurance company intends to stop performing a certain class of insurance for which it has been licensed, it has to apply to the regulatory authority for a change of licence for the pursuit of insurance operations. Also, if the company wants to expand its insurance operation, the same procedure is applied.[132]

*132.* Revocation of the licence is also regulated by the LI if the company is not registered in the Central Register of Business Entities within sixty days following the day of granting the licence or if the company fails to commence its business operations within six months following the day of granting the licence for carrying out insurance operations.[133]

132. *See*: Article 35, LI.
133. *See*: Article 37, LI.

# Chapter 3. Supervision

*133.* The insurance sector in Montenegro is highly regulated, so the provisions on insurance supervision are numerous and encompass the supervision of all active subjects in insurance operations and all affiliated legal entities. Supervision in the area of insurance is a matter of public interest, since insurance contracts are long-term contracts, which consequently means that a long period of time can pass from conclusion of the contract until its realisation, so that the ability of the insurer to fulfil its obligation is of utmost importance, which requires the supervision of the state authorities. In general, there are two types of supervision in the insurance industry: internal, which is done within the insurance company by the set of rules prescribed by the law, and external, which is done by the regulatory authority. This is the division of supervision observed from the point of view of the organisation that performs the supervision.

*134.* Internal supervision is entrusted to actuaries and internal auditors working in the insurance companies. Internal auditors conduct internal supervision and present their quarterly and annual reports directly to the board of directors of the insurance company. Internal revision is regulated by the LI, the company's articles of association and the general act of the insurance on the conduct of internal supervision.[134]

*135.* External supervision is entrusted to the regulatory authority – the Montenegrin ISA.

*136.* The other division of supervision may be performed during solvency control of the insurance companies and supervision of the general terms and tariffs established and passed by the insurance companies. Supervision of tariffs and general terms and conditions does not exist in all areas of insurance.

## §1. Solvency Control

*137.* Solvency control is conducted during the entire existence of an insurance company, even in the phase of incorporation. In the phase of incorporation, solvency control refers to the minimal initial pecuniary capital that needs to be paid in order to meet the criteria set by the Law on Minimum Initial Capital. In this phase, the Capital Market Authority is also included in the solvency control, since this public authority is the one involved in all incorporations of joint-stock companies, which controls the issuance of shares of a joint-stock company and other securities representing a share in the capital or membership rights in companies.[135] This regulatory authority issues a confirmation of the successful issuance of securities, which is one of the documents that is checked by the ISA in the process of licensing the insurance company.

134. *See*: Articles 108–114, LI.
135. Law on the Capital Market, OJM, No. 1/18.

*138.* Solvency control during the course of business operations in insurance is comprised of supervision over the conducting of activities in accordance with the granted licence; the liquidity and solvency of the insurance company; technical reserves; the performance of obligations from the existing contracts; the deposit and investment of insurance funds; and so on. The ISA has adopted several regulations regarding solvency control, of which the one on the method of calculating the solvency margin is the most important one in the solvency control.[136] The supervision is done through direct or indirect supervision of the ISA.

*139.* Indirect supervision is supervision that is carried out through the submissions of monthly, quarterly or annual reports, the monitoring and analysis of these reports, data and notifications that the insurance company is required by law to submit to the regulatory authority. The ISA has adopted the Regulations on the content of reports and other notifications and data submitted to the ISA and on the method and deadlines of their delivery, which regulate the content and the method of submission of these reports.[137]

*140.* Direct supervision is direct insight into the operations of the insurance company, which is performed by the insurance inspectors of the ISA. Based on the performed supervision (direct or indirect), the regulatory authority may impose supervision measures in accordance with the LI and submit reports to the competent authorities in cases of reasonable suspicion that the established illegalities and irregularities contain features of a criminal offence or misdemeanour. The ISA adopted a regulation that determines a more detailed way of performing the supervision referred by the insurance companies.[138]

*141.* The solvency margin is the amount of funds that the insurance company must provide in order to permanently fulfil its obligations underinsurance contracts, and this is one of the parameters that is being closely monitored by the ISA. The LI has several provisions on the solvency margin: the way of determination of the solvency margin, assurance of the solvency margin, the capital ratio and solvency margin, guarantee capital, insurance company measures to ensure solvency, and measures of the regulatory authority with the aim of the financial recovery of the insurance company.[139]

*142.* According to the LI, the insurance company is obliged to calculate the solvency margin in the manner determined by the ISA and to ensure in its operations that the solvency margin is always at the level determined by the ISA. The insurance company is obliged to maintain capital at a level at least equal to the solvency margin, and the guarantee capital must be no less than one-third of the solvency

136. OJM, No. 14/13.
137. OJM, No. 56/21.
138. Regulation on the closer way of supervising the business of insurance companies, OJM, No. 115/22.
139. *See*: Articles 96–99a, LI.

margin. The LI prescribes two sets of measures: the measures of the insurance company that must be implemented in the case of solvency problems and the ones that may be undertaken by the regulatory authority with the aim of financial recovery for the insurance company.

*143.* The insurance company must undertake measures to ensure solvency. In the case of a decrease in the capital or the guarantee capital to below the level set in the LI, the insurance company must notify the regulatory authority in writing without delay and within fifteen days of the date of determination of that decrease must adopt a programme of measures, without delay, in order to reach the required amount of capital or guarantee capital.[140]

*144.* The ISA has at its disposal the measures that it can undertake in order to achieve the financial recovery of the insurance company. In the event that the rights of the insured are threatened due to the compromised ability of the company to fulfil its obligations under the insurance contract, the regulatory authority may order the insurance company to take one of three measures.[141]

*145.* The first measure is to adopt a financial plan for a period of at least three years, with a proposal for measures to maintain or rehabilitate the company's financial condition. This financial plan shall contain: an estimate of the costs of implementing the insurance; a detailed assessment of the income and expenses from direct insurance business; a proposal of a balance sheet and income statement; a calculation of the solvency margin, capital and guarantee capital; assessment of the necessary funds to cover all insurance obligations; and a reinsurance policy. The second measure, based on the financial plan, may be to order the insurance company to provide capital in an amount greater than the amount determined by this law. The third measure may be to prohibit the insurance company from freely disposing of its assets. Also, the LI gives the ISA the possibility to prohibit or limit the payment of dividends to the shareholders of an insurance company if the payment of the dividend would impair the solvency of the insurance company or if it assesses that the payment of the dividend would endanger the interests and rights of the insured or insurance beneficiary.[142]

*146.* Other measures that may be taken by the ISA are the measures granted by the general rules on supervision. In exercising supervision over the operations of an insurance company, the ISA may impose one of six possible measures: (1) warn the insurance company in writing and request for the irregularities established in its operation to be corrected by a specified deadline; (2) order measures to correct illegalities and irregularities; (3) order special measures against responsible persons in the company; (4) order the transfer of the insurance portfolio to another insurance

140. *See*: Article 99, LI.
141. *See*: Article 99a, LI.
142. *See*: Article 104, LI.

company; (5) introduce an interim administration in the company; or (6) revoke the licence for the carrying out of specific or all insurance activities.[143]

*147.* The ISA may impose the first measure on the insurance company if the irregularities established in its operation do not affect directly and substantially the financial operations of the company or the rights of insured persons or insurance contract beneficiaries and could have a substantial effect on the financial operations of the company and the rights of insured persons or insurance contract beneficiaries.

*148.* The second group of measures may be undertaken in order to correct illegalities and irregularities in the insurance company's operations. If the ISA establishes that the insurance company has breached the risk management rules prescribed by the law, it will order the insurance company to ensure:

- the co-insurance and reinsurance of excess risks above the self-insured retention;
- the payment of claims, the contracted insured sums, and execution of insurance-related obligations; capital in the prescribed amount;
- the stipulated technical reserves;
- the liquidity of the company;
- the depositing and investing of funds of technical provisions in line with the prescribed amount and structure; the depositing and investing of capital funds in line with the prescribed amount and structure;
- the alignment of the capital and solvency margin, or the guaranteed capital and solvency margin; the meeting of obligations pertaining to risk management established under this law.

In addition, the ISA may:

- prohibit the entering into of new insurance contracts for specific or all classes of insurance and the expansion of undertaken obligations;
- order the termination of an insurance contract, insurance brokerage contract or insurance agency contract if application thereof would cause damage to the company;
- limit the risk level to be assumed by the company;
- prohibit the execution of certain payments; prohibit transactions with specific shareholders, members of managing bodies of the company, related parties, or other legal persons;
- order the appointment of an adviser for segments of operations where illegalities and irregularities are established;
- order a change of the organisation of work; order the collection of receivables; prohibit or limit temporarily the disposal of assets;
- order the updating of business books, the inventory of assets and liabilities, reconciling receivables and liabilities, and assessment of balance and off-balance items;

143. See: Article 129, LI.

- order the improvement of electronic data processing systems;
- order the improvement of the organisation and manner of carrying out the internal audit;
- order the undertaking of other activities in accordance with law.[144]

*149.* The third group of measures are special measures against responsible persons in the insurance company, which may be instituted against board members, executive directors or persons with special authorisations who have failed to act in accordance with the law, the general acts of the company, imposed measures, or who have committed repeated breaches of the obligation to report to and notify the regulatory authority. The measures may be the dismissal of a member of the Board of Directors, the Executive Director of the company, or a person with special authorisations, or a temporary prohibition from performing insurance business for a member of the board of directors, the executive director or a person with special authorisations. If there is a criminal proceeding for the described activities underway, the ISA may propose that such a person be suspended until the termination of criminal proceedings. In the case that the employment relationship was terminated due to one of the reasons described above, such a person may not be employed or otherwise participate in the activities of a person related to the insurance company for a period of five years, starting from the day such a measure was imposed.[145]

*150.* The fourth measure may be imposed when the regulatory authority establishes illegalities and irregularities in the operations of an insurance company that may jeopardise or are already jeopardising its ability to meet its obligations arising from the pursuit of insurance activities. In this case, the ISA may order the company to transfer its insurance portfolio to another insurance company.[146]

*151.* The fifth measure may be the institution of an interim administration in an insurance company for a period of up to one year if: the company fails to meet its obligations under insurance contracts or will not be able to do so at maturity; the assets of the company are not sufficient to provide contractual protection to the insured persons or creditors of the company; part of the assets recorded in business books or other company records, or the assets under the company management are not appraised and stated in the prescribed manner; the capital is at such a level, or its level is decreasing to such a degree, that it may have harmful consequences for insured persons or creditors of the company; the company has established or stated the results of its operations in an incorrect or illegal manner; or the company fails to act in compliance with the measures imposed by the regulatory authority.[147] The provisions on the interim administration are numerous, but we will present the ones relevant for solvency, which pertain to an increase in the share capital for the assurance of economic stability of the insurance company. If the ISA, on the basis of the report of an interim administrator, estimates that the share capital of the company

144. *See*: Article 130, LI.
145. *See*: Article 146, LI.
146. *See*: Article 133, LI.
147. *See*: Article 134, LI.

needs to be increased with new monetary investments in order to ensure matching of the capital and solvency margin of the insurance company or to correct the reasons for the illiquidity of the company, it may order the interim administrator of the company to convene a general meeting of shareholders and to propose the adoption of a decision on such an increase of the share capital. The interim administrator must publish the notification no later than eight days after the day of receipt of the order from the ISA. In this notification, shareholders must be warned about the legal consequences of failing to adopt the decision on the increase in capital or of the unsuccessful issuing of shares in the notification about the convening of the general meeting of shareholders.[148]

*152.* As the toughest measure, the measure of revocation of the licence for the carrying out of specific or all insurance activities may be undertaken by the ISA if: the company fails to maintain capital in the prescribed amount; illegalities and irregularities in the operations of the company are established, and further carrying out of insurance activities would jeopardise the interests of the insured persons and other insurance beneficiaries; the company does not conduct its business activity in accordance with trade rules, good business practices and business ethics; the company fails to comply with a measure imposed by the regulatory authority within the prescribed deadline, or fails to correct the reasons for imposing such a measure; the company fails to enable supervision; etc. Licence revocation does not release the insurance company from its obligations under the insurance contracts.[149] These are the cases of optional revocation of the licence, so there are instances in which the LI prescribes mandatory licence revocation.[150]

## §2. Supervision of Tariffs and Insurance Conditions

*153.* Supervision of the tariffs and insurance conditions is not part of the standard procedures in the licensing of insurance companies, and there is no general obligation of the insurance company to present its tariffs and terms and conditions to the supervising authority for prior supervision before it can start concluding insurance contracts based on those tariffs. This type of supervision is used only as an exception in the one area of insurance in which there is an obvious public interest in supervision.

*154.* This exception exists in the area of compulsory traffic insurance, where insurance companies are obliged to present their tariffs and conditions for validation. There was a five-year transitional period for the application of this provision of the Law on Compulsory Insurance in Traffic, after which all insurance companies had to present their individual tariffs and conditions for supervision. During this transitional period, all insurance companies were, as members of the Association of Insurers, obliged to prepare a joint proposal of terms and conditions and a premium

148. *See*: Article 140, LI.
149. *See*: Article 144, LI.
150. *See*: Article 145, LI.

tariff, as well as the technical bases for calculation of the premium in line with actuarial principles, insurance profession rules and the general principles regulating the insurance business, and submit the same to the Regulatory Authority for approval within 180 days of the date of this law entering into force.[151]

*155.* Since the Law on Compulsory Insurance in Traffic was introduced in 2012, this provision is no longer in force; now, the general provisions of this law are the ones being implemented. Now, insurance companies are free to determine the insurance terms and conditions and premium tariffs in accordance with the bases for calculation of the premium and the premium structure (premium system) for compulsory traffic insurance, but they must submit them to the ISA sixty days prior to the commencement of their application for the purpose of verification of their compliance with the law and professional rules.[152]

*156.* Insurance companies must also submit the premium tariffs and premium systems, including the technical bases for the calculation of the tariff to the ISA, for the purpose of verifying their compliance with the law, actuarial principles and professional rules. This request must be accompanied by the opinion of a certified actuary on the sufficiency of the insurance premium for the permanent settlement of all liabilities under the compulsory insurance contract and insurance administration costs, as well as a three-year business plan of the company illustrating the sufficiency of the calculated premiums. The ISA may propose adjustments to the premium tariffs, premium system or technical basis for the calculation of the tariff, if it finds that they are not compliant with the law, actuarial principles and professional rules.[153] The rules described in this paragraph will cease to be in force after Montenegro's accession to the EU.[154]

151. *See*: Article 69, LI.
152. *See*: Article 10, LMIT.
153. *See*: Article 10, paras 3–6, LMIT.
154. *See*: Article 69a, LMIT.

# Chapter 4. Technical Reserves and Investments

## §1. Technical Reserves

*157.* A technical reserve is a reserved part of the funds that an insurance company must establish and is intended to cover the obligations that could arise based on the carrying out of insurance operations. The amounts of funds are determined at the end of the accounting period based on the rules of actuarial mathematics, statistical data and insurance practices. The criteria and manner of calculation of technical reserves are determined by the regulations of the ISA. There are several types of technical reserves that need to be formed depending on the field of insurance in which the insurance company is operating. In that regard, there is a differentiation between companies in life insurance, non-life insurance, credit insurance and unit-linked insurance.

*158.* All insurance companies must establish reserves for unearned premiums, reserves for outstanding claims, reserves for bonuses and discounts, and other technical reserves. These are the only types of reserves that non-life insurance companies have to establish. Life insurance companies and companies that are engaged in insurance of a multi-annual duration, where savings funds are accumulated for risk coverage in the forthcoming years of insurance and where probability tables are applied, as well as calculations applicable to life insurances, must establish mathematical reserves in addition to the previously stated reserves.[155] An insurance company engaged in credit insurance activities must establish a risk equalisation reserve for this class of insurance in addition to the reserves common to all types of insurance companies. An insurance company engaged in insurance activities where an insured person undertakes an investment risk (unit-linked insurance) must establish special technical reserves for such insurance.

*159.* Unearned premiums are established from the total insurance premium, separately for each class of insurance, in proportion to the duration of insurance, and are used to cover insurance obligations that will occur in the forthcoming accounting period.[156] Outstanding claims are established in an amount equal to the assessed liabilities for claims incurred and reported but not paid and for claims incurred but not reported in the current period. If claims for certain classes of insurance appear in the form of annuities, the outstanding claims are established in a capitalised amount that represents the amount of all future obligations.[157] Bonus-malus reserves are established up to the level of compensations and other payments the insured persons and other insurance beneficiaries are entitled to and which arise from: the right to participate in profit or other rights under an insurance contract (bonus); the rights to a partial reduction of a premium (discounts); and the right to compensation of a

155. *See*: Article 83, LI.
156. *See*: Article 84, LI.
157. *See*: Article 85, LI.

part of a premium resulting from an unused period of insurance coverage due to premature contract termination (cancellation).[158]

*160.* A mathematical reserve is established in an amount equal to the present value of the future liabilities of an insurance company, reduced by the present value of future obligations of a policyholder (insurance premium) and is calculated separately for each insurance contract.[159] Risk equalisation reserves are used for the equalisation of unbalanced occurrences of claims in such classes of insurance where significant discrepancies in the annual amount of claims can be expected based on statistical data.[160] Other technical reserves are established with respect to specific future liabilities and risks against large claims caused by earthquakes or floods, claims from nuclear liability insurance, producer liability for pharmaceutical products, as well as other liabilities and risks for which reserves were not established in life insurance, non-life insurance and credit insurance.[161]

## §2. Investment

*161.* Assurance of the real value of monetary assets is one of the problems that need to be addressed by the insurance company. The conditions and limitations of the investment of the reserve deposit are regulated by the LI and other acts of the ISA. The rules respect the need for investment of idle (unused) funds but are aimed at ensuring that insurance companies maintain constant liquidity and pay claims and other obligations in a timely manner. The idle funds of technical reserves are determined by reducing the total technical reserves on the day of determination by the due obligations from those funds. The special process of supervision is established regarding the investment of idle funds, so it is the obligation of the insurance company to present to the ISA quarterly reports on the depositing and the investment of the funds.[162]

*162.* A restriction on the depositing and investing of the technical reserves is set by the LI, so insurance companies in Montenegro may deposit and/or invest these funds in: securities issued by Montenegro, central banks and the governments of foreign countries that have at least an 'A' rating or its equivalent awarded by widely-accepted, internationally recognised rating agencies; bonds or other debt securities traded on the organised security market in Montenegro; bonds, or other debt securities not traded on the organised securities market, if the issuer is a legal person with its registered office in Montenegro; shares traded on the organised securities market in Montenegro; and with banks that have their head offices in Montenegro.

158. *See*: Article 86, LI.
159. *See*: Article 87, LI.
160. *See*: Article 88, LI.
161. *See*: Article 88a, LI.
162. *See*: Article 89, LI.

The LI has authorised the Ministry of Finance to establish limitations of the technical provisions for deposits and investments and to prescribe other types of depositing and investing of technical provisions funds, that are, with respect to safety, yield and marketability, adequate for depositing and investing.[163]

*163.* The ISA has adopted the Rules on depositing and investing funds from the technical reserves of the insurance company, which have widened the list of investment and deposit opportunities, and set limitations on each investment and/or deposit. These Rules have granted the possibility of investment in immovable property, debt securities issued by another country or central bank of an EU Member State or Organization for Economic Cooperation and Development (OECD) Member State or international financial organisation, or securities guaranteed by another country or central bank of an EU Member State or OECD Member State, bonds and other debt securities issued by municipalities in Montenegro or EU Member States or OECD Member States, debt securities of foreign legal persons traded on a stock exchange market in the countries where they are registered, shares of foreign legal persons, interests of reinsurers in technical reserves, loans to legal entities secured by a lien on real estate, investment units of investment funds that are registered in Montenegro, an EU Member State or an OECD Member State. The funds of the mathematical reserve may be invested in advances and loans given to policyholders up to the amount of the purchase value of the insurance based on a life insurance contract. Funds of technical reserves may be deposited and invested in the property of persons related to the insurance company, in total up to 20% of the total amount of technical reserves, and individually up to the limits established by the Rules. All these investments are regulated and may be made only if they meet the conditions described in detail in the Rules on investment.[164]

*164.* The limits of total deposit and investment are set in the Rules, so the insurance company may invest up to: 30% into immovable property; 30% in total in bonds and other debt securities whose issuer is a local self-government unit in Montenegro, an EU Member State or an OECD Member State, and bonds and other debt securities for which a local self-government unit in Montenegro, an EU Member State or a state member of the OECD has issued a guarantee to; 30% in other bonds, debt securities and shares; 100% in the deposits in banks with a business office in Montenegro; 25% in bonds, or other debt securities that are traded on the regulated securities market in Montenegro; 30% in shares traded on the regulated securities market in Montenegro; 5% in bonds, or other debt securities that are not traded on the regulated securities market, if the issuer is a legal entity based in Montenegro; 3% in the business account of the insurance company; 25% in investment units of investment funds that are registered in Montenegro, an EU Member State or an

163. *See*: Articles 90 and 91, LI.

164. *See*: Article 6 of the Rules on depositing and investing funds of technical reserves of the insurance company, OJM, No. 141/22.

OECD Member State, and for investments in investment funds managed by the same management company or investment funds are interconnected entities up to 15%; 5% in loans to legal entities.[165]

*165.* Also, the rules set the limits of individual investments, so insurance companies may invest up to: 10% in one real estate, or in several real estates that are connected to each other and represent one investment; up to 20% in the securities of the same issuer, bonds and other debt securities whose issuer is a local self-government unit in Montenegro, an EU Member State or an OECD Member State, and bonds and other debt securities for which a local self-government unit in Montenegro has issued a guarantee to an EU Member State or a Member State of the OECD; 10% in other bonds, debt securities and shares of the same issuer bonds and other debt securities; 20% in deposits with one bank based in Montenegro; 5% in bonds, or other debt securities that are traded on the regulated securities market in Montenegro; 5% in shares of one issuer traded on the regulated securities market in Montenegro; up to 1% in bonds, or other debt securities of one issuer that are not traded on the regulated securities market, if the issuer is a legal entity with its head office in Montenegro; up to 10% in investment units of one investment fund; and 1% in loans of one legal entity.[166]

*166.* When investing the funds of the mathematical reserve, special rules apply in relation to those described in the previous paragraphs, so that the restrictions on the total level are up to: 25% in shares traded on the organised securities market in Montenegro; 40% in real estate; 30% in advances and loans given to policyholders together up to the amount of the purchase value of the insurance based on a life insurance contract. These restrictions also apply to the total technical reserves formed by the life insurance company.[167]

*167.* Funds of special reserves for benefits secured by an insurance contract that are directly related to investment values are deposited and invested with the following limits up to 50% in the investment units of one investment fund; and 70% in the investment units of investment funds that are managed by the same management company or if the investment funds are interconnected entities. In this particular case, the total net assets of an individual fund may not be less than EUR 100 million.[168]

*168.* With the new ISA rules on depositing and investing funds in technical reserves, the insurance companies now have more opportunities to invest the funds since the provision on investment from the LI is supplemented by a new type of

---

165. *See*: Article 7, para. 1, item 1, Rules on depositing and investing funds of technical reserves of the insurance company, OJM, No. 141/22.
166. *See*: Article 7, para. 1, item 2, Rules on depositing and investing funds of technical reserves of the insurance company, OJM, No. 141/22.
167. *See*: Article 8, Rules on depositing and investing funds of technical reserves of the insurance company, OJM, No. 141/22.
168. *See*: Article 8, Rules on depositing and investing funds of technical reserves of the insurance company, OJM, No. 141/22.

investment and a clearer set of limitations for individual investments is given so that the control of the investment of the insurance companies by the ISA may be more efficient.

## Chapter 5. Accountancy

*169.* The field of accountancy in Montenegro is regulated by the Law on Accountancy[169] and the Law on Auditing.[170] These laws govern the conditions and manner for keeping business books, the preparation and presentation of financial statements, as well as the conditions and manner for conducting procedures and performing audits of financial statements and other issues important for accounting and auditing. The Law on Auditing also prescribes the obligation of some companies to have internal auditors, but the LI also contains some provisions on auditing that are relevant.

*170.* According to the provisions of the Law on Accounting, legal entities are obliged to prepare financial statements according to the International Accounting Standards (IAS) or according to the International Financial Reporting Standards (IFRS), which were published by the International Accounting Standards Board (IASB) and determined and published by the state administration body responsible for financial affairs, or the legal entity entrusted with the performance of those affairs, and which were obtained from the appropriate authority, and which the International Federation of Accountants (IFAC) obtained the right to translate and publish.[171] Insurance companies are obliged to, in written and electronic form, prepare and submit annual and quarterly financial reports to the ISA. These reports are published on the website of the ISA. The content, deadlines and methods of preparation and submission of insurance company reports are prescribed by the ISA.[172] The Law on Accounting also prescribes the content of the auditing report.[173] The rules of this law are relevant for the operation of insurance companies.

*171.* The obligation to audit insurance companies is set by the Law on Auditing, as these are legal entities of public interest.[174] Regardless of the classification of legal entities as micro, small, medium or large, insurance companies have the same obligation as large companies, since large companies are also companies of public interest according to the Law on Auditing. One of the obligations set forth in the Law on Auditing is not mandatory for all companies, but it is the obligation of insurance companies in particular, and this is to appoint an auditing committee of at least three members, of which at least one member must have knowledge in the field of accounting and auditing and must not be an employee, shareholder or member of the management body of the insurance company.[175] The audit committee: follows the procedure of financial reporting; monitors the effectiveness of the legal entity's internal control and internal audit; monitors the audit of annual and consolidated financial statements prescribed by law; monitors the independence of the engaged

169. OJM, Nos 145/21 & 152/21.
170. OJM, No. 1/17.
171. *See*: Article 5, Law on Accounting.
172. *See*: Article 18, Law on Accounting.
173. *See*: Article 13, Law on Accounting.
174. *See*: Article 29, Law on Auditing.
175. *See*: Article 30, Law on Auditing.

authorised auditors or audit companies, which perform the audit, as well as contracts for the use of additional services in accordance with the law; makes recommendations to the assembly of the joint-stock company or to the founders, on the selection of the company for auditing or authorised auditor; and considers the plans and annual reports of internal control, as well as other issues related to financial reporting and auditing.[176]

*172.* According to the provisions of the Law on Auditing, a large legal entity is required to have an internal auditor or a separate organisational unit that conducts internal audits,[177] but the system in the insurance companies regulated by the LI is to have a separate organisational unit that will operate autonomously and independently, based on the provisions of the Articles of Association, and is directly responsible for its work to the Board of Directors of the company.[178] So, the system of internal auditing in insurance companies that is in implementation in Montenegro is the one prescribed in the LI. The internal audit of the insurance company assesses: the adequacy and effectiveness of the internal control systems in the insurance company; the compliance of the insurance company's operations with the law, regulations and the company's established policies and practices; the adequacy and application of the prescribed risk control policies and procedures; the quality and reliability of the electronic data processing systems; and the accuracy, timeliness and reliability of the accounting, financial and other reports and records.[179]

*173.* The conditions for nomination of the internal auditor in the insurance companies, the annual internal audit work programme, internal audit reports, and the rules on notification to the insurance company's board of directors if an internal audit finds that an insurance company is not acting in accordance with the risk management rules and the insurance company, is thus threatened by illiquidity or insolvency or realises that the safety of the company's operations or the interests of insured persons are compromised, are prescribed in the LI.[180]

*174.* The annual financial report, together with the opinion of an authorised actuary and the opinion of an external auditor, must be discussed and adopted at the insurance company's general shareholders' meeting.[181] According to the LI, auditing of the financial reports of the insurance company will be done in accordance with the law governing auditing of financial reports, unless otherwise prescribed by the LI for certain issues.[182]

*175.* The special rules on audits in the LI refer to the appointment of the auditor at the general meeting of the shareholders, which is subject to the prior approval of the ISA. The auditor must not be related in any way to the insurance company, may

176. *See*: Article 31, Law on Auditing.
177. *See*: Article 33, Law on Auditing.
178. *See*: Article 108, LI.
179. *See*: Article 110, LI.
180. *See*: Articles 110–114, LI.
181. *See*: Article 106, LI.
182. *See*: Article 168, LI.

not provide consulting or tax services to this company, and may not be nominated as auditor for more than four consecutive years. The auditor is considered a related party if more than half of the auditor's revenue in the previous year was made by auditing the financial reports of such an insurance company. If there is a breach of these rules, the ISA may order a new audit.[183]

*176.* The content of the auditor's report and its obligations to notify the ISA are prescribed by the LI, along with authorising the ISA to prescribe a more detailed content of the external auditor's report.[184] The deadlines for submission of the auditor's report are set in the Law on Auditing, so the insurance companies are required to submit to the administrative body responsible for taxes an audit report with the auditor's opinion on the financial statements, in paper and electronic form, no later than 30 June of the current year for the previous year.

*177.* During the supervision, the ISA may request the external auditor's report to be verified by another auditor appointed by the regulatory authority if there are reasons to doubt the correctness of the external auditor's opinion. If the new auditor confirms the report, the cost of the audit is borne by the ISA, but if not, the cost is borne by the first auditor, and the ISA has the obligation to notify the authority that is in charge of supervision of auditors of the established omissions and irregularities in the audit report and the external auditor's work during the audit of the insurance company.[185] The summary of the audited financial report shall be published in at least one printed media outlet distributed in the entire territory of Montenegro within thirty days of the day of adoption.[186]

183. *See*: Article 168, LI.
184. *See*: Article 169, LI.
185. *See*: Article 171, LI.
186. *See*: Article 172, LI.

## Chapter 6. Taxation of the Company

*178.* In the Montenegrin tax system, insurance companies, like any other legal entity that performs activities for the purpose of obtaining profit, are obliged to pay corporate taxes, as regulated by the Law on Corporate Tax.[187] The basis for corporate taxes is the taxable income of the company.[188] The taxable profit is determined by adjusting the taxpayer's profit shown in the income statement in the manner provided by the law. Losses resulting from business relations, excluding those resulting in capital gains and losses, may be transferred forward against the profit generated in future assessment periods but not exceeding five years.[189]

*179.* Corporate income tax rates in Montenegro are progressive. The tax rate on the amount of taxable profit up to EUR 100,000.00 is 9%; from EUR 100,000.01 to EUR 1,500,000.00, the tax is EUR 9,000.00 + 12% of the amount exceeding EUR 100,000.01; and on amounts over EUR 1,500,000.01, the tax is EUR 177,000.00 + 15% of the amount exceeding EUR 1,500,000.01.[190]

*180.* The tax period for which the profit tax is calculated is the financial year, which is a calendar year, except in the case of liquidation or commencement of activities during the year.[191]

187. OJRM, Nos 65/01, 12/02 & 80/04 and OJM, Nos 40/08, 86/09, 40/11, 14/12, 61/13, 55/16, 146/21 & 152/22.
188. *See*: Article 6, para. 1, Corporate Tax Law.
189. *See*: Article 25, Corporate Tax Law.
190. *See*: Article 28, Corporate Tax Law.
191. *See*: Article 39, Corporate Tax Law.

# Part II. The Insurance Contract – General

## Chapter 1. Generalities

### §1. Characteristics of the Insurance Contract

*181.* Insurance contracts are regulated by the LO and are usually categorised as: named, consensual, mutually binding, onerous, causal, formal, continuous, successive, adhesion, aleatory and *uberimae fidei* contracts. It may be a contract of commercial trade or a civil contract, depending on the status of the contracting party seeking to cover the risk. The norms on insurance contracts in the Montenegrin Law on Obligations correspond to the old Yugoslavian Law on Obligations from 1978.

*182.* An insurance contract is considered a named contract, since it is regulated in the LO, which is the primary legislation in the field of contracts and also defines an insurance contract. The basic definition of an insurance contract in the Law of Obligations is the following: By a contract of insurance, a contractor of insurance shall assume the obligation to pay a specific amount to an insurance organisation (insurer), while the organisation shall assume the obligation, should an event take place that represents the case covered by insurance, to pay to the insured person, or to a third party, compensation, the stipulated amount, or to do something else.[192]

*183.* The insurance contract is a consensual contract since concurrence of the wills of the contracting parties is needed for the creation of the contract. All other acts of the parties are not necessary for the creation of the contract. One of the contracting parties – the insurer – is highly limited by the law, which states that only the insurance organisation may assume the obligation to provide compensation for the realisation of risk. However, there are almost no limitations on the other contracting party, except for those limitations that are required for the conclusion of all contracts, so any legal entity and natural person may be the other contracting party in the insurance contract.

*184.* The insurance contract is a mutually binding contract. This means that the obligation of one party is the basis for the obligation of the other party. Both parties are debtors, the insurer – for the obligation that can arise in the case of the realisation of the insured risk, and the insurance contractor – for the obligation of paying premiums.

192. *See*: Article 994, LO.

*185.* The onerousness of the insurance contract is evident since the obligation of the insurer is opposed by the obligation of the contracting party to pay premiums. The difference between onerous and favouritism contracts is significant because there is a difference in the general rules on the interpretation of the provisions of these two types of contracts.[193] Also, it is evident that an insurance contract is a causal contract, since the grounds for the obligations of both sides are evident within this contract.

*186.* According to the provisions of the LO, an insurance contract is a formal contract, since it is concluded after the contracting parties sign an insurance policy or list of coverage. Following the general rule of formal contracts, even the offer made to the insurer must be in written form.[194] As a general principle, the informality of the contracts is evident in the Montenegrin Law on Obligations, but in the case of an insurance contract, the written form is the rule, since the legislators consider that there is a need for protection of the private interests of the contracting parties in insurance. There are some exceptions to the rules on the formality of the insurance contract.

*187.* As some of the obligations of the insurance contracts are spread over the whole contract duration, the insurance contract is a continuous contract. The obligation of the insured party to present any changes in circumstances relevant to the risk assessment is present throughout the entire contract duration, as is the obligation of the insurer to be ready to pay in the event of the risk realisation. One of the consequences of the continuous nature of the insurance contract is in the rules on withdrawal, so the withdrawal has effects only from the moment of the withdrawal. Any obligations that arise before withdrawal from the contract are fully valid and must be fulfilled.

*188.* An insurance contract is very often a successive contract, since the obligations of the parties can have a periodical character. This is most evident in the obligation of the insurance contractor, since this party usually has the obligation to periodically pay the matured part of the premium. A special set of rules exists for successive contracts, since the influence of time can have serious effects on the performance of this type of contract, so these contracts may be modified or terminated due to the change in circumstances. When there is a change in the circumstances regarding the risk of the insurance, the general rules do not apply, since special rules are instituted in the part of the law dealing with insurance contracts.[195] Also, the successiveness of the contract has an effect on the statute of limitations of successive obligations.[196]

*189.* Whereas insurance contracts are concluded daily and *en masse*, there has been a certain standardisation and equalisation of contractual conditions, so the

193. *See*: Article 99, LO.
194. *See*: Article 998, paras 1 and 2, LO.
195. *See*: Articles 1011–1013, LO.
196. *See*: Article 381, LO.

insurer is the one that adopts the terms and conditions that will apply to all contracts and the contracting party can only agree to their use. This feature classifies insurance contracts as adhesion contracts, thus creating the need for the protection of the other contracting side in insurance contracts. The supervision of the terms and conditions is one of the mechanisms used for providing balance, while the others are the use of imperative legal norms that protect the contracting party and that cannot be changed by the insurer. Also, there are special rules on the interpretation of these types of contracts that go in favour of the economically weaker side in the contract and cannot influence the content of the terms and conditions.[197]

*190.* One of the main characteristics of an insurance contract is that it is an aleatory contract. At the moment of contract conclusion, the contracting parties do not know whether the obligation of one party will arise, since this is contingent upon the occurrence of the uncertain circumstance, and they do not know what the amount of that obligation will be, if there is the realisation of that uncertain circumstance. The other contracting party does not know if it will suffer some loss, but this party knows its obligation – the payment of the premium. The question is whether the premium is economically justified. In an insurance contract, the insured party is trying to avoid the loss and is entering into the contract to be sure that in the case of an unfavourable event, the loss will be covered by the insurance. In this regard, there is a difference between insurance and gambling contracts, since this contracting party does not seek the *alea*, this party is not entering into a contract because it expects a gain from the realisation of the uncertain circumstance, but on the contrary, it is trying to protect itself and to receive the amount in accordance with the rules on indemnification.[198] Uncertainty of the occurrence is one of the conditions for the conclusion of an insurance contract, so an insurance contract is void if, at the time of its conclusion, the insured event has already occurred, it is in the process of occurring, or it is certain that it will occur, or if the possibility of its occurrence has already ceased at that time.[199] Consequently, this means that the *alea* is the focal point of the insurance contract and its main characteristic.

*191.* An insurance contract is an *uberimae fidei* contract, and the good faith of the contracting parties in relations before, during and after the contract conclusion is of the utmost importance. Bona fide is one of the main principles in the LO and is consequently reflected in insurance relations. By some accounts, an insurance contract requires a higher level of bona fide than all other contracts.[200] This characteristic has consequences for both sides of the insurance contract. The contracting party has obligations to report all the relevant circumstances for risk assessment, and the insurer has the obligation to be efficient and speedy in the calculation and payment of damages.[201]

197. *See*: Article 98, LO.
198. *See*: Predrag Šulejić, *supra,* p. 170.
199. *See*: Article 995, para. 2, LO.
200. *See*: Jasna Pak, *Pravo osiguranja (Insurance Law),* Univerzitet Singidunum, Beograd, 2011, p. 190.
201. *See*: Predrag Šulejić, *supra,* p. 175.

## §2. Interpretation of an Insurance Contract

*192.* The provisions concerning the interpretation of contracts in the Montenegrin Law on Obligations are of a general nature, meaning that these rules apply regardless of the kind of contract in question,[202] so they apply to the interpretation of the insurance contract.

*193.* The first rule is that the terms of a contract must be implemented in the way they are worded. When controversial provisions are interpreted, the literal meaning of the terms employed should not be followed. The interpreter should instead inquire into the joint intention of the contracting parties and understand the provision in accordance with the principles of the Law of Obligations.[203] The joint intention of the contracting parties shall be established according to what one of the parties has actually declared and how the other party was supposed to understand it. If this is impossible to establish, one should inquire what the intention of a reasonable person of the same character in the same situation would be. A particular meaning of the intention of one side, of which the other party could not have been unaware, constitutes the interpretation of that particular meaning.[204]

*194.* The circumstances relevant for interpretation are the circumstances in which it was concluded, preceding negotiations, the conduct of the contracting parties subsequent to the conclusion of the contract, the nature and purpose of the contract, the interpretation that has already been given to similar clauses by parties and the practices they have established between themselves, the meaning commonly given to provisions and expressions in specific professions or branches of activity, as well as the principles of good faith and fair dealing.[205]

*195.* When a contract is concluded in conformity with a form printed in advance or prepared and proposed in some other way by one of the contracting parties, any unclear provisions shall be interpreted so as to benefit the other party.[206] This rule applies in the interpretation of almost all insurance contracts, since almost all are concluded by the use of the pre-printed text of the contract.

*196.* A special rule is set as a supplementary rule in the interpretation of contracts so that the unclear provisions in a contract without consideration should be interpreted in a way that is less burdensome for the debtor, while in the case of an onerous contract, it should be in such a way that establishes an equitable relationship between mutual considerations.[207] The part of this rule on onerous contracts can benefit the interpretation of insurance contracts in cases where the use of the previous rule does not yield results.

---

202. *See*: Articles 95–100, LO.
203. *See*: Article 95, LO.
204. *See*: Article 96, LO.
205. *See*: Article 97, LO.
206. *See*: Article 98, LO.
207. *See*: Article 99, LO.

*197.* Additional rules on out-of-court interpretations of the scope and meaning of terms by a third party are established by the LO, but they can be implemented only if the contracting parties have agreed on them. In a dispositive legal norm, the LO establishes the limitation on a party's actions before the courts or competent authorities prior to obtaining this interpretation, unless the third person refuses to provide an interpretation of the contract. But this limitation can be otherwise specified by the contract.[208]

## §3. Categories of Insurance Contract

*198.* The LO, as a general law in insurance operations in Montenegro, provides the rules on two different types of insurance contacts: property insurance and life insurance. The law not only provides the general rules that should be applied to all types of insurance regulated by this law but also mentions that not all types of insurance are regulated by this law, so navigation, claim and reinsurance, in particular, are excluded from the application of the general rules.[209] Bearing this in mind, the classification of all insurance contracts in Montenegro can be based on property (with liability insurance) and life insurance.

*199.* Contracts of marine insurance are regulated by the LMIN as a special contract.

## §4. General Principles

*200.* The general principles of all types of insurance are set out in the LO. These provisions contain the rules on: the definition of the insurance contract; the insured event; exclusion of some types of insurance; possible deviations from the provisions on insurance; the rules on contract conclusion; the policy and the list of cover; the unauthorised conclusion of a contract on behalf of another person; insurance for another person's account or for the account of the party interested; the insurance agent's limitations in concluding contracts; the obligations of an insured, or of an insurance contractor; the obligations of the insurer; and the duration of the insurance.

208. *See*: Article 100, LO.
209. *See*: Article 996, LO.

# Chapter 2. Insurable Risk

## §1. Definition of Risk

*201.* In legal theory, risk is recognised as one of the basic elements of insurance,[210] even though the same authors do not agree on other basic elements of insurance. The LO does not give a definition of risk, although risk is one of the most important terms for understanding insurance and is an important element of the insurance contract. Even though the Montenegrin Law on Obligations was adopted in 2008, it follows the old LO of the former Yugoslavia from 1978 and has the same provisions and omissions in defining risk and insured events.

*202.* In the Montenegrin Law on Obligations, there is no differentiation between the insured event and risk, and, in fact, when the law defines the insured event as a future event, uncertain and entirely independent of the contracting party's will,[211] it is actually defining the risk, since the risk represents the possibility of the contingent event occurring and the insured event is the realisation of the risk covered by the insurance.[212] So, the mistake of the old LO is still present in Montenegro. The adoption of the Montenegrin Law on Obligations was a political decision, but this was also the case in all other former Yugoslav countries, and the new LO followed the old text, which was the work of academics.

*203.* Property insurance may be concluded by any person who has an interest in preventing the insured event from occurring, as he would otherwise suffer some material loss. Only a person who, at the time of the occurrence of the damage, has a material interest in ensuring that the insured event does not occur can have rights under the insurance contract.[213] In the LMIN, the concept of insurable interest prevails as well. The insured may only be a person who has or can expect to have a justified material interest (insurable interest) that the insured event will not occur. The insured may claim compensation for the damage that is covered by the insurance only if they had an interest in the insured object at the time of the occurrence of the insured event or if they acquired it after that moment.[214]

*204.* In the LMIN, the risks are numbered, so unless otherwise specified in the insurance contract, navigation insurance covers the risks to which the insured object is exposed during navigation, namely: navigation accident, natural disaster, explosion, fire and robbery. The insurance contract can also cover other risks to which the insured item is exposed during the insurance period, such as theft and non-delivery, manipulative risks, war and political risks, etc.[215]

210. *See*: Predrag Šulejić, *supra*, p. 83; Jasna Pak, *supra*, p. 195.
211. *See*: Article 995, para. 1, LO.
212. *See*: Predrag Šulejić, *supra,* pp. 84 and 109; Jasna Pak, *supra*, pp. 195 and 197; Vladimir Mrijanski, *Ugovor o osiguranju (Insurance Contract),* Pravni fakultet u Novom Sadu, Novi Sad, 2007, p. 15.
213. *See*: Article 1021, LO.
214. *See* Article 729, Law on Maritime and Inland Navigation.
215. *See*: Article 749, LMIN.

§2. ELEMENTS OF RISK

*205.* The legally relevant elements of the risk are the possibility of its occurrence, the uncertainty of its occurrence, the independence of the risk from the will of the interested parties and the legality of the risk.

*206.* The possibility of the occurrence of the risk is a necessary element since the basic rule of contract law is that contracts that are impossible are void.[216] If there is no possibility of the risk occurrence, there is no *alea* in the insurance, since there is no uncertainty of risk. Impossibility eliminates uncertainty, but it does not work the other way around. If something is possible, it does not mean that it is certain that it will occur.[217] In that regard, the impossibility and uncertainty of the risk are interconnected.

*207.* The uncertainty of the occurrence of the risk means that it is not certain whether a risk will be realised in a specific person, but there is a probability that it might occur based on the law of large numbers. Also, uncertainty exists when we know that a risk must occur but do not know when it will occur. Either way, there is the presence of uncertainty, which is more than enough for the aleatory nature of the insurance contract.

*208.* Because the uncertainty of the risk is a prerogative in insurance contracts, one might presume that the parties will conclude contracts only for the possibility of risk occurring in the period after the contract is concluded, but it is not unusual for the parties to cover the time period preceding the conclusion of the contract. The LO does not forbid the conclusion of contracts for the time period prior to the moment of concluding the contracts, but it contains specific rules, in this case, that are relevant for the possibility of the occurrence of a risk in the period preceding or following the conclusion of the insurance contract.

*209.* The sanction of nullity is prescribed in the situation where, at the moment of the conclusion of the contract, the insured case has already materialised, or is at the point of occurring or if it is certain that it is going to occur, or if, even at that time, there was no possibility of its occurring.[218] All situations described in this provision have the same consequence: there is no uncertainty of risk occurrence anymore, so the same sanction is prescribed for all.

*210.* The same sanction of nullity is prescribed in a situation in which the parties are stipulating that the insurance shall cover a specified period of time preceding the conclusion of the contract, but only in the case if, at the moment of its conclusion, the interested party was aware that the case covered by the insurance had already taken place or that even then the possibility of it taking place had ceased

216. Predrag Šulejić, *supra*, p. 85.
217. *Ibid.*
218. *See*: Article 995, para. 2, LO.

to exist.[219] Awareness by the contracting parties of the relevant circumstances is of the utmost importance, since, in this case, the parties must be unaware of the actual situation.

*211.* Consequently, the LO regulates two out of four possible cases where there is no more uncertainty of the occurrence of the risk, the risk is realised before the contract conclusion, or the possibility of its occurrence has ceased to exist. There are no rules for situations where the risk is actually occurring at the moment of the conclusion of the contract, but the damages are not yet realised, and the risk, according to the regular course of things, is imminent.[220]

*212.* The risk must be independent of the interested parties' exclusive will. This is an extension of the uncertainty of the risk principle. If it is the interested party in the insurance contract that causes the realisation of the risk by their own will, the risk is not uncertain to this party. The rules regarding the wilful realisation of risk are mandatory and cannot be changed by the provisions of the insurance contract. So, if the contractor of the insurance, the insured person (policyholder), or the beneficiary of the insurance caused the event covered by the insurance by their intentional misconduct or fraud, the insurer shall have no obligation whatsoever.[221]

*213.* With this provision, the LO has pointed out that it is the interested parties that have an interest in the materialisation of the insurable risk, so the effects of the provisions on wilful realisation of the risk to the contractor, policyholder or beneficiary are limited to them. No other party's conduct can be relevant for this provision, since no other party can have an interest in risk realisation.

*214.* The degree of culpability of the interested party for the wilful realisation of the risk is significant. In cases of wilful realisation of the risk, there is always the same sanction against the contractor of insurance or policyholder if they are the same person. They will not have any rights against the insurer in this case. But there is the option for the beneficiary of the insurance contract in the case of mandatory traffic insurance to realise their rights against the insurer even in the case of wilful action by the insured person. The contract on mandatory liability traffic insurance also covers liability for damage caused to third parties due to the use of a motor vehicle by a person who intentionally caused damage. The insurer will pay the intentionally caused damage to third parties, but the insurer will have the right to recover the entire paid amount of damage, interest and associated costs from the person responsible for the damage.[222] So, in this case, the obligation of the insurer against the claim of the damaged third party exists, but the law constitutes the right of recourse of the insurer against the responsible party. We can conclude that in this

219. *See*: Article 995, para. 3, LO.
220. *See*: Predrag Šulejić, *supra*, p. 86.
221. *See*: Article 1017, LO.
222. *See*: Article 31, para. 1, LMIT.

case, the intent can be directly excluded by the provisions of the general rule or indirectly excluded by presenting the insurer with the rights of recourse towards the person who caused the realisation of the risk intentionally.[223] According to the LO, the statute of limitations of the insurer's claim under the right of recourse is three years after the party sustaining injury or loss became aware of the injury and loss and of the party inflicting damage, but such a claim shall expire five years after the occurrence of injury or loss. If the loss is caused by a criminal offence, where a longer expiration period is prescribed for the criminal prosecution, the claim for compensation against the person liable expires at the time of expiration of the limitation period set forth in the statute of limitations of the criminal prosecution.[224] This longer statute of limitations is considered a privileged limitation period for subrogation claims in relation to the perpetrator of the criminal act and in relation to the responsible person whose responsibility is derived from the criminal responsibility, who is responsible for the damages based on his culpability.[225]

*215.* It is similar in the case of risk realisation caused by gross negligence of the interested party, when a party fails to act with the level of care that a person of average physical and intellectual capabilities and moral properties would employ in the same situation under the same or similar circumstances. So, the elements of consciousness, willingness and consent to harmful consequences are missing. By traditional rules, gross negligence is equated with intent and is usually accepted as an exclusion of the insurer's liability in insurance contracts.[226] But again, in the cases of mandatory traffic insurance, there is an exception, since generally gross negligence is covered by the insurance, and there are a limited number of cases in which the gross negligence of the insured creates an exclusion of the obligation of the insurer under the contract. An exclusion is present: in the case where a person drives a vehicle under the influence of alcohol above the approved limit, narcotic drugs, psychoactive drugs or other psychoactive substances; in the case where a person has avoided or refused a breathalyser and testing; in the case where a person drives without a driving licence, and similar.[227] In these exclusion cases, the law constitutes the right of redress of the insurer against the responsible party, as in the case of intentional cause of the insured event. Before the Supreme Court of Montenegro, a case was argued in which the insurer's right of recourse was in question due to the culpability of the insured. In this particular case, in the criminal proceedings against the insured, the cause of the accident was determined to be a natural illness

223. *See*: Predrag Šulejić, *supra*, p. 90.

224. *See*: Articles 385 and 386, LO.

225. *See*: Legal Position of the Supreme Court of Montenegro on Limitation of Recourse and Subrogation Claims in Insurance of 1 Dec. 2017.

226. The Supreme Court of Montenegro has reiterated that the insurer is not obliged to compensate for the damage to a vehicle that was insured under the comprehensive insurance policy if the driver was driving at double the speed limit when the damage occurred. In the general terms and conditions for comprehensive motor vehicle insurance it is stipulated that the comprehensive insurance policy does not cover damage caused by gross negligence of the driver, which also includes driving at double the speed limit, as in this particular case. Therefore, all the courts that deliberated this case concluded that there is no obligation for the defendant to compensate the plaintiff for damages. *See*: Supreme Court of Montenegro, Rev. No. 357/19.

227. *See*: Article 31, para. 1, LMIT.

of the insured, which caused a loss of consciousness, which was the subsequent cause of the accident. In the civil proceedings, it was not proven that the first defendant was responsible for the damage because it was not established that he was culpable for the accident. All courts that deliberated this case held the same position that the natural illness of the insured could not be interpreted as a case in which the insured could lose their rights under the insurance contract, which would provide the insurer with the right of recourse. The Supreme Court reiterated that, in order for the insurer to have the right of recourse against the insured, it is necessary that the insurer has paid compensation to the person injured in the traffic accident and that the owner, user, or any driver, as persons whose civil liability is covered by liability insurance, is responsible for the accident according to the provisions of the LO, and that the traffic accident occurred, in the case when the driver drove the vehicle without a driving licence. In a situation where there is no liability on the part of the insured for the damage caused, the insured cannot lose their insurance rights in accordance with the provisions of Article 4 of the Conditions for Insuring Users, i.e., owners of motor vehicles, against liability for damages caused to third parties.[228]

*216.* Simple negligence, defined as a failure to exercise the caution that would be employed by an exceptionally contentious person with above-average capabilities or a person professionally conducting certain activities, is covered by the insurance, regardless of the type of insurance. But there is always the problem of determining if the person was acting with gross or simple negligence, which must be established in each particular case.

*217.* Last, but not least, is the question of the legality of the risk. All risks must not be contrary to the mandatory provisions of the law, public order or the ethical rules of society. This would be the case with the insurance of monetary penalties in criminal or misdemeanour penalties, since the purpose of the penalty is to affect the person responsible.[229]

## §3. Excluded Risk

*218.* The other types of limitation of the risk, besides the wilful realisation of the risk are possible, so risks are limited in property insurance in cases where the damages were caused by the defects of the insured item,[230] or the damages were caused by war operations, insurrections or riots.[231] In the case of the wilful realisation of the risk, there is no option of yielding from this provision in insurance contracts, but the other two risks mentioned above may be insured if the parties agree on their coverage, since these exclusions of the risks, even though prescribed by the LO, are of a yielding kind.

---

228. *See*: Supreme Court of Montenegro, Rev. No. 1273/17.
229. *See*: Predrag Šulejić, *supra*, p. 95.
230. *See*: Article 1027, LO.
231. *See*: Article 1028, LO.

*219.* The list of statutory risk exclusions in life insurance is more extensive, so the following risks are excluded: suicide of the insured; intentional killing of the insured; deliberately causing an accident; and war operations. Other risks may be excluded by the contractual provisions of the insurance contract.

*220.* The life insurance contract may not cover the risk of suicide for the insured if it happens in the first year of insurance. According to the statutory provisions, in the event of a suicide occurring within three years of the date of the contract conclusion, the insurer is not obliged to pay the insured amount to the beneficiary but only the mathematical reserve of the contract.[232] The LO clearly states this rule for the suicide of the insured within three years of the day of conclusion of the life insurance contract. After that period, there are no mandatory rules regarding the suicide of the insured.

*221.* If the beneficiary intentionally caused the insured's death, the insurer is released from the obligation to pay the beneficiary the insured sum, but the insurer must pay the mathematical reserve of the contract to the insurance contract holder, and if he/she is the insured, to his/her heirs, if at least three annual premiums have been paid up to that point.[233]

*222.* Intentional causing of an accident by the insured is another reason for the release of the insurer from the obligation.[234]

*223.* The risk of accident or death caused by war operations in life insurance may be insured if the parties agree on their coverage, since this exclusion of the risks, even though prescribed by the LO, is of a yielding kind. If the risk of death is excluded, there is an obligation for the insurer to pay the mathematical reserve from the contract.[235]

*224.* In the LMIN, the excluded risks are also prescribed. So, any damage caused directly or indirectly by the intentional action of the insured is excluded from the insurance. If the insurance contract does not stipulate otherwise, damages are caused directly or indirectly due to: gross negligence of the insured; deliberate action or gross negligence of a person for whose actions, by law, the insured is responsible; and the occurrence of war risks. The last provision does not apply to damages caused by deliberate action or gross negligence of a ship's crew, as well as damages caused by the actions and omissions of the insured, such as the captain or other crew member or pilot, in the navigation and handling of a ship.[236]

232. *See*: Article 1046, LO.
233. *See*: Article 1047, LO.
234. *See*: Article 1048, LO.
235. *See*: Article 1049, LO.
236. *See*: Article 752, LMIN.

## Chapter 3. Formation of the Insurance Contract

*225.* The conclusion of an insurance contract does not differ much from the creation of any other contract. An insurance contract is concluded after the concurrence of the wills of the contracting parties occurs. There are six articles in the LO that are especially related to the conclusion of an insurance contract. All other issues that are not regulated by these provisions are regulated by the general rules of the LO on the formation of contracts.

*226.* Also, we must bear in mind that in the case when the contracting party is a natural person, the rules on consumer protection also apply, so there can be some special obligation in all phases – from the conclusion to the realisation of the insurance contract – specially regulated by the separate set of rules regarding consumer protection.

### §1. Precontractual Phase

*227.* An insurance contract is concluded by an offer and acceptance of the offer between the contracting parties. An offer is a proposal for the conclusion of a contract made to a specific person, which contains all the essential elements of the contract so that the contract can be concluded by accepting it. Also, a proposal for the conclusion of a contract that can be made to an unspecified number of persons and contains the essential ingredients of the contract for which it is intended to be concluded is valid as an offer, unless it results otherwise from the circumstances of the case or customs.[237] The offeror may be either an insurer or an insurance contractor. It depends on who initiates the conclusion of the contract. In practice, it is usually the insurance contractor who initiates the conclusion of an insurance contract, and in the special rules on insurance contracts, the LO starts from the assumption that the offeror is the contracting party.[238] Even though the contracting party usually initiates the conclusion of the contract, they are also usually unaware of the necessary elements of the offer that are relevant for the conclusion of the insurance contract. This problem is usually overcome by the insurers preparing questionnaires or a form pre-printed for the contracting party to fill out that can serve as its offer. Sending price lists, tariffs and other notices, as well as advertisements made through the media, flyers or in any other way, does not represent an offer to conclude a contract, but it represents only an invitation to make an offer under the published conditions.[239]

*228.* A special rule on the formation of insurance contracts prescribes the provisions on the offer for the conclusion of the insurance contract. So, a written offer made to an insurer to conclude an insurance contract binds the offeror, if he/she has not specified a shorter term, for a period of eight days from the day, the offer was

237. *See*: Article 26, LO.
238. *See*: Article 998, para. 2, LO.
239. *See*: Article 28, LO.

received by the insurer, and if a medical examination is required, then for a period of thirty days.[240] This is a special rule regarding the duration of an offer binding on the contracting party.

*229.* The LO also contains the rules for the acceptance of an offer. The general rules apply to acceptance of the offer and to the insurance contract.[241] The general rules also regulate the silence of the offered, which cannot be constituted as acceptance. A special rule is established in cases where there is no formal act of acceptance or rejection of the offer within the timeframe in which the offer binds the contracting party. If the presented offer of the contracting party does not deviate from the conditions under which the insurer provides the proposed insurance, it will be considered that the insurer has accepted the offer and that the contract has been concluded when the offer has reached the insurer.[242]

*230.* There are obligations of the insurer and the contractor of the insurance in the precontractual phase that need to be fulfilled. We can differentiate between the obligations set in the LO and the ones set in the other laws regulating the insurance contract, such as the LI and the Law on Mandatory Insurance in Traffic (LMIT).

*231.* The precontractual obligations of the contracting party are to provide all the information to the insurer pertaining to the calculation of risk, which will be described in the part pertaining to the obligations of the insured. The other obligation can be to pay the first premium of the insurance as a realisation of the special form of contract, which is concluded by the payment of the first premium. Even the LO foresees that, by the general terms and conditions of the insurance, it may be regulated that the insurance contract between the parties may be concluded without the issuance of an insurance policy and that this contractual relationship in insurance will be formed after the first premium is paid by a contracting party.[243]

*232.* The LO contains the obligation of the insurer to warn the contracting party that the general and special insurance conditions are an integral part of the contract and to provide the contracting party with their text if these conditions are not printed on the policy itself.[244] This obligation is a precontractual obligation of the insurer and is the only one prescribed by the LO, but it is again treated as the precontractual obligation of the insurance company in the LI.

*233.* One of the precontractual obligations is that the insurer is obliged to accept the offer of the contracting party for the conclusion of the mandatory traffic insurance contract. Since the conclusion of these contracts is mandatory by law for the

240. *See*: Article 992, para. 2, LO.
241. *See*: Articles 34–49, LO.
242. *See*: Article 992, paras 3 and 4, LO.
243. *See*: Article 1000, LO.
244. *See*: Article 999, para. 3, LO.

users of vehicles, the obligation of the insurance companies to conclude these contracts is derived from the obligation of the users.[245]

*234.* The LI contains the list of obligations of the precontractual information that the insurance company, insurance intermediary, and insurance agent must provide to the contracting party. Before concluding any insurance contract, the insurance company is obliged to familiarise the contracting party with the general and special conditions of the insurance and to provide information on:

- the name of the company, the legal-organisational form and the head office, and the name of the subsidiary that is concluding the contract;
- the period of validity of the contract;
- the manner and conditions for terminating the contract;
- the amount and method of payment of the insurance premium, the amount of contributions, taxes, and other costs charged in addition to the insurance premium, and the total amount of the payments;
- the deadline by which the offer is binding on the insurance company;
- the right to terminate and conditions for terminating the contract or deviating from the contract;
- the method of resolving complaints;
- the law applicable to the insurance contract;
- information that the insurance policyholder may withdraw from the individual life insurance contract within thirty days, at the latest, from the date of receipt of the insurance company's notification of the conclusion of the contract, whereby the insurance policyholder does not bear the obligations arising from that contract.[246]

*235.* Before concluding a life insurance contract, additional information must be provided to the insurance contractor on: the basis and criteria for participation in profit and the method and terms of payment; the table of redemption values; the right to capitalise the life insurance contract and the right from that insurance; the tax regulations related to the life insurance; for contracts where the insured assumes the investment risk (unit-link insurance), the fund prospectus and the investment structure.[247]

*236.* All the information must be delivered to the insurance contractor in written form, in a clear and comprehensible manner, in the language of official use in Montenegro. There is also the obligation of the insurance company to make information about the insurance product available in a timely manner to persons who perform insurance representation work for that company and to insurance intermediaries to whom they make an offer for concluding an insurance contract.

245. Predrag Šulejić, *supra*, p. 214.
246. *See*: Article 81d, para. 1, LI.
247. *See*: Article 81d, para. 2, LI.

*237.* The LI establishes a relationship between the rules on consumer protection and the insurance law, so the provisions of the law regulating consumer protection apply accordingly to the provision of information in accordance with the described rules in the part that is not regulated by the LI.

*238.* Since the contracting party is the one making the offer, most likely based on information derived from the advertisement of the insurance business, the obligations of the insurance companies in marketing their products are of special importance. According to the LI, marketing activities and information about insurance companies and the products they offer on the market must contain clear, true and complete information based on reliable data. Marketing information is defined as all information communicated to potential consumers through advertisements in the press, radio, television, personal visits, telephone calls, websites, electronic media or any other way from which the intention of promotion arises. The obligations of the insurance companies to provide this information are that:

- they must not conceal or display information in a way that misleads potential consumers;
- they must provide a complete, accurate, clear and true description of the product, prescribed obligations, revenue projection and possibility of loss, as well as a description of the risk arising from such a product;
- they must not state false or unverified indicators about the business of the insurance company, its position on the market and the products it offers;
- they must ensure that all information, in its appearance, content and form, is presented identically.

If another company is providing the information, the insurance company is still responsible for the information provided.[248]

## §2. Formation and Commencement of Contracts

*239.* By the provision in the article dedicated to the formation of a contract in the LO, the insurance contract is concluded when the contracting parties sign the insurance policy or the list of coverage.[249] Since there is the option of silence by the insurer, not rejecting or accepting the offer of the contracting party, if the offer does not deviate from the conditions under which the insurer provides the proposed insurance, it will be considered that he has accepted the offer and that the contract has been concluded, when the offer has reached the insurer.[250] These rules represent a significant deviation from the general rules of concluding a contract, which pertains to the fact that a contract is concluded the moment the acceptance of the offer reaches the offeror.[251]

248. *See*: Article 81f, LI.
249. *See*: Article 998, para. 1, LO.
250. *See*: Article 998, para. 2, LO.
251. *See*: Article 21, para. 1, LO.

*240.* The moment of commencement of the insurance contract's effects is defined in the LO by the yielding provision of the law. So, unless otherwise agreed, the insurance contract takes effect starting from the twenty-fourth hour of the day marked in the policy as the start date of the insurance period until the end of the last day of the period for which the insurance was contracted.[252] The LMIN has almost the same provision, but it is supplemented by an additional rule: the time of commencement of the contract is calculated according to the official time of the place where the insurance policy was issued, and if no policy is issued, this is calculated according to the official time in the place where the insurance contract was concluded.[253]

*241.* Since there is a possibility that an insured event can occur on the day of the contract conclusion, it may be disputed between the parties if the insured event occurred prior to the conclusion of the contract. This is why the rules of the law are set like this, in order to prevent the misuse of the rules of insurance by an unscrupulous contractual party.[254] These are rules that attempt to presume the will of the parties, so they are free to change them. The change of the moment of contract commencement is then subjected only to the rules on risk uncertainty that need to be followed by both contracting parties, and of course, it is prudent to take such measures of assurance that will prevent the possibility of a dispute at the moment of the occurrence of the insured event. Sometimes, the general rules and conditions on certain types of insurance prescribe some special rules on the commencement of the insurance contract, as in the case of livestock insurance, where the general terms ask for a specified period of time after the conclusion of the contract as a waiting period.[255]

*242.* The commencement of the insurance contract may be conditioned by prior payment of the premium. The obligation of the insurer under the insurance contract will not exist if the insurance case was realised after conclusion of the contract but prior to the premium payment. The validity of the insurance contract is dependent on the premium payment.[256] These are the general rules established by the LO.

*243.* On the contrary, the LMIN contains slightly different rules. The policyholder is obliged to pay the premium to the insurer immediately after concluding the insurance contract, unless otherwise agreed. The insurer is not obliged to hand over the issued insurance policy to the policyholder before the policyholder pays the due premium. During the liquidation of the damage, the insurer may deduct from the insurance compensation the amount of the premium that is still owed. Failure to pay the premium on time does not release the insurer from its obligations under the insurance contract and does not give it the right to terminate the insurance contract, unless otherwise agreed. If the insurance contract is concluded with the insurance

252. *See*: Article 1019, LO.
253. *See*: Article 747, para. 2, LMIN.
254. Predrag Šulejić, *supra*, p. 206.
255. *Ibid.*, p. 207.
256. *See*: Article 1010, LO.

premium being subsequently determined, the amount of the premium is determined in an appropriate amount, proportional to the severity of the risk. The policyholder is obliged to pay the insurer a premium for the concluded insurance even when the insured object ceased to be exposed to the insured risks before the conclusion of the insurance contract, provided that the insurer was not aware of this at the time of the conclusion of the insurance contract.[257]

## §3. Insurance Policies

*244.* An insurance contract may be accompanied by a large number of documents such as: an insurance policy, a list of coverage, certificates of contract conclusion, cover notes, slips and others. The insurance policy is by far the most important insurance contract document that can serve many purposes. Even in cases where the insurance contract is not a formal contract, the insurance policy is the document that is issued by the insurance company upon conclusion of the insurance contract. According to the LO, in cases regulated by the general terms and conditions of the insurance, it may be set that the insurance policy will not be issued and that the contract will be concluded by payment of the premium by the contracting party.[258] But this rule, set as a possibility, proves that these cases will be exceptional.

*245.* In the Montenegrin legal system, an insurance contract is a formal contract, meaning that there is an obligation on the parties to conclude the contract in written form. The LO states that an insurance contract is concluded when the contracting parties sign the insurance policy or the list of coverages.[259] The issuance and signing of the insurance policy are mandatory, and the insurance policy may only be temporarily replaced by the list of coverage, in which the essential components of the contract are entered.[260]

*246.* The LO has a provision on insurance policy content that prescribes its mandatory content, so the insurance policy must state: the contracting parties, the insured object/person, the risk covered by the insurance, the duration of the insurance and the period of coverage, the amount of the insurance or that the insurance is unlimited; the premium or contribution, the date of issue of the policy and the signatures of the contracting parties.[261] In one case argued before the Supreme Court of Montenegro, the insurer declined the payment upon the insured event in the case of a border motor insurance policy, stating that it was not signed by the insured. The court decided that the fact that the insured's signature is not visible on the photocopy of the policy is irrelevant and that the insurer was obliged to submit to the court the original of the policy from which it could be reliably determined

257. *See*: Article 740, LMIN.
258. *See*: Article 1000, LO.
259. *See*: Article 998, para. 1, LO.
260. *See*: Article 999, para. 2, LO.
261. *See*: Article 999, para. 1, LO.

whether the policy was also signed by the insured. The court argued that, even if this were the case, the insurer could not invoke this because it came about through the insurer's omission, which does not release it from the obligation to compensate for the damage.[262] In addition to the mandatory elements that every policy must have, a life insurance policy must indicate: the first name and surname of the person whose life is covered by the insurance, their date of birth, and the event or term on which the right to demand the payment of the insured amount depends.[263]

*247.* Also, the LMIT, in the case of a traffic insurance policy, grants the ISA the authority to regulate the content of the policy at the proposal of the Montenegrin Association of Insurers.[264] The LO does not differentiate between the insurance contract and the insurance policy and only prescribes the content of the insurance policy. Also, by the provisions of the LMIT, there is an equation of the insurance contract and the insurance policy, since the provision states that the 'insurance contract/insurance policy is uniform for the territory of Montenegro'.[265] Even though one of the most important characteristics of an insurance policy is that it is proof of the existence of the insurance contract, it can serve many other purposes. On the contrary, the LMIN does differentiate between an insurance contract and an insurance policy. Under the provisions of this law, the insurer is obliged to hand over the duly issued and signed insurance policy to the policyholder at the policyholder's request, which should contain all the provisions from the concluded insurance contract that determine the insurer's obligation to compensate for insurance damage.[266]

*248.* Since there is a precontractual obligation of the insurance company to warn the insurance contractor that the general and special insurance conditions are an integral part of the contract and provide him/her with its text, if those conditions are not printed on the policy itself, the fulfilment of this obligation may be noticed on the insurance policy.[267] And usually, in practice, insurance policies contain a provision that states that the contracting party was warned about these facts by the insurance company. However, the insurance policy usually contains the provision that the conditions of insurance were provided with the policy, which usually is not the case, so the insurance contractor does not know which provisions he/she is agreeing to. But the insurers have written proof stating the opposite.

*249.* An insurance policy is also a document that provides proof of the content of an insurance contract. The LO contains provisions on discrepancies between the general or special conditions and the policy provisions that regulate that the policy provision will be applied, and, in the event of a discrepancy between the printed policy provision and its handwritten provision, that the handwritten provision will

262. *See*: Supreme Court, Rev. No. 1184/16.
263. *See*: Article 1040, para. 1, LO.
264. *See*: Article 27, para. 2, LMIN.
265. *See*: Article 27, para. 1, LMIN.
266. *See*: Article 735, LMIN.
267. *See*: Article 999, paras 3 and 4, LO.

be applied.[268] It should be obvious that the LO gives much importance to the insurance policy and gives special notice to the changes in the printed text of the insurance policy; hence, the rules on handwritten changes recognise the importance of these changes due to the manner and speed of the conclusion of the insurance contract.

*250.* For the insurance contractor, the insurance policy may be a legitimation document, since it is easier to prove the capacity of the creditor in the insurance contract by presenting the insurance policy to the insurance company. The insurance policy often serves other commercial relations, since the presentation of the policy is a requirement for realisation of the rights from some other contract, as in the case of a documentary accreditive, or as a proof of the fulfilment of other contractual obligations, as is the case of a Cost, insurance, and freight (CIF) clause sales contract.

*251.* In the case of marine insurance, there is no obligation on the part of the insurer if the insurer has issued and handed it over to the policyholder until the presentation of that policy, if the insured makes it probable that the policy has been lost or destroyed, or before receiving appropriate security from the insured.[269] This rule serves to protect both parties in marine insurance contracts and to prevent mistakes in the payment form of the contract.

*252.* There are no rules on the number of original copies of the policy that may be issued by the insurer at the request of the policyholder in the LO, but the LMIN has a special provision: if an insurance policy is issued in two or more original copies at the request of the policyholder, it should be stated on each such copy how many originals of the policy were issued.[270] Subsequently, the same law regulates the rules on fulfilment of the obligation of the insurer in cases of the issuance of multiple original copies of the policy. The insurer is released from its insurance obligation if it conscientiously makes a payment to the policyholder and – if the policy is issued in multiple original copies – to the submitter of one of the original copies which makes their right to insurance compensation probable under that policy.[271]

*253.* The contracting parties can agree that the insurance policy may be issued to a specific person, by order, or to the bearer.[272] Again, there are some specificities for a life insurance policy that can be issued to a specific person or by order, but it may not be issued to a bearer. For the policy endorsement to be valid, it must contain the name of the beneficiary, the date of endorsement and the signature of the endorser.[273]

268. *See*: Article 999, para. 5, LO.
269. *See*: Article 735, para. 4, LMIN.
270. *See*: Article 735, para. 2, LMIN.
271. *See*: Article 735, para. 5, LMIN.
272. *See*: Article 999, para. 6, LO.
273. *See*: Article 1040, paras 2 and 3, LO.

*254.* The rights under an insurance contract are transferable, unless the possibility of such a transfer is expressly excluded in the insurance contract. So, it is possible to transfer the rights from an insurance contract, but before the damage occurs, they may be transferred only to persons who have an insurable interest. If an insurance policy has been issued, the transfer of insurance rights is done by endorsing that policy or in another appropriate way. The matter of the rights of the insurer against the original contracting party is regulated as well. The assignment of rights to the insured object to another person does not entail the transfer of rights from the insurance if there is no express or tacit agreement between the insured and the acquirer of rights.[274]

*255.* According to the LO, in case of alienation of the insured item, as well as the item regarding use of which the liability insurance was concluded, the rights and obligations of the insurance contractor are transferred by law to the acquirer, unless otherwise agreed. If only one part of the insured items, which do not form a separate entity in terms of insurance, is alienated, the insurance contract is terminated according to the law itself with regard to the alienated items.[275]

274. *See*: Article 736, LMIN.
275. *See*: Article 1034, LO.

## Chapter 4. Obligations of the Insured

*256.* Montenegro's insurance theory and legislature distinguish several types of persons that can be related to the insurance contract on the side opposite the insurer. So, the LO distinguishes between the insurance contractor, the insured, the insured party and the insurance beneficiaries. The term 'insurance contractor' is generally used to describe a person who enters into an insurance contract on their own behalf and then incurs the obligation of premium payment to the insurer. If this party acts in their own name and on his behalf, the insurance contractor may be insured at the same time. The main difference between the insurance contractor and the insured is that the insurance contractor is the party that has obligations towards the insurer, and the insured is the party that has all the rights under the insurance contract.

*257.* The term 'insured party' is only used in the area of personal insurance. This term differs from the term 'insured', since this party is acting as the insured by contracting the insurance in his name on his behalf. This means that this contracting party has signed the insurance contract in their own name and has insured his personal assets, such as life or health, for example, but has denominated the beneficiary of that contract. The beneficiary of this contract is the person who, in the event of the risk realisation, has all the rights, which have been transferred to them by the insured party. If the insured party does not denominate the beneficiary, and the insured event is the death of this party, the benefits from the insurance contract will be a part of their inheritance and will be divided among their heirs. The peculiarity of the life insurance contract is that it may be concluded by one person – the insurance contractor – who is insuring the life of another person. In this case, the insured party is neither the contracting party nor the beneficiary. This is a case that is specially regulated by the LO, which requires the fulfilment of certain conditions for the validity of such a contract.[276]

*258.* Last but not least are the insurance beneficiaries. This is the term used in the area of personal insurance for those persons who will acquire certain rights in the case that the insured event is realised.

*259.* So, these are the terms that will be used in the following chapters in order to portray a certain person and their position and rights under the insurance contracts.

### §1. Description of Risk

*260.* The description of risk is the obligation of the insurance contractor. This obligation exists in the precontractual phase of the contract conclusion since information on the risk is necessary for the decision of the insurer on the contract conclusion and in the phase of the realisation of the insurance contract, since the

276. *See*: Article 1043, LO.

insurance contract is a long-term contract and the risk can change during its existence. So, the LO has ascertained two distinct obligations of the insurance contractor regarding the description of the risk: one in the precontractual phase and one in the phase of contract duration.

*261.* The insurance contractor is obliged to report to the insurer, at the time of the contract conclusion, all circumstances that are material in assessing the risk and that were known, or could not have been unknown, to the insurance contractor.[277] This obligation is viewed as an absolutely fundamental obligation of the insurance contractor in the insurance contract.[278] The insurance contractor is obliged, in the case of property insurance, to notify the insurer of every change in circumstances that may be relevant for assessing the risk and, in the case of life insurance, only if the risk has increased because the insured person has changed their occupation.[279] So, the LO differentiates between life and property insurance contracts and presents this obligation as absolute only in the case of property insurance contracts.

*262.* Although there is the same obligation from the insurance contractor's point of view, there are significant differences in the legal consequences that will occur in the case of a breach of each of these obligations. In that regard, we will present these two cases.

## I. Obligation to Report the Circumstances Material for the Risk Assessment

*263.* At the time of the contract conclusion, all circumstances that are material in assessing the risk and that were known, or could not have been unknown, to the insurance contractor had to be presented to the insurer in order for his deliberation. This obligation is imposed on the insurance contractor during negotiations for the conclusion of the contract, in the interest of the insurer, so that the insurer can assess the risk and decide whether they want to conclude the contract or whether they can cover some of the risks. Sometimes, there is no question if the insurer wants to conclude the contract, but rather if the insurer can or under what conditions they can conclude this contract and assume the coverage of the risks. Maybe the risk is too great for a simple insurance contract, but the insurer would conclude this contract with high risks under a higher premium, ascertain the co-insurance or reinsurance, and disperse the risk horizontally or vertically. In any case, all the relevant information must be presented to the insurer in order for the insurer to make a rational decision and risk assessment.

*264.* The question that inevitably arises is: how should the insurance contractor know which circumstances are important for risk assessment? In some cases, the

277. *See*: Article 1004, LO.
278. *See*: Nikola Dožić, Dužnost prijavljivanja okolnosti značajnih za ocjenu rizika i prevare u osiguranju, Osiguranje i nkanada štete, XVI Međunarodni naučni skup – Udruženje za odštetno pravo, 2013, p. 115.
279. *See*: Article 1011, LO.

insurance contractor is the only one who can know what risks the property will be exposed to, so only they can inform the insurer of the circumstances on the basis of which they will assess the risk. However, in most cases, the insured does not even know on what basis the insurers are assessing the risk, so they cannot know which circumstances are important for risk assessment. How then can those persons fulfil the obligation imposed on them by law? Usually, insurers draw up questionnaires, especially for mass insurances, in which the questions to which the insurance contractor should answer are specified. But the insurance contractor's obligation does not consist only of honestly filling out the questionnaire. If the contractor knows of any additional circumstances that are not mentioned in the questionnaire, which may be of importance to the insurer and the upcoming risk assessment, the contractor must additionally inform the insurer about them. Today, in order for the insurance contractor to fulfil this obligation, they must honestly and completely answer all questions about the facts that are known to them and that exist before the conclusion of the contract (because after the conclusion of the contract, the contractor will be obliged to inform the insurer of any changes in the risk), which have an impact on the severity of the risk, and which are not known to the insurer at the time of concluding the insurance contract. The contractor is not obliged to inform the insurer of notorious facts, as well as facts about which the insurer knew or could reasonably be assumed to know.[280]

*265.* The consequences of not complying with this obligation depend on the conscientiousness of the insurance contractor, i.e., whether the contractor violated the reporting obligation intentionally or unintentionally, as well as the nature of the facts that were intentionally inaccurately reported or concealed, whether the insurer would have entered into the conclusion of the contract if they had known the true situation.

*266.* In the event of a deliberate false report or concealment of facts important for the risk assessment, the insurer is given the right to demand the annulment of the contract if facts of such importance were kept silent or falsely presented that the insurer would not enter into the conclusion of the contract. At the same time, the insurer has the right to keep the received premiums and claim the premiums due to them until the day of cancellation of the contract. The right to cancellation is conditioned by compliance with the statutory limitation period.[281] The law does not contain provisions on what happens when the insured has intentionally falsely reported or kept silent about facts that are of such a nature that the insurer would nevertheless agree to conclude a contract under modified conditions, i.e., for a higher insurance premium. In this case, there would be room for an analogous application of the rules related to unintentional incorrect reporting or concealment of facts in the part that concerns the insurer's right to request an increase in the premium or termination of the contract. The insurance policyholder's negligence would also justify the analogous application of the aforementioned rules. In the case of negligence on the part of the policyholder (even though facts that are not decisive

280. Predrag Šulejić Predrag, *supra*, pp. 225–226.
281. *See*: Article 1005, LO.

for the formation of the decision on the conclusion of the contract have been kept silent or falsely presented), the question of the existence of the insurer's obligation to pay damages when the insured event occurred before the termination of the contract or before reaching an agreement on an increase in the premium arises. If we keep in mind that it was the insurer who chose to increase the premium, of course, if the occurrence of the insured event was not the fault of the insured, the insurer would have the obligation to pay, even though the contractor acted negligently. Because the contractor's negligence is not enough to cause the exclusion of the obligation of the insurer, who themself agreed to the existence of the contract under the amended conditions, in this case, the insurer would have the obligation to pay compensation, reduced in proportion to the difference in the premiums paid and the premiums that should have been paid. However, if we look at the case where the insurer chose to terminate the contract or the insured event occurred before the insurer became aware of the inaccuracy of the facts or of their concealment, there is no consent from the insurer for the continued validity of the contract, so, in combination with the policyholder's negligence, the question of the existence of his liability for damages must be established. It can be considered that in this case, there is no obligation of the insurer to compensate for damages, however, there is no right for the insurer to keep the premiums received, but they are obliged to return part of the premiums related to the period after the termination of the contract or after the occurrence of the insured event, if the insured event occurred before the insurer became aware of incorrect or silent facts. Due to the fraudulent intent of the policyholder, which existed at the time of the conclusion of the contract, the insurer's obligation would be excluded.

In the Supreme Court Bulletin, there is only one case concerning Article 1005 of the LO and its relation to Article 1006. In this case, the courts deliberated on the possible rights of the insurer, who, at the time of the contract conclusion, was aware of the fact that the insurance contractor had falsely reported the facts relevant to the risk assessment. The Supreme Court of Montenegro concluded that, in the case where the insurer was aware of the incorrect presentation of the facts at the time of the contract conclusion, the insurer had the right to refuse the conclusion of the contract or to ask for an increase in premiums, but the insurer did not opt for either of these options. The court argued that, in the event that the insurer believed that this incorrect reporting of the facts was intentional, the insurer had the option to ask for an annulment of the contract, but they did not have the right to ask for a rescission of the contract, so the Supreme Court confirmed the decisions of the lower courts, which determined the insurer's obligation under the insurance contract in this case.[282] Legal theory in Montenegro acknowledges the different theories and different legal solutions in comparative legislation, such as in the case of the German LI, which in this case would grant the insurer the right of contract termination,[283] but there were no other cases in which the Montenegrin courts deliberated on this question. The decisions of all lower courts in this case were on the same grounds as those of the Supreme Court.

282. *See*: Supreme Court of Montenegro, Rev. No. 105/14 of 17 Dec. 2014.
283. *See*: Šulejić, *supra*, p. 227.

*267.* In the case of an unintentionally incorrect application or failure to provide the necessary notification, the insurer is granted the right to choose between termination of the contract and a proposal to increase the insurance premium in proportion to the increase in risk within thirty days of the day of learning about the inaccuracy or incompleteness of the application. In order to terminate the contract, the insurer is obliged to notify the insured in writing, and termination of the contract occurs after the expiration of a period of fourteen days from the date of delivery of that notification. If the insurer wants to use the right to increase the premium, they must inform the policyholder, who has fourteen days to decide whether they agree to the premium increase. If the policyholder has not informed the insurer about his consent, the contract is ended by force of law at the end of this period. In that case, the insurer does not have the right to retain all premiums received but must return those related to risk coverage after termination of the contract.[284]

*268.* The provisions on the consequences of incorrect reporting or concealment of circumstances relevant to the risk assessment are also applied in cases of insurance concluded in the name of and on behalf of another, or for the benefit of a third party, or for another's account, or for the account of whom it concerns, if these persons knew of the inaccuracy of the application or the concealment of circumstances of importance for the risk assessment.[285]

*269.* If the insurer, at the moment of entering into a contract, was aware, or could not have been unaware, of circumstances relevant to assessing the risk, which were incorrectly notified or suppressed by the insurance contractor, they will not have the right to invoke on the incorrectness of the application or the fact of suppression. The same applies in the event that the insurer becomes aware of these circumstances during the course of the insurance period but fails to use their legal rights.[286] This rule was reiterated in the judgment of the Supreme Court of Montenegro, stating that the insurer may not invoke the right based on the inaccuracy or incompleteness of the report in the event of the insurer's own negligence because the insurer should have asked the policyholder about the actual state of the stock of goods, if this is an important circumstance for risk assessment, as well as requesting accounting documentation on the state of the stock, which means that it was not necessary to visit all facilities in order to check the stock.[287]

## II. Obligation to Report the Changes Within the Circumstance's Material for the Risk Assessment

*270.* During the duration of the insurance contract, the insurance contractor is obliged to inform the insurer of changes in risk, i.e., about the facts that the insurance contractor had to communicate to the insurer when concluding the contract.

284. *See*: Article 1006, LO.
285. *See*: Article 1007, LO.
286. *See*: Article 1008, LO.
287. *See*: Supreme Court of Montenegro, Rev. IP No. 176/15.

This obligation is of a contractual nature, with special legal consequences. Changes in risk may refer to an increase, decrease or cessation of the risk, which may be of a temporary or permanent nature. In this sense, different legal consequences are foreseen for these situations, and different rules also apply in the case of property and life insurance.

*271.* As the contract has already been concluded, it is a different legal situation that is specially regulated and has special legal consequences. This can refer to an increase, decrease or cessation of risk, which can be permanent or temporary in nature. In the precontractual phase, there are only two options, since the cessation of the risk in the precontractual phase leads to different solutions.

*272.* It is appropriate to distinguish between the situations of a reduction or increase of risk because it is natural that the same consequences cannot be predicted for both risk changes. Thus, our legislator has foreseen different solutions for situations where there is an increase or decrease in risk and about which the insurer has not been informed. Also, the legislator makes a distinction between property insurance and life insurance. Thus, if there is an increase in risk after concluding a life insurance contract, the policyholder is obliged to inform the insurer about the increase in risk only if it is conditioned by a change in the insured's occupation. If it is a matter of property insurance, the contractor must inform the insurer of any change in circumstances relevant to the risk assessment.[288]

*273.* The legislator also made a distinction in the issue of an increase in the risk by an act on the part of the insurance contractor, and in that sense, the legislator provided different rules for an increase in risk that have taken place without the legislator's participation. The insurance contractor is given a period of fourteen days to notify the insurer of an increase in risk that has occurred without his participation, while if the increase in risk is conditioned by some of his actions, he is obliged to notify the insurer of this increase without delay.[289]

*274.* A difference was also made regarding the nature of the change in risk. If the risk increased so much that the insurer would not have agreed to conclude the insurance contract if that risk had existed at the time of the conclusion of the contract, the law leaves it with the possibility of terminating the contract. If the increase in risk is of such a nature that the insurer would still conclude the contract even with such a predicted risk, albeit with a higher insurance premium, the insurer has the right to propose a new insurance premium rate to the insurance contractor. The proposal to change the premium is submitted to the insurance contractor, who may accept the new premium within fourteen days. If the insurance contractor rejects this offer before the end of this period, the contract is terminated by law. The contract is terminated by force of law and upon expiry of the set period if the insurance contractor does not notify the insurer of the acceptance of the new premium.[290]

---

288. *See*: Article 1011, para. 1, LO.
289. *See*: Article 1011, para. 2, LO.
290. *See*: Article 1011, paras 3–5, LO.

*275.* However, the insurer's right to request a change in the amount of the insurance premium is conditioned by the existence of a preclusion term in which the insurer has the right to request this increase, which, in the event of non-acceptance of the offer, may result in termination of the contract. The term in which the insurer can exercise the right to increase the premium is thirty days, which is calculated from the day of realising that there is an increase in risk. It does not matter how the insurer found out about the increased risk, i.e., whether they learned about the increase from the insurance contractor, from a third party or in some other way. It is important that the insurer knows about the increased risk, so the deadline left is considered to be enough to assess the new circumstances. However, the thirty-day period will not benefit the insurer, who, before the expiration of this period, has somehow agreed to extend the contract. In the law, cases of agreeing to the extension of the contract are specified as receiving the insurance premium, payment of compensation for an insured event that occurred after an increase in risk, etc.[291]

*276.* If, in the meantime, before notifying the insurer of the increased risk or after the notification but before the insurer had the opportunity to terminate the contract or reach a new agreement with the insurance contractor on the amount of the premium, the insured event occurs, the compensation, which the insurer must pay according to the existing contract, will be reduced in proportion to the difference between the premiums that have been paid and the premiums that should have been paid according to the increased risk.[292]

*277.* In the event of a reduction in risk after the conclusion of the insurance contract, the legislator has given the insurance contractor the right to request a corresponding reduction in the premium. If the insurer does not agree to reduce the premium, the insurance contractor has the right to terminate the contract. The right to reduce the premium, if the insurer agrees to the reduction, is calculated from the day when the insurer is requested to reduce the premium.[293] If the insurer rejects the premium reduction, the insurance contractor will have time to conclude a new insurance contract with some other insurer under conditions that are more favourable for the contractor, and at the time of the conclusion of the second contract, the contractor will have the option of terminating the first insurance contract. If the contractor acts in this way, they do not have to have the uncovered risk for the period of time needed for the second insurance contract conclusion.

## III. Special Rules for Life Insurance Contracts

*278.* The rules on life insurance have some special provisions relevant to risk assessment. These rules are an exception to the general provisions on the consequences of incorrect applications or of suppressing the circumstances relevant for

291. *See*: Article 1011, para. 6, LO.
292. *See*: Article 1012, LO.
293. *See*: Article 1013, LO.

the assessment of risk and pertain to incorrect reporting of age in life insurance contracts. The sanctions for the breach of obligation on the risk description are different, so they will be presented separately. In that sense, a life insurance contract shall be void, and the insurer shall be obliged in any case to repay all received premiums should, at the moment of its conclusion, the age of the insured person be incorrectly stated, if their real age exceeds the limit up to which the insurer, by their terms and tariffs, normally enters into life insurance contracts.[294]

*279.* If it should be incorrectly reported that the insured person is of a lower age, but their real age does not exceed the limit up to which the insurer normally enters into life insurance transactions, the contract shall be valid, but the insured amount shall be reduced in proportion to the stipulated insurance premium and the insurance premium provided for the life insurance of a person of the age of the insured person.[295]

*280.* Should the insured person be of a younger age than reported in the application to enter into a contract, the insurance premium shall be reduced by a corresponding amount, while the insurer shall be obliged to repay the difference between the insurance premiums received and the premiums they are entitled to.[296]

*281.* So, among all cases, only in one, the sanction for the breach of obligation is the voidance of the contract. In other cases, the contract is considered valid, and there are additional rules that regulate the situation of incorrect age reporting.

## §2. Payment of Premium

### I. General Rules on Premium Payment

*282.* The premium is one of the basic obligations of the insurance contractor towards the fulfilment of the insurance contract. It represents the sum of money the contractor has to pay to the insurer as a price for covering the risks. Although this is the obligation of the insurance contractor, the insurer is obliged to accept the payment of the premium by any other person with a legal interest in the fact that the premium is paid.[297] So, by this provision, not only is the obligation of the insurance contractor to pay the premium established but the obligation of the insurer to accept the premium payment is also established. In this case, a third interested party has offered a premium payment.

294. *See*: Article 1041, para. 1, item 1, LO.
295. *See*: Article 1041, para. 1, item 2, LO.
296. *See*: Article 1041, para. 1, item 3, LO.
297. *See*: Article 1009, para. 1, LO.

*283.* The place of payment of the insurance premium is the place of the head office or the place of permanent residence of the insurance contractor, unless another place is designated by the contract.[298]

*284.* The premium may be paid as a lump sum or within the stipulated time limits periodically. If the contracting parties agree on the payment of the premium as a lump sum, it must be paid upon the conclusion of the contract.[299] The lump sum premium is an exception, since the majority of insurance contracts are long-term contracts. Only for short-term contracts can the premium be determined in advance and the rule on lump sum premiums applies. Usually, premiums are paid periodically over a longer period of time during the existence of the insurance contract.

*285.* Also, the payment of the premium may represent the conclusion of the insurance contract if the contracting parties agree that the payment of the first premium will represent the conclusion of the contract. So, the LO stipulates that, according to the terms of insurance, it may be regulated in which cases a contractual relationship in insurance shall ensue due to only the payment of the premium.[300] This is considered to be the real form of the insurance contract, since the existence of the insurance contract is dependent on the act of paying the premium.

*286.* The commencement of the insurance contract may depend on the payment of the first premium. So, we must differentiate the situation in which the payment of the premium exists at the moment of entering into a contract or after entering into a contract, since the consequences of failing to fulfil the obligation are different.

*287.* If the contracting parties stipulate that the insurance premium must be paid upon entering into a contract, the duty of the insurer to pay compensation, or the amount specified by contract, shall commence on the day following the day of payment of the insurance premium. Failure to fulfil the obligation of the insurance contractor is followed by the non-existence of the insurer's obligation under the contract.[301] The jurisprudence in this matter is clear. The Supreme Court of Montenegro reiterated that the payment of insurance premiums is a deferred condition for a valid insurance contract to take effect.[302] One of the cases was especially interesting since the insurance contractor, who was obliged to pay the first premium upon entering into a contract, paid neither the first nor any of the other monthly determined premiums before the harmful event took place. They paid only one premium nine days after the day of the harmful event and then took the case to the courts. It must be noted that the reasoning of the second-instance court – that the insurance contract is valid because it was stipulated that the premiums would be paid monthly – was disputed by the Supreme Court. On the contrary, the Supreme

298. *See*: Article 1009, para. 3, LO.
299. *See*: Article 1009, para. 2, LO.
300. *See*: Article 1000, LO.
301. *See*: Article 1010, para. 1, LO.
302. *See*: Supreme Court of Montenegro, Rev. No. 152/2008.

Court pointed out that in this case, since the first premium was paid after a harmful event had taken place, there was no obligation on the insurer to pay out the damages.[303]

*288.* If, however, the contracting parties stipulate that the insurance premium must be paid after entering into the contract, the duty of the insurer to pay the compensation or the amount specified by contract shall commence from the day determined in the contract as the day of commencement of the insurance.[304] Failure to fulfil the obligation of the insurance contractor is not followed by the same sanction as in the previous case. The consequences of a failure to make a premium payment upon its maturity are regulated. The premium must be paid by the insurance contractor or by an interested person after its maturity. If not, the insurer can send a registered letter to the insurance contractor notifying the latter of the maturity of the premium. If the premium is not paid within the thirty-day period from the day the insurance contractor received such a letter from the insurer, the contract will be terminated by law. This means that no other declaration or action of the contracting parties is needed for the termination of such a contract. If the insurer sends this letter in advance of the premium maturity, the time limits will count from the day of maturity of the insurance premium.[305] In this time period, the obligation of the insurer is valid, and in the case of the risk realisation, the insurer will have to pay the compensation. In this case, the insurer may deduct the amount of the premiums that have already matured from the amount of his obligation.

*289.* The LO regulates one other case in which the contract will be terminated by law. If the premium is not paid within one year, counting from its maturity, the contract will be terminated by the law, regardless of whether the insurer has notified the insurance contractor or not.[306] The LO has put this limit for reasons of legal certainty.

*290.* The question of forcible collection of the premium is the second question that is important. In all the cases described, in non-life insurance, there is a possibility of judicially seeking the premium. In the case of a premium that must be paid for the commencement of the obligation of the insurer, he can ask only for the future period of insurance. The contract is concluded for a set period, but since the commencement of the obligation of the insurer is dependent on the premium payment, after the claim is made, the insurer may only seek the premium for the remaining period of the contract.[307] In the other case, when the payment of the premium is an obligation not related to the commencement of the obligation of the insurer, after the premium maturity, the insurer may claim not only the amount of the mature premium but also the amount of the interest on the pecuniary obligation. We must point

303. *See*: Supreme Court of Montenegro, Rev. No. 935/19.
304. *See*: Article 1009, para. 2, LO.
305. *See*: Article 1009, para. 3, LO.
306. *See*: Article 1009, para. 4, LO.
307. Slobodan Perović and Dragoljub Stojanović, *Komentar Zakona o obligacionim odnosima*, Knjiga druga, Gornji Milanovac, 1980, p. 807.

out that these rules on the commencement of the contract and the rules on the payment and consequences of non-payment of the premium after its maturity do not apply to life insurance contracts or to marine insurance contracts.

## II. Special Rules for Marine Insurance Contracts

*291.* The LMIN has special rules regarding the commencement of the obligation of the insurer and the failure to fulfil the obligation of premium payment.[308] In marine insurance contracts, the insurance contractor is obliged to pay the premium to the insurer immediately after concluding the insurance contract, unless otherwise agreed. There is no obligation on the part of the insurer to hand over the issued insurance policy to the insurance contractor before the latter pays the due premium. During the liquidation of the damage, the insurer can deduct from the insurance compensation the amount of the premium that is still owed.

*292.* Another specificity is that the LMIN prescribes the possible situation of the conclusion of an insurance contract without determining the premium. In this case, the premium will be subsequently determined proportionally to the severity of the risk. In marine insurance contracts, failure to pay the premium on time does not release the insurer from their obligations under the insurance contract and does not give the insurer the right to terminate the insurance contract, unless otherwise agreed.

*293.* The insurance contractor is obliged to pay the insurer a premium for the concluded insurance even when the insured object has ceased to be exposed to the insured risks before the conclusion of the insurance contract, provided that the insurer was not aware of this at the time of the conclusion of the insurance contract.[309]

## III. Special Rules for Life Insurance Contracts

*294.* Unlike the rules in non-life insurance, the obligation to pay a premium in life insurance contracts is an optional obligation. There is no guarantee that the insurer may claim the agreed premium before the courts.[310] This is not an example of natural obligations that do not create any obligations under the law. In the event that the insurance contractor has paid the premiums, they may not ask for the premiums to be returned because the contractor has fulfilled their obligation under the provisions of the life insurance contract. This is the part that resembles a case of

308. *See*: Article 744, LMIN.
309. *See*: Article 744, para. 6, LMIN.
310. *See*: Article 1042, para. 1, LO.

natural obligations, but there are some consequences of non-payment of the premiums, including the lowering of the inured sum, and in some cases, the contract may be suspended.[311]

*295.* These rules are set in such a way for many reasons, among which are the goals of the life insurance contract and because this is a contract that is adjusted to the capabilities of the insured.[312] A life insurance contract is a long-term contract, so many years may pass and many of the circumstances may change after the conclusion of the contract, especially on the side of the insurance contractor, who undertakes the obligation under the contract to pay the premium for a long period of time. The circumstances may change in such a way that the insurance contractor does not have any income and may not be able to pay the life insurance premiums. So, forcible collection of the premiums would represent a harsh sanction.

*296.* According to the LO, should an insurance contractor of a life insurance contract fail to pay some of the insurance premiums when they are due, the insurer shall not be entitled to demand payment by instituting legal proceedings. The law has devised a special procedure in respect of the procedure that needs to be undertaken in order to reduce the obligation of the insurer or to repudiate the contract.

*297.* The insurer must invite the contractor, by letter sent by registered mail, to pay the premium due within the time limit that is indicated in this letter. This time limit may not be shorter than one month, calculated from the day of the letter's delivery date. The payment may be made either by the insurance contractor or by a third interested party. The legal implication of the failure to pay the premiums that are due differs depending on whether at least three annual insurance premiums have been paid up until that moment. If at least three annual insurance premiums have been paid, the insurer may only state to the insurance contractor that the insurer is going to reduce the amount of insurance to the level of the repurchase value of insurance. In the opposite case, an insurance contractor may only repudiate the contract.[313]

*298.* Special attention has been devoted to the question of the occurrence of the insured event prior to the repudiation of the contract or reduction of the insured amount. The law states that, in this case, if the procedure was underway when the insured event occurred, the insurer is protected, so the legal consequences are the same as in the case where the procedure was finished.[314]

311. Predrag Šulejić, *supra*, p. 484.
312. *Ibid.*, p. 485.
313. *See*: Article 1042, para. 2, LO.
314. *See*: Article 1042, para. 3, LO.

## §3. OBLIGATIONS IN THE CASE OF THE INSURED EVENT

*299.* The LO stipulates the obligation of the insured to notify the insurer within three days of the occurrence of the insured event in non-life insurance.[315] This obligation does not exist when it comes to life insurance because, in this contract, the insured is the person whose life is insured, so the insured event is realised upon the death of this person. It is not possible to foresee this obligation at the expense of the beneficiary from the insurance contract because the beneficiary from the insurance contract is not a contractual party in order to have obligations from the contract. This person does not have to know about the existence of this contract or about the fact that they are the beneficiary of this contract. Consequently, the beneficiary does not need to know that the realisation of the risk from the life insurance contract has happened, even in cases where the beneficiary is familiar with their designation as the life insurance contract beneficiary.

*300.* The law has devised this obligation at the expense of the insured, not of the insurance contractor, bearing in mind the fact that compensation can be paid to the insured, who does not have to be the insurance contractor at the same time. Therefore, in this case, the legislator has restricted the obligation to the person who benefits from the payment of the insured sum. In the case of insurance for the benefit of a third party, the insurance beneficiary should fulfil this obligation of notification.[316]

*301.* The content of the notification about the occurrence of the insured event is usually regulated by the insurance conditions and is done on the form that the insured fills out on the insurer's premises at the time of the notification of the insured event.[317] The law does not prescribe the content of the application, but depending on the type of insured case occurring, it is left to the fact that the general or special conditions of the insurance foresee the facts that need to be reported and the way in which they will be reported to the insurer.[318] Usually, insurers prepare the forms on which the application will be made. In motor liability insurance, there is the form of the European Accident Report Form for Motor Vehicles, which the insurer is obliged to hand over to the insured at the conclusion of the insurance contract and which the insured and the injured person may use as a compensation claim under this insurance.[319]

*302.* If the insured fails to fulfil this obligation, they are obliged to compensate the insurer for the damage the insurer suffered as a result of not being informed of the occurrence of the insured event.[320]

---

315. *See*: Article 1014, para. 1, LO.
316. Slobodan Perović and Dragoljub Stojanović, *supra*, p. 478.
317. Predrag Šulejić, *supra*, p. 240.
318. Slobodan Perović & Dragoljub Stojanović, *supra*, p. 479.
319. Drago Pavić, *Ugovorno pravo osiguranja – Komentar zakonskih odredbi*, Zagreb, 2009, p. 224.
320. *See*: Article 1014, para. 2, LO.

*303.* The term for the fulfilment of this obligation is three days from the date of the occurrence of the insured event. The duration of this term depends on the non-existence of other provisions in the insurance terms or in the insurance contract that would provide for a longer term. The provision on the extension of the term would not be void because the term is extended in the interest of the insured.[321] By fulfilling this obligation within the set deadline, the insured will enable the insurer to take appropriate measures in order to reduce the damage, and the insured also avoids complaints from the insurer that the insured did not pay enough attention to the insured object and the legal consequences that go with this complaint.[322]

*304.* What are the consequences of missing the deadline for notifying the insurer of the occurrence of the insured event? In this case, the insured does not lose the right to compensation because the deadline is not a limitation period. The insured is only obliged to compensate the insurer for any damage that would occur to the insurer's property due to the insured's failure to report because the damage may occur due to non-reporting or damage, or it may increase after the occurrence of the insured event due to non-reporting this fact to the insurer within the deadline. The insurer will deduct that damage from the amount of compensation paid to the insured. The fault for failure to report is assumed in this case, but under the insurance conditions, it is usually limited to intent or gross negligence.[323] In one case before the Appellate Court of Montenegro, the decision of the lower court was revoked, since this court had concluded that the three-day deadline for the notification of the insurer on the occurrence of the insured event was of a preclusive kind, which consequently led this court to reject the claim of the insured, due to the loss of rights. The Appellate Court reiterated that the sanction of loss of rights was prohibited by the provision of Article 1015, which stipulates that the provisions of the contract that provide for the loss of the right to compensation or the insurance amount are null and void if the insured does not perform any of the prescribed or contracted obligations after the occurrence of the insured event.[324]

*305.* It is interesting that the legislator, immediately after prescribing this obligation and the rules on compensation for damages in the event of failure of notification, provided a provision that determines the nullity of all contractual provisions that provide for the loss of the right to compensation or the insurance amount if the insured does not perform one of the obligations prescribed by the law or any contractual obligations. Such provisions would be against the goal of the insurance and therefore cannot produce a legal effect.

*306.* The insured is obliged to prove: that the damage is a consequence of the occurrence of the risk; the existence of the damage; and the amount of the damage, which is increasingly difficult to prove over time. If the insured does not report the occurrence of the insured event, thus preventing the insurer from establishing these

321. Slobodan Perović & Dragoljub Stojanović, *supra,* p. 478.
322. Drago Pavić, *supra,* p. 223.
323. Slobodan Perović & Dragoljub Stojanović, *supra,* p. 480.
324. *See*: Decision of the Appellate court of Montenegro, Pž. No. 742/13.

facts, the insured will not lose his right to compensation because of this. The insured will only be obliged to prove the mentioned facts.[325]

*307.* Proving the occurrence of the insured event in Montenegrin law is up to the insured, who must provide the insurer with all the notices and explain the circumstances so that the damage can be assessed. In some cases, as in the case of motor liability insurance, proving the occurrence of the insured event also requires the submission of an official report from an official body (the police) that proves the occurrence of the damage, while for smaller amounts of damage, this is not required, but the damage liquidator may determine the existence of the damage themselves, or this will be done by the court in the proceedings. It is also stated in the literature that the police report is reliable evidence of the occurrence of the accident,[326] but the European Accident Report Form for Motor Vehicles is used in cases where the total amount of damages is low enough to justify not using the more reliable evidence of the accident occurrence.

325. Slobodan Perović & Dragoljub Stojanović, *supra*, p. 480.
326. *Ibid.*, p. 441.

## Chapter 5. Obligations of the Insurer

### §1. Non-life Insurance

*308.* The obligations of the insurer differ with regard to the type of insurance. The major difference in the insurer's obligation is due to the application of the principle of compensation in non-life insurance as a general rule. This principle underlines the entirety of non-life insurance, meaning that the insured may not receive a payment higher than the loss incurred on the insured property by the realisation of the insured event.

*309.* Property insurance may be contracted by any person having an interest in ensuring that the insured event does not take place, since otherwise such a person would suffer a material loss. The insurance rights may pertain only to persons having material interest that the insured event does not take place at the moment of the occurrence of the damage. Redress of damages inflicted on the property of the insured due to the occurrence of the insured event shall be provided for, and the amount of compensation may not exceed the loss suffered by the insured person by the occurrence of the insured event.[327] When the event covered by the insurance takes place, the insurer must pay the compensation or the amount specified by contract within the stipulated time limit, which may not exceed fourteen days, calculated from the day that the notification was received by the insurer of the occurrence of the insured event. But should some time be needed to establish the existence of the insurer's obligation or its amount, the time limit described will begin to run from the day of establishing the existence of the insurer's obligation and its amount. The insurer will be obliged to pay the undisputed part of their obligation as an advance payment until the determination of the full obligation. If the insurer breaches their obligations, they will owe the insured person default interest from the day of receipt of notification about the occurrence of the insured case, as well as to redress the damages incurred to the latter thereby.[328]

*310.* The limitation of the amount of compensation may be negotiated, so the clauses of a contract, in which the amount of compensation is limited to a sum that is lower than the amount of damage, are valid. Loss of profit may be taken into consideration only if this is provided by the contract, and in the case of crop insurance or insurance of other agricultural products, the amount of damage shall be determined in relation to the value such crop would have at the time of harvest, unless otherwise provided by the contract.[329]

---

327. *See*: Article 1021, paras 1 and 2, LO.
328. *See*: Article 1016, LO. The Supreme Court of Montenegro has reiterated that when it is not possible to determine the existence and scope of the insurer's obligation within the period referred to in Art. 1016, para. 1 of the LO, then the deadline does not begin to run from the day when the insurer received the notification that the insured event occurred, but from the day when the existence of its obligation and its amount were determined. In that regard, the insurer who did not breach the insurance contract is not obliged to compensate the insured for damages in the name of unrealised profit. *See*: Supreme Court of Montenegro, Rev. No. 1302/15.
329. *See*: Article 1022, paras 3–5, LO.

*311.* The LO also contains provisions on consecutive damages, so should several insured events take place one after the other in the course of the same period of insurance, the insurance compensation for each one of them shall be determined and paid off entirely by taking into consideration the total amount insured, without reducing it by the amount of compensation previously paid within such a period.

*312.* The value of the insured object may be agreed upon by the contracting parties, and compensation for damages must be determined with that value in mind. Only if the insurer is successful in proving that the value stipulated is excessively higher than the real value and that there is no justified ground for such a difference will the agreed value not be the basis for the calculation of the insurer's obligation. The justified grounds for such a difference in value are also determined by the law, for instance, insuring a used object at the value of a new one or insuring a subjective, personal value.[330]

*313.* In the Montenegrin legal system and insurance practice, matters of over-insurance, under-insurance, and multiple and double insurance are especially regulated by the rules of the LO.

## I. Over- and under-Insurance

### *A. Over-Insurance*

*314.* Over-insurance is regulated almost the same way as in other countries. It is usually assessed as a danger for the insurer, so legislation in almost all countries contains provisions that sanction this behaviour in order to avoid intentionally causing an insured event.[331] Over-insurance exists when, at the time of the contract conclusion, the value of the insured object is determined to be higher than the actual value of the object. The Montenegrin LO differentiates between the possibility of intentionally and unintentionally causing the insured object to have a higher value.

*315.* In the first case, at the time of contract conclusion, one party intentionally contracts an insurance amount higher than the actual value of the insured item. Bearing in mind the rules on compensation for damage and the rules on the purpose of property insurance, contracting for a higher value of items constitutes fraud. The law gives the other party the possibility of requesting annulment of the contract.[332]

*316.* Over-insurance may also occur due to the insured's ignorance when the insured does not know the true value of the object, but this can also occur when the insured wants to avoid under-insuring the item, so they conclude the insurance of

330. *See*: Article 1022, para. 7, LO.
331. Predrag Šulejić, *supra*, p. 343.
332. *See*: Article 1029, para. 1, LO.

the item for an insurance amount that is greater than the value of the item. Therefore, a distinction is made between malicious over-insurance (bad-faith over-insurance) and unintentional over-insurance. Only in the case of malicious over-insurance does the Montenegrin LO foresee the sanction of nullity of the contract, while in the case of unintentional over-insurance, the contract remains in force, the insurance amount is reduced to the actual value of the item, and the premium is reduced in proportion to that established value.[333]

*317.* The consequence of over-insurance is the right of the conscientious party to request the annulment of the contract. However, in practice, insurers rarely decide to request cancellation of the contract because the intention to conclude this contract with the intent of over-insuring the object is a subjective circumstance that is difficult to prove. It could also be argued that paying a higher premium for the resulting damage is a sufficient sanction for a non-conscientious party. Thus, the general terms and conditions of insurance do not provide for the right of the insurer to request cancellation of the contract in cases of over-insurance.[334]

*318.* It is interesting that our legislator does not use the term 'insurance contractor' in defining over-insurance, which would limit the possibility of fraud to the claims of the owner of the item regarding its value. The legislator uses the term 'one party', by which they intend to show that the fraud, in this case, may be committed by both contracting parties. When defining the consequences of over-insurance when both contractual parties are conscientious, the legislator uses this term and provides for the contract to remain in force and for the premiums and insurance sums to be proportionally reduced in relation to the correctly determined value of the item. However, in the third paragraph of this article, the legislator states: 'In both cases, the conscientious insurer keeps the received premiums and has the right to an unreduced premium for the current period.' How can we then interpret this paragraph? The law provided for a solution only in the case of the conscientiousness of the insurer, either in the case of conscientiousness or in the case of unconscientiousness of the policyholder. With that, the law has regulated three out of four possible cases. The fourth possibility would be that the insurer is unconscientious and the policyholder is conscientious. So, one can imagine a situation in which the insurer would be the one who determines the value of the insured item in order to collect a higher insurance premium and therefore value the item at a higher value. In this case, the policyholder may not know the true value of the item and may be forced to accept the insurer's estimate in order to insure it. In the case of a contract concluded in this way, if no adverse consequences occur, the insurer would charge a higher insurance premium.

*319.* The case of over-insurance known to both contracting parties has also been discussed in the theory of insurance law since there have been cases in practice realised not by the will of the contracting parties but by the asking of the creditor in mortgage loans where both parties knew that the value of the insurance sum was

333. Jasna Pak, *supra*, pp. 266–237.
334. Slobodan Perović & Dragoljub Stojanović, *supra*, p. 505.

too high for the specific object of insurance, but willingly entered into the contract, knowing that in the case of risk realisation, the insurance sum would never be paid out in the contracted amount.[335]

*320.* Since the insurance contract is a long-term contract, the situation arises when, during the duration of the contract, a change in the value of an object can happen, e.g., *when* there is a decrease in its value. In the case of a reduction of the value of the insured object, each contracting party has the right to request a reduction of the insurance sum and the insurance premium from the day he submits the request.[336] This usually occurs as a result of wear and tear due to use, a price drop, a reduction in the number and value of the insured items, alienation of some of the insured items due to a decrease in the value of the item as a result of the occurrence of the insured event if the item is not repaired or replaced.[337]

### *B. Under-Insurance*

*321.* According to the general provisions regulating the purpose of property insurance, the limitation of the amount of compensation is negotiable and the clauses of a contract, in which the amount of compensation is limited to a sum that is lower than the amount of damage, are valid. In these cases, the object is under-insured and special provisions of the LO apply.

*322.* The LO connects the under-insurance to the beginning of the relevant period of insurance. So, in the case where the value of the insured object was higher than the amount of insurance at the beginning of the relevant period of insurance, the amount of compensation owed by the insurer shall be proportionally reduced, unless otherwise provided by the contract.[338]

*323.* Application of the principle of proportionality, in this case, means that the insurance amount is calculated when the product of the value of the object of insurance and the incurred damage is divided by the value of the object insured. The application of this principle insures that the amount received by the insured is proportional to the value of the object and the value of the insurance. But these rules are of a yielding kind, since otherwise they may be agreed upon by the parties, and this agreement will not be in conflict with the principle of compensation since the damage suffered is real but the initial value of the object is determined to be lower than the real value. This exceptional case of this rule is constituted by the LO. In a case where it is stipulated by the insurance contract that the relationship between

335. Nikola Dožić, *Nesavjesnost obije ugovorne strane kod nadosiguranja imovine*, XXI Međunarodni naučni skup – Udruženje za odštetno pravo, 2018, p. 421.
336. *See*: Article 1030, LO.
337. Predrag Šulejić, *supra*, p. 343.
338. *See*: Article 1033, para. 1, LO.

the value of the object and the amount of insurance shall have no relevance in determining the amount of compensation, the insurer shall be liable to pay the entire compensation up to the amount of the insurance.[339]

## II. Subrogation

### A. *General Rules on Subrogation*

*324.* The LO contains some general rules on performance through subrogation. There is a distinction made between contractual and statutory subrogation, as well as a general distinction between personal (subrogation of the parties) and real (subrogation of the object) subrogation.

*325.* Contractual subrogation exists in the case of the performance of another person's obligation when each party rendering performance may stipulate with the creditor, prior to the performance or in the course of it, that the claim that is being performed should be transferred to him, together with all, or only some, of the accessory rights. A creditor's rights may also be transferred to the party who has rendered the performance on the grounds of a contract between the debtor and the party rendering performance concluded prior to the performance. The subrogation of the rights of the creditor by the party rendering performance shall take place at the moment of the performance.[340]

*326.* Statutory subrogation exists in a case where an obligation is fulfilled by a person having some legal interest in the matter, and then the creditor's claim shall be transferred to that person by the operation of the law itself at the moment of performance, together with all accessory rights.[341] As a general rule, it is established that a party who has rendered performance and to whom the claim was transferred may not request from a debtor more than has been paid to the creditor.[342]

*327.* The LO also contains provisions on: subrogation in cases of partial performance and transfer of accessory rights;[343] evidence and instruments of securing the claim;[344] exemption from liability of a creditor for the existence and collectability of the claim.[345]

339. *See*: Article 1033, para. 2, LO.
340. *See*: Article 306, LO.
341. *See*: Article 307, LO.
342. *See*: Article 310, LO.
343. *See*: Article 308, LO.
344. *See*: Article 309, LO.
345. *See*: Article 311, LO.

*B. Subrogation in an Insurance Contract*

*328.* In the area of insurance contracts, special rules of subrogation are established by the LO. There are different rules regarding personal and real subrogation.

*329.* Personal subrogation may exist in cases in which the insured has suffered a loss and a third person is responsible for the damage. In this case, the insured is the party that has suffered the loss. By the general rules, the insured may choose between two persons from whom they may claim compensation. The liable person is the one that must pay the damage, but if the object was insured, the insurer may also set their claim against the insurer.

*330.* The insured in this case may choose, but they may not cumulate the claims and ask both the tortfeasor and the insurer to cover the claim in full because this is a breach of the principle of compensation. Since there is more certainty in the collection of the claim from the insurer, it may be expected that the insured will, in most cases, aim their claim towards the insurer. If the insured chooses to set their claim with the insurer, the tortfeasor may not be released from their obligation to pay the damages caused, so the rights of the insured will be transferred to the insurer, so upon the payment of compensation from insurance, the insurer shall acquire, by law, all the rights of the insured person against the person liable for damage on whatever ground, up to the total amount of compensation.[346] The LO does not require any form for the realisation of subrogation rights, so the payment of the insurer is sufficient for the subrogation. There is no obligation on the part of the insurer to inform the liable person of the subrogation. The rights of the insurer are limited by the amount of their payment to the insurer and by the amount of damages that the liable persons must pay to the insured. The insurer may not claim their expenses in determining the amount of payment to the insured or the expenses of the proceedings.

*331.* The transfer of the rights from the insured to the insurer is a prerequisite for payment by the insurer. If the transfer of rights is entirely or partially impossible through the fault of the insured person, the insurer shall be released correspondingly from their obligation towards the insured person.[347] So, the insured is liable for the transfer possibility and must not be culpable for the impossibility of the transfer of rights, or they will lose their rights under the insurance contract. The courts have reiterated that, for the transfer of rights to the insurer, no special legal transaction is required and that the grounds for third-party liability are irrelevant. The Supreme Court has pointed out that subrogation represents the institution of property rights, on the basis of which all the rights of the insured towards the third party, who is responsible for the damage on any grounds, are transferred to the insurer upon payment of damages.[348]

346. *See*: Article 1036, para. 1, LO.
347. *See*: Article 1036, para. 2, LO.
348. *See*: Supreme Court of Montenegro, Rev. No. 53/18.

*332.* If the insurer did not pay the full amount of the damages, the insured may claim the difference between the paid amount by the insurer and the damage suffered by the insured from the liable person. Although the insurer has paid a part of the damage, their right by subrogation may not supersede the right of the insured toward the liable person, so the insured person shall be entitled to reimbursement from the liable party's means for the remaining part of compensation prior to the payment of the insurer's claim on the grounds of rights that have been transferred to them.[349]

*333.* This rule was set in order to ensure that the transfer of rights from the insured person to the insurer may not be to the detriment of the insured person, since the insured is the only one who has the right to full compensation. In the event that the liable party cannot pay the whole sum of the damage, the insured, who has received partial remuneration of damages, may claim the rest from the liable party. In the event the insured succeeds, their damage will be remunerated in full, but there is the question of the claim of the insurer, who may ask for the amount the insurer paid to the insured from the liable party. If the liable party is in a poor financial condition, it is questionable if the insurer will succeed in the claim. But in this case, there is no fault on the part of the insured, and the insurer may not ask for the part of the damages they have paid out. Consequently, this is one of the reasons why the insurance is concluded, since there is always the possibility of not being able to collect on the claim from the liable person. However, an out-of-court settlement between the insurer and the injured party means that the claim against the insurer and the insured is settled, even though the out-of-court settlement did not cover the entire damage.[350]

*334.* It may be the case that the liable person is insured against the liability for the damages they incur to third parties, so the claim may be set against the insurer of the liable person. The only limitation to the success of the subrogation claim in this case would be that the insurer of the damaged is also the insurer of the liable person. In this case, there could be grounds for the success of the claim if the insurance of liability could be voided on the grounds of the culpability of the insured, so consequently, the liable person would have to bear the amount of damage they have caused.

*335.* The rules of transfer of an insured person's rights to the insurer will not apply in some cases determined by law. There will be no subrogation of the insurer if the damage was caused by a relative in the direct line of descendancy with the insured person, a person under the care and responsibility of the insured person, a person living with the insured person in the same household, or a person who is an employee of the insured person.[351] In these cases, if the transfer were allowed, the insured would again suffer damages, since they would consequently be the ones who would suffer from the realisation of the rights of the insurer after subrogation.

349. *See*: Article 1036, para. 3, LO.
350. *See*: Supreme Court of Montenegro, Rev. No. 720/11.
351. *See*: Article 1036, para. 4, LO.

There are two exceptions to the application of this rule. The first is in a case where the person caused the damage by intentional misconduct, and the second is in a case where a particular person who is liable is insured against liability, so that the insurer may demand redress of the amount paid to the insured person from the latter's insurer.

*336.* Real subrogation exists in cases where there is a change in the object of the legal transaction and the identity and regulation of the transaction stay the same. This can happen when the insured object is owned by one person who has given some interest in this object to a third person, such as in the case of security rights. This third person, third to the insurance contract, has some rights towards the insured object and is an interested party in the case of the insured event occurring. The LO has constituted a special provision regarding these types of cases so that, after the occurrence of an insured event, a right of security and other rights existing previously in relation to the insured object shall have as their subject the compensation owed, both in the case of insuring one's own objects and in the case of insuring another person's objects because of a duty to keep and restitute them, so that the insurer shall not be able to pay compensation to the insured person without the consent of the holder of such rights.[352]

*337.* In this case, the insurer will be relieved of their obligation if they pay out the sum after receiving the consent of the holder of the security or another right to the insured object because these persons have the right to claim payment directly from the insurer.[353] If the insurer pays out the claim without the consent of the holder of these rights, the insurer will still be liable to them for the entire amount of damages. They will also be relieved of this obligation in the case where they had paid out the claim but did not know and were not aware of the rights of the holder.[354] Thus, the insurer should be informed about the existence of these rights by the insured to the insured object. The rules of security rights apply here, so in the case of the insurer's payment without the consent of the holder: the insurer will be liable up to the insured amount if the claim is higher or to the amount of the claim if it is lower than the insured sum; the insurer will be liable only to the person who by the rules of security rights has the priority for payment (as in the case of a mortgage, the first person who was recorded in the land register) if their claim is above the limit of the insurance.

*338.* Similar to this is the matter of insurance policy *vinculation*. In this case, the provision is entered into the insurance contract on the assignment of the right of recovery, usually by the creditor of the object owner, upon approving the credit to the owner, since the insurance of the object purchased on credit is the usual means of security in these types of contracts. In this case, the creditor would have a direct claim towards the insurer in the event of the insured event occurring, and the payment of the insurer would represent the performance of the obligation of the insured

352. *See*: Article 1035, para. 1, LO.
353. *See*: Article 1035, para. 2, LO.
354. *See*: Article 1035, para. 3, LO.

towards the creditor in their credit contract. The similarity with real subrogation is that in this case, the insurer will have to pay the direct claim of the creditor, but in this case, there is no real subrogation because the insured is transferring only his future uncertain claim to the creditor. When the insured event occurs, the insurer's obligation is to pay the calculated damage in full, up to the value of the insured object, if the sum insured is equal to or higher than the value of the insured object. This means that the insurer is obliged to pay not only the remainder of the debt towards the bank but the whole amount of the damage. This was the subject of the Supreme Court ruling, which had to reiterate this obligation of the insurer, who had paid only the amount still owed to the bank.[355]

## III. Multiple Insurance

### *A. Multiple and Double Insurance*

*339.* The insured does not have to insure the object for its full value, i.e., it is allowed to insure items at a value lower than the true value of those items. Also, after the insurance has been concluded in this way, the insured may conclude a contract with another insurer on the insurance of this object up to the amount of its real value. In this case, we are talking about multiple insurances where there is an obligation for each insurer to pay its part of the insurance sum. There is no violation of the principle of indemnification, which is why each of these contracts is valid.[356]

*340.* If an object is insured with two or more insurers against the same risk, for the same interest, and at the same time, and the sum of the insurance sums exceeds the value of the object, each of the contracts concluded in this way, if the insurance contractor did not act negligently, is valid. In this case, it is double insurance, and each insurer has the right to claim the insurance premium, but the insured has the right to claim compensation from each of them individually, but not in a total sum higher than the amount of the damage.

*341.* After the occurrence of the insured event, the policyholder is obliged to inform each insurer of the names and addresses of the other insurers, as well as the insurance sums of the individual contracts concluded with them. The amount to be paid by each of them is calculated in proportion to the sum of the individual insurance with the total sum of all insurances. If one of them has paid more, that one has the right to demand payment from the other insurers. If the insurance amount is not indicated in any contract or if unlimited coverage is provided, that contract is considered to have been concluded for the highest insurance amount. When one of the insurers is unable to pay the amount to which that insurer has committed itself in the contract, the others will be responsible for that insurer in proportion to the others' parts.[357]

355. *See*: Supreme Court of Montenegro, Rev. No. 957/14.
356. Slobodan Perović & Dragoljub Stojanović, *supra*, p. 507.
357. *See*: Article 1031, paras 1–6, LO.

*342.* Non-compliance with the obligation of notification is not sanctioned by Montenegrin legislation. In some legal systems, failure to fulfil this obligation is subject to strict consequences, even up to releasing the insurer from the obligation, if the failure to notify is the result of intent.[358]

*343.* If the insurance contractor concluded a contract that created double insurance but did not know about the previously concluded contract (the contract was concluded by someone else), they may, within one month from the day they learned about that insurance, demand a corresponding reduction in the insurance sum and the premiums of a later concluded contract, with that insurer having the right to retain the premiums received and entitled to premiums for the current period.[359] If the insured does not inform the insurer about other contracts, the insured is negligent. However, double insurance usually occurs due to ignorance of an already existing insurance contract for that item, so the insured shows their conscientiousness by reporting the fact of double insurance.[360]

*344.* The negligence of a double insurance contractor is sanctioned by leaving the possibility for the insurer to request cancellation of the contract, whereby the insurer will have the right to keep the received premiums and request an unreduced premium for the current period.[361] Therefore, the legislator has provided for a sanction only in the cases where the policyholder was negligent when creating the double insurance. Negligence does not have to exist at the time of the conclusion of the contract that created the double insurance. It is possible that the policyholder was conscientious at the time of double insurance, i.e., the policyholder did not know about the existence of another insurance contract at the time of creation.

*345.* So, if, after learning about the existence of a previously concluded contract, the insurance contractor does not request a reduction within the deadline, then negligence of the contractor occurs. The contractor then does not have the right to request a reduction of the sum and the insurance premium, and the insurers have the right to request the full amount of the premiums, although their liability in the event of the insured event would be less.

*346.* It must also be mentioned that, in practice, it can happen that the total insurance sums exceed the value of the insured object, but that there is no double insurance: when one person concludes an insurance contract with a high deductible amount, and another concludes a contract for a value that does not exceed the deductible amount. By simply adding the sums of insurance, it would appear that there is double insurance, but in essence, the value of the sums of insurance that the insurers will be obliged to pay does not exceed the value of the insured object.[362]

358. Slobodan Perović & Dragoljub Stojanović, *supra*, p. 508.
359. *See*: Article 1031, para. 7, LO.
360. Jasna Pak, *supra*, p. 239.
361. *See*: Article 1031, para. 9, LO.
362. Jasna Pak, *supra*, p. 239.

*347.* The principle of indemnification applied in the field of property insurance prohibits the insured from cumulating the compensation of insurance sums from several insurance contracts, thus obtaining more than the amount of damage. When a person has concluded several insurance contracts so that the total value exceeds the value of the item, with the intention of obtaining an illegal benefit, the same rules will apply as for additional insurance of items with one insurer.[363]

### *B. Co-insurance*

*348.* The LO regulates co-insurance in the same part dealing with undesirable cases in non-life insurance. There is only one provision intended to point out that, in the case of co-insurance, there are no similar consequences as in the case of undesirable over-insurance. So, should a contract of insurance be concluded with several insurers who agree on the joint bearing and distribution of risk, each insurer designated in the insurance policy shall be liable to the insured person for the entire compensation.[364] By this provision, the joint and several liability of the insurers involved is constituted by the law.

## §2. Life Insurance

*349.* Life insurance is the second part of the major division between non-life and life insurance in the Montenegrin legal system.[365] In that regard, special provisions of the LI are instated in order to organise a system by which a separate company needs to be formed if someone would like to operate on the non-life and life insurance markets in Montenegro.[366] The basic forms of life insurance contracts are: insurance against death; survivorship insurance for a certain period of time; and mixed insurance contracts that usually cover both risks – death and survivorship. Unlike a non-life insurance contract, where the principle of compensation is applicable, in life insurance contracts, the obligation of the insurer is to pay a previously determined amount of money.

*350.* Besides these contracts, which are always considered life insurance contracts, the LI allows for an insurance company engaged in life insurance activities to also perform activities related to associated accident insurance and voluntary health insurance with respect to healthcare expenses, provided that these classes of insurance refer to the person who has concluded the life insurance contract.[367] But unlike life insurance contracts, the characteristics of these contracts are that, in the case of accident insurance and payment of medical expenses, this may have a compensatory character. But, usually the contracts contain provisions on the fixed

---

363. Predrag Šulejić, *supra*, p. 349.
364. *See*: Article 1032, LO.
365. *See*: Article 10, LI.
366. *See*: Article 19, para. 2, LI.
367. *See*: Article 20, LI.

amounts that will be paid out by the insurer in case of hospital treatment or temporary incapacitation for work, which are agreed upon during the contract conclusion. In these cases, there is no compensatory payment, since the amount of the insurer's obligation is predetermined and the actual amount of losses incurred by the insured is irrelevant. According to the provisions of the LO in contracts of insurance for persons (life insurance and accident insurance), the amount of insurance to be paid by the insurer on the occurrence of the insured event shall be determined in the insurance policy by agreement between the contracting parties.[368]

*351.* So, in the case of life insurance contracts, there is no implementation of a system of compensation and, subsequently, no implementation of the rights of subrogation of the insurer, since there is no prohibition of accumulation of the insured sum and the payments received from the liable party. Basically, the rules pertaining to the relationship between the insured amount and the insured interest and the rules on over-insurance and under-insurance do not apply in life insurance. The LO is very clear on this, so in the case of life insurance, an insurer paying the insured amount shall have no right whatsoever to compensation against a third party liable for the occurrence of the insured event. The right to seek compensation from a third liable party for the occurrence of the insured event belongs to the insured person or beneficiary, independently of their right to the insured amount. The only limitation to these rules is set in cases of insurance covering the consequences of accidents stipulated as liability insurance, where these rules will not apply.[369]

*352.* Also, a specificity of insurance contracts is that there is no limitation in contract conclusion pertaining to the material interest of the insurance contractor, so the contractor is free to conclude the contract without any material interest. A major limitation that exists in this matter affects the validity of the life insurance contract insuring the third party's life. The validity of the contract is dependent on the written consent of that third party upon the conclusion of the insurance contract and on the insurance amount. This consent may be a part of the insurance policy or may be the subject of a separate document.[370] The age limit of the third party is the next limitation, so in a case where a minor is the third party in the life insurance contract against death, this person must be over 14 years of age, and the contract is then dependent on the written consent of this person's legal representative and the written consent of the insured person themself. Life insurance against the death of minors younger than 14 and persons completely deprived of business capacity is prohibited. The insurer must repay the insurance contractor all the insurance premiums received under such a contract.[371]

*353.* The last and other major difference between life insurance and non-life insurance is in the certainty of the risk and the possibility of the insured event occurring. In a life insurance contract, it is evident that the risk of death will occur, but

---

368. *See*: Article 1036, LO.
369. *See*: Article 1045, LO.
370. *See*: Article 1043, LO.
371. *See*: Article 1044, LO.

it is uncertain when it will occur, and this is enough uncertainty for the legality of the insured risk. In the case of a life insurance contract for the whole life of the insured, it is evident that the insured event will occur, but the time of its occurrence is uncertain.

*354.* In addition to the elements that are constituents of every insurance policy, a life insurance policy must include indications of the first name and surname of the person whose life is insured, their date of birth, and an event or time limit, which are prerequisite for requesting payment of the amount insured. This policy may be made out to a specific person or to order, but it may not be made out to the bearer. The endorsement of the insurance policy made out to order is valid if it contains an indication of the name of the beneficiary, the date of endorsement, and the signature of the endorser.[372]

*355.* In a life insurance contract, there are several more rights of the insurance contractor that may be realised prior to the occurrence of the insured event. These are the rules on repurchase of the policy, advance payment and the insurance policy as a security.

*356.* At the demand of the insurance contractor of the life insurance contract concluded for the lifetime of the insured person, the insurer is obliged to pay to the latter the repurchasing value of the insurance policy, if at least three annual insurance premiums have been paid. The terms and conditions for this request, as well as the method for calculating that value, must be in the insurance policy, all in accordance with the terms and conditions of the insurer. This right is guaranteed to the insurance contractor and may not be realised by the beneficiary or by the creditors of the negotiator, but upon his request, it will be paid out to the beneficiary if his designation is irrevocable. The exception is made in case the insurance policy is transferred to the creditor as a security, in which case he will have the right to demand the payment of the repurchase value if his claim has not been settled at maturity.[373]

*357.* An insurance contractor of life insurance that is concluded for the lifetime of the insured person may request from the insurer advance payment of the amount insured, up to the amount of the repurchase value of the policy. This advance payment may be subsequently repaid by the insurance contractor. The obligation of the insurance contractor is to pay the interest against the advanced payment, and in the event that the contractor is late with the payment of the interest due, the insurer will proceed as if the insurance contractor has requested a repurchase. The terms of granting, the possibility of returning, the amount of the interest rate, and the consequences of a failure to pay the interest due must be indicated in the insurance policy as provided by the terms and conditions of the insurance.[374]

---

372. *See*: Article 1040, LO.
373. *See*: Article 1051, LO.
374. *See*: Article 1052, LO.

*358.* The obligations of the insurer in a life insurance contract also differ from the general rules on insurance contracts in the case of giving the life insurance policy as a security. In this case, this transfer of rights has effects on the insurer only if he has been notified in writing that the policy has been given as a security to the specific creditor. One of the limitations for the transfer of the life insurance policy is set in the case of a policy made out to order so that the security will have effect only if the transfer was made by the endorsement.[375]

375. *See*: Article 1053, LO.

# Chapter 6. Insurance and Third Parties

## §1. Designation of the Beneficiary in Life Insurance Contracts

*359.* By the legal definition of an insurance contract, there are only two parties in this contract: the insurance contractor and the insurer, in the phase of the contract conclusion. In the same definition, in the phase of the realisation of the insurance contract, if an event takes place that represents the case covered by the insurance, the insurer has the obligation to pay to the insured person or to a third party compensation, the stipulated amount, or to do something else.[376] So, the definition of the insurance contract assumes that the obligation of the insurer may be to pay the stipulated amount to the insured person, who may be the insurance contractor but does not have to be, or to a third party.

*360.* The insurance contractor may negotiate and conclude the contract in their own name and on behalf of a third person. In this case, it is clear why we have insisted on precise terminology and differentiation of the term 'insurance contractor'. In this case, the insurance contractor has all the obligations under the insurance contract, and the third party has all the rights under the contract. The third person, in this case, does not partake in the conclusion of the contract, nor are they represented by the insurance contractor. In this case, they are truly a third party in the contract, who may be directly named as a third party or by presenting the criteria for determination of that third party in the contract, meaning that it can be determined who they are.

*361.* Designating a beneficiary who will acquire the rights from the contract is a standard in life insurance contracts. So, the insurance contractor may designate a beneficiary in the contract itself, at the time of the contract conclusion, or in other legal transactions after the conclusion of the life insurance contract. The insurance contractor may make this designation even in their will, so there is no prior knowledge of the insurer about the designated beneficiary until the death of the insurance contractor.[377] In the case of a life insurance contract that relates to the life of a person other than the insurance contractor, that other person must give their written consent for the designation of the beneficiary.[378] So, besides the obligation of obtaining the written consent needed for the insurance contractor to conclude the life insurance contract that relates to the life of another person, for the designation of a beneficiary in this contract, additional written consent is needed by the person whose life is insured.

*362.* The simplest way of designating a beneficiary is by designating his name. But, the designation of a beneficiary is valid even if that designation contains data

376. *See*: Article 994, LO.
377. *See*: Article 1054, para. 1, LO.
378. *See*: Article 1054, para. 2, LO.

necessary for the designation. So, it is possible that the beneficiary is only determinable at the moment of designation.[379] The insurance contractor may designate that their children, descendants or spouse will be the beneficiaries. This designation would mean that all their children at the moment of the contractor's death are beneficiaries, and the benefit shall also accrue to those who are born after the moment of their designation of their children as beneficiaries. If a spouse is designated as a beneficiary, this will be interpreted so that the person who is, at the moment of death, the spouse of the insurance contractor will be the beneficiary. It is irrelevant who was the spouse of the beneficiary at the moment of the designation of the beneficiary if it is a case of designation by affiliation through marriage.[380]

*363.* The other question is how the way of sharing the benefit will be determined when several beneficiaries are designated. If the insurance contractor has determined the precise amounts or percentages of shares of each of the beneficiaries, then there is no need for additional deliberation. Two situations are possible. First, when all the designated beneficiaries are successors of the insurance contractor, their children or their descendants, if there is no determined way of distributing the benefits among them, such distribution shall be done proportionally to their inheritance shares. Second, when all the designated beneficiaries are not successors of the insurance contractor on the grounds of inheritance, if there is no determined way of distribution of benefit among them, the amount insured shall be distributed in equal shares.[381]

*364.* Is the designation revocable, and when will we consider that the designated beneficiary has refused the benefit? These questions need further deliberation. The designation of a beneficiary is revocable by the insurance contractor and only by them. This is a personal right of the insurance contractor and may not be inherited by their successors, nor may it be transferred or used by their creditors. The insurance contractor may revoke the clause on benefit only until the beneficiary comes to acknowledge it by stating, in any way whatsoever, their intention to accept the benefit – after which the clause becomes irrevocable. In two cases, the LO allows revocation of the beneficiary clause even after acceptance. First, revocation is allowed if the beneficiary has attempted to murder the insured person. The second case depends on the existence of consideration, so if the benefit is granted without consideration, the revocation shall be subjected to provisions regulating the revoking of a gift.[382] Revocation of a gift is generally possible if the recipient of a gift, by their behaviour towards the donor or towards a person close to the donor, demonstrates grave ingratitude or if the donor has insufficient means of sustenance. Grave ingratitude is shown particularly in cases where the gift recipient has committed against the donor or a person close to the donor (spouse, parent, child) a

379. *See*: Article 1054, para. 3, LO.
380. *See*: Article 1054, para. 4, LO.
381. *See*: Article 1055, LO.
382. *See*: Article 1056, paras 1–3, LO.

criminal offence, gravely violated some statutory duty towards the donor, or intentionally provoked significant damage to their property.[383]

*365.* So, revocation may be done up until the acceptance of the beneficiary but no later than the realisation of the insured event. In a life insurance contract, the insured event is the death of the insurance contractor, so after this moment, it is impossible for the insurance contractor to revoke the beneficiary. The beneficiary may consent upon notification of their designation. But they must acknowledge their acceptance of the benefit intended for them within one month of the death of the negotiator of insurance. The beneficiary shall be considered to have refused the benefit intended for them if they fail, after the death of the negotiator of insurance, at the invitation of their successors, to acknowledge its acceptance within one month.[384]

*366.* The rights of the beneficiaries are personal rights, and they may be realised by a direct claim to the insurer. According to the provisions of the LO, the beneficiary is the only one entitled to request the insured amount from the moment of contract conclusion, regardless of the way and time of them being designated as the beneficiary and regardless of whether they have stated their acceptance prior to or after the death of the insured person. So, in this case, the LO constitutes a legal fiction that the beneficiary has the right from the moment of contract conclusion, even though they were designated a beneficiary at a later moment, and maybe their acceptance of this designation came after the death of the insurance contractor. This means that the LO has tied the right to the insured amount from this contract only to the beneficiary, so the insurance contractor or any other person did not have any rights towards the insurer at any moment from the contract conclusion. Also, the beneficiary is entitled to request payment of the insured amount directly from the insurer.[385]

*367.* In the same article pertaining to the rights to direct action of the beneficiaries, the LO has regulated the claims of the beneficiaries in the case when the insurance contractor has designated their descendants as the beneficiaries. Although these norms do not pertain to the direct actions of the beneficiaries, they are of importance to the status of the beneficiary if they are the descendants of the insurance contractor and to the relationship between the insured amount and the total estate of the insurance contractor. The successors of the insurance contractors do not need to become heirs of the insurance contractor, or rather, they do not accept the inheritance in the probate proceedings. After the insurance contractor has designated their children, their descendants and, generally, their successors as beneficiaries, each one of these beneficiaries shall be entitled to a corresponding part of the insured amount, even if they have renounced the inheritance.[386] Although special rules apply regarding division of the insured amount among the beneficiaries, who are at the same

383. *See*: Article 586, para. 2, LO.
384. *See*: Article 1054, para. 4, LO.
385. *See*: Article 1057, para. 2, LO.
386. *See*: Article 1057, para. 3, LO.

time the heirs of the insurance contractor, by these provisions of the LO, the legislator wanted to point out that these two capacities (heir and beneficiary) are not interconnected in a way that would hinder the beneficiary from realising their rights if they have renounced the inheritance.

*368.* Another provision of that article is related to the question of whether the insured amount represents a part of the total estate of the insurance contractor. The insured amount to be paid to the beneficiary does not enter into the total estate of inheritance of the insurance contractor, even if the beneficiaries are the contractor's own successors.[387] The question here is, if the insured sum represents a part of the total estate of the insurance contractor, will the creditors of the insurance contractor have any rights towards the insured sum? The LO contains detailed provisions blocking any claim by the creditors towards the insured amount contracted for the beneficiary. Since the problem here may be the over-indebtedness of the insurance contractor, who was paying insurance premiums that were disproportionally high compared to their possibilities at the moment of payment, the LO states that some rights of the creditors may be given to them but not towards the insured amount. In the case described, the creditors may request a part of such payments of the premium, exceeding the possibilities of the insurance contractor, if the requirements by which the creditors are entitled to oppose the debtor's legal actions are met.[388] In this case, the insurer would have the obligation to pay the entire amount of the insured sum but would have to pay some of the funds to the creditors in the amount of the part of the premiums exceeding the possibility of the insurance contract.

*369.* Assignment of the insured amount by the beneficiary is possible and allowed by the LO under certain conditions, even prior to the occurrence of the insured event. So, a beneficiary is allowed to transfer to another their right to the insured amount, even prior to the occurrence of the insured event, but the beneficiary will need written consent from the insurance contractor. This written consent from the insurance contractor must contain the name of the proposed assignee, and in the case where the insurance relates to the life of another person, the same consent must be obtained from that person as well.[389]

*370.* The LO also deals with the question of the death of the designated beneficiary prior to the maturity of the insured principal or annuity. In the case where the beneficiary was designated without consideration and died prior to the maturity of the insured principal or annuity, the insurance benefit does not belong to the beneficiary's successors but to the next beneficiary. If there are no other designated beneficiaries, then the benefit belongs to the estate of the negotiator of the insurance.[390] In the opposite case, this provision could be interpreted as meaning that if that beneficiary was designated with consideration, the benefits would be inheritable by the successors of the designated beneficiary.

---

387. *See*: Article 1057, para. 1, LO.
388. *See*: Article 1058, LO.
389. *See*: Article 1059, LO.
390. *See*: Article 1060, LO.

*371.* The designation of the beneficiary is the logical and expected outcome of the conclusion of the life insurance contract, so it is the acceptance of the designation by the beneficiary and, in general, the realisation of the designation in the case of the insured event occurring. But there is the possibility that the insurance contractor does not designate the beneficiary at all, or it may happen that the clause on determining the beneficiary remains ineffective due to the revocation or refusal of the designated person or due to some other reason, and the insurance contractor fails to determine another beneficiary. In all of these cases, the legal consequence is the same: the insured amount shall belong to the estate of the insurance contractor, and its part shall pass, together with their remaining rights, to their successors.[391]

*372.* One of the problems that the LO has anticipated is the payment of the insured amount by the insurer to an unauthorised person. Since the designation of the beneficiary may happen up until the death of the insurance contractor, it could be that the insurer was unaware of the designation. In the event that the insurer pays the insured amount to a person who would be entitled to it if the negotiator of insurance failed to designate the beneficiary, he will be released from his obligation under the contract of insurance if, at the moment of payment, he was not aware, or could not have been aware, that the beneficiary was designated by a will or by some other act not related to his knowledge, but the beneficiary shall be entitled to request repayment from the person who has accepted the amount insured.[392] By this provision, the designated beneficiary is deprived of their rights towards the insurer and the direct claim, since the insurer made the payment to the unauthorised person in good faith. But the beneficiary has the option to request payment from the person who has accepted the amount insured. By the provisions of the LO, the same rules also apply in the case that the problem of unauthorised payment was caused by the replacement of the beneficiary, in the case that the insurer was unaware of that replacement.[393]

*373.* Since the life insurance contract with the designation of the beneficiary, or without it, is a contract in favour of a third person, the question is: what are the objections that the insurer can make in opposition to the designated beneficiary claim? By the general rules of the LO, an insurer can raise against a third person all defences that they are otherwise entitled to against a contracting party on the grounds of a contract by means of which the benefit for the third person has been stipulated. Other objections that the insurer could raise against the contracting party by means of legal relations outside of the insurance contract in question may not be raised against the designated beneficiary.[394] But the insurer may invoke the question of compensation for their obligation towards the designated beneficiary, even though this claim of the insurer towards the designated beneficiary is not related to the specific insurance contract.[395]

---

391. *See*: Article 1061, LO.
392. *See*: Article 1062, para. 1, LO.
393. *See*: Article 1062, para. 2, LO.
394. *See*: Article 145, LO.
395. Predrag Šulejić, *supra,* p. 492.

## §2. Personal Right of the Person Sustaining Damage and Direct Action

*374.* The general rules of the LO on the defences of the insurer contain some of the rules that are relevant for the direct action of third parties. As a general rule, the insurer is entitled, against the request by the bearer of the policy, as well as against the request of any other person referring to it, to set up all defences otherwise at their disposal on the grounds of the contract towards the person with whom they have concluded the contract of insurance. The exception is that in the case of mandatory liability insurance, the insurer is not entitled to raise against the claim for indemnity brought by a third party such defences to which they would be entitled against the insured. As an exception, according to the LO, the insurer may raise only those defences that originated prior to the occurrence of the insured event against a claim by the third party in the case of voluntary liability insurance and claims by holders of specific rights on the insured object whose rights have been passed, by operation of the law, from the destroyed or damaged object to the insurance compensation.[396] So, in the general rules on direct claims of third parties, the LO differentiates between the existence of voluntary and mandatory insurance against liability, and the provisions are more in the favour of the claimant in cases of mandatory insurance, since the law does not give the insurer the opportunity to raise the defences that it would have against the insured.

*375.* Under the special provisions of the LO, in the cases of liability insurance, the insurer is liable for damage caused by the insured event only if the third party sustaining damage requests compensation.[397] By this provision of the LO, a direct claim of the third party that sustained damage is established as a rule in the area of insurance against liability. The benefits of this direct claim are numerous, among which we can emphasise the simplification of the procedure for damage compensation and its expediency. The obligation of the insurer is limited by the amount of insurance, but again, the LO accepts the expenses of litigation over the liability of the insured person as expenses that will be covered by the insurer within the amount of the insurance.[398]

*376.* In the case of liability insurance, the person sustaining damage may request compensation for loss sustained due to an event falling within the sphere of liability of the insured person directly from the insurer, but only up to the amount of the insurer's obligation.[399] The obligation of the insurer exists only for cases that may fall within the sphere of the insured person's liability and again only to the extent of the amount of the insurer's obligation. For all claims that are higher than the insurer's liability, there is only the option of claiming the rest from the insured person who is liable for the damages. This may be achieved by a joint claim or by a subsequent claim after the procedure with the insurer has taken place.

---

396. *See*: Article 1018, LO.
397. *See*: Article 1037, para. 1, LO.
398. *See*: Article 1037, para. 2, LO.
399. *See*: Article 1038, para. 1, LO.

*377.* This person sustaining damage has their own right to compensation from the insurance, from the day of the occurrence of the insured event, so that any subsequent change in the insured person's rights against the insurer shall have no effect on the right of a person sustaining damage to compensation.[400] By the former law on mandatory traffic insurance, a passenger who voluntarily entered the vehicle that caused the damage and who was aware of the fact that the vehicle was being driven by a person who had not passed their driving test was not entitled to compensation for the damage.[401]

## §3. Direct Action in Mandatory Traffic Insurance

*378.* The LMIT contains special provisions regarding the direct actions of persons suffering damage caused by traffic. Based on a compulsory insurance contract, a direct claim may be submitted to the insurer or to the Insurance Association with regard to the fact that the damage was caused by the insured and a known vehicle. In all cases where the damage was caused by the insured vehicle, the insurer who signed the contract in question is the one that will have the obligation to pay the damage. The cases in which the damaged party may present their claim to the Insurance Association are rather limited to those when the damage was caused by an uninsured vehicle, an unknown vehicle, or a vehicle insured by a company whose licence has been revoked or which has been subject to the initiation of liquidation or bankruptcy proceedings.[402] Also, one other provision of the LO is relevant here: owners of motor vehicles are jointly and severally liable for damage inflicted on third persons.[403] Third parties who suffer damage in a collision of two motor vehicles have the right to demand compensation from both joint and several debtors, regardless of the degree of their fault. The Supreme Court of Montenegro rejected the arguments of the insurer that the lower courts had to determine the degree of fault of the individual insured person in the case of a claim by a third person sustaining damage.[404] In another case, the Supreme Court pointed out that when damage is caused to a third party in a motor vehicle collision, the third injured party enjoys coverage up to twice the insured amount, since each insurance organisation is liable up to the limit of its liability. When the insurance limit has been paid, the injured party may claim up to the total damage only directly from the liable motorist.[405]

*379.* The LMIT contains detailed provisions on the procedure for the realisation of the direct claims. The insurance company or the Insurance Association is obliged to submit to the claimant, within sixty days of the day of receipt of a duly completed claim, a detailed offer for compensation if the liability for compensation and the amount of the claim are not disputable, or a detailed response if the liability for

---

400. *See*: Article 1038, para. 2, LO.
401. *See*: Supreme Court of Montenegro, Rev. No. 104/14.
402. *See*: Article 12, paras 1 and 2, LMIT.
403. *See*: Article 173, para. 4, LO.
404. *See*: Supreme Court of Montenegro, Rev. No. 35/07.
405. *See*: Supreme Court of Montenegro, Rev. No. 1002/16.

compensation or the amount of the claim is disputable. If the deadline is breached by the insurance company or by the insurance agency, the claimant may exercise their right to compensation for the damage by filing a lawsuit before a competent court.[406] In this manner, the LMIT constitutes the procedure that needs to be followed before making the claim in the court proceedings. If the claimant files a lawsuit before the deadline has expired, the court must reject the claimant's lawsuit as premature. This prior proceeding before the insurance company gives the insurance company the option of settling the claim out of court and gives them enough time to pay out the claim before the expenses of the court proceedings start to pile up. But not all situations are treated the same way, since some of the claims could be of such a nature that the period of time prescribed above is not enough for the company to assess the claim. In the event that the insurance company cannot assess the claim in such a way that it can pay out the final amount of compensation within the deadlines described above, it must offer to pay out the undisputed portion of its liability as an advance payment.[407] After the decision is made and the compensation is determined, the insurance company or the Insurance Association has eight days to pay out the agreed sum, unless otherwise specified in the agreement. Failing this obligation creates the obligation for the debtor to pay out the default interest rate to the claimant for the period from the expiry of the deadline for compensation payment to the day of actual payment.[408]

*380.* Since the claim, under the provisions of the LMIT, may be brought by the party suffering the damage, the question of defences of the insurance companies is again relevant. In response to the claim brought by the party suffering damage, the insurance company cannot present all the defences it could present to the insured person due to his failure to adhere to the law or contract based on the law or insurance contract.[409] This is especially relevant since all insurance contracts contain provisions of their termination due to the conduct of the insured person. The existence of these facts could be relevant to regulation of the future relations between the insurance company and the insured person, but it may not be the grounds for repealing the claim of the damaged party. The LMIT also constitutes the substitute rights of the insurance company against the person liable for the damage with respect to the amount of compensation paid, interest on the amount of compensation paid, and loss adjustment expenses, if the liability of the company has not been incurred pursuant to the terms and conditions of the compulsory traffic insurance contract.[410]

406. *See*: Article 12, paras 3 and 4, LMIT.
407. *See*: Article 13, LMIT.
408. *See*: Article 15, LMIT.
409. *See*: Article 16, para. 1, LMIT.
410. *See*: Article 16, para. 2, LMIT.

## Chapter 7. Termination of an Insurance Contract

*381.* Termination of insurance contracts may occur for many different reasons. Legal theory differentiates termination due to: performance of the contract, contract term expiry, cancellation of the contract, contract nullity, contract rescission, initiation of insolvency proceedings, and other causes.

### §1. Termination of an Insurance Contract in the Event of Contract Performance

*382.* As with any other contract, an insurance contract is concluded in order to be fulfilled, although the aleatory element is evident in this contract, so both parties are hopeful that there will be no need for its fulfilment of the obligation of the insurer. We can again differentiate between the situations in life and non-life insurance with regard to termination of the contract. In the case of the realisation of the insured event, in non-life insurance, if the object that is insured ceases to exist, the purpose of the insurance contract is realised, since there cannot be any other realisation of the risk. In the case where the realisation of the insured event damaged the insured object, there is a purpose in continuing the insurance relations. After the insurer's performance, the conditions are met for the termination of the contract by means of performance. Partial destruction of the insured object does not create grounds for the termination of the contract by means of performance. In the case of the occurrence of the insured event in life insurance contracts, meaning the death of the insured person, their total disability, or their surviving a particular moment, the same consequences of the contract termination are envisioned. Upon the performance of the insurer in the life insurance, in these cases, the contract is terminated by means of performance.[411]

*383.* Partial destruction of the insured object, or in the case of the life insurance contract, partial disability of the insured determined in a percentage lower than 100%, does not create grounds for termination of the contract by means of performance. In these cases, the contract continues to exist, but it may be subjected to changes in the conditions of the insurance, mainly in a reduction of the premiums, since, after the occurrence of the event, the risk in these cases is significantly lower.

*384.* These situations must be differentiated from those in which the object that is insured ceases to exist, the death of the insured or their total disability occurs, or by an event that is not covered by the insurance contract. In these cases, if this situation occurred during the period of coverage by the insurance contract and the destruction was the consequence of an uninsured event and there was no intent or gross negligence on the part of the insured, the insurance contract is terminated. In the event of the partial destruction of the insured object, the contract will continue to exist for the remaining part of the insured object, with the need for changes in

411. Predrag Šulejić, *supra*, p. 257.

the contract due to the lowering of the object's value. The intent or gross negligence of the insured in these cases is relevant for the realisation of the right of the insured to ask for prepaid premiums for the remaining term of the contract, since, in this case, the insured object was destroyed by the intent of the insured.[412] The LO contains two provisions that regulate these cases. So, if an insured object or an object whose use is the basis for concluding the liability insurance is lost in the course of the insurance period due to an event not provided for in the insurance policy, the contract shall cease to be valid for the future, while the insurer shall be obliged to provide restitution to the negotiator of the insurance part of the insurance premium, proportionate to the remaining time period.[413] The question of the validity of the insurance contract may be raised in cases where one of several objects encompassed by the contract has been lost due to an event not provided for in the insurance policy. In this case, the insurance will remain valid regarding the remaining objects, but necessary amendments may be introduced because of the reduction of the subject of insurance.[414]

## §2. Termination of an Insurance Contract in the Event of the Expiry of the Term

*385.* Termination of an insurance contract in the event of the expiry of the term is one of the most common cases of termination of an insurance contract, which affects the termination of the contract automatically. The moment of the expiration of the term can be precisely determined, or it can be determinable. Precise determination exists in situations where the contract or statute contains provisions on the last day of the term. The LO contains special provisions on the duration of non-life insurance contracts that differentiate between situations where the term of the contract is stipulated in the policy and cases where there is no determination of the duration of the insurance contract.

*386.* In the first case, unless otherwise stipulated, the contract of insurance shall begin to take effect twenty-four hours from the day designated in the insurance policy as the day of commencement of the insurance and shall continue to be effective until the end of the last day of the time limit stipulated for the insurance. In the second case, if an insurance time limit is not provided by the contract, each party is entitled to a rescission of the contract, becoming effective on the day of maturity of the insurance premium, after notifying the other party accordingly in writing, three months before the maturity of the premium, at the latest.[415] The LO provision in the second case treats the question of contract term and the right of contract cancellation since this is a case in which there is no term defined, so the natural end of the insurance contract is the cancellation of the contract. In the judgment of the Appellate Court of Montenegro, this rule was reiterated by stating that if the duration of

412. *Ibid.*, p. 258.
413. *See*: Article 1025, para. 1, LO.
414. *See*: Article 1025, para. 2, LO.
415. *See*: Article 1019 paras 1 and 2, LO.

the insurance is not determined by the contract, each party may terminate the contract before the expiration of the current insurance year by notifying the other party in writing no later than three months before the expiration of the current insurance year.[416]

*387.* A determinable term can be defined as the occurrence of an event or the starting or finishing of a certain action. Determinable terms are more common in transport insurance since it may be stipulated by the contract that it is valid from warehouse to warehouse, for specific transport, etc.[417]

*388.* In the event of an insurance contract term expiring, the effects of the contract are terminated *pro-futuro*, so all the effects of the contract in the past are invalid. There is a question of the effects of the damages on the insured object that are realised after the termination of the contract, but where the initial event occurred during the duration of the insurance contract and was covered by the insurance. These damages may be construed as the danger that has begun to be realised on the insured object and may be treated as the insured event that constitutes the insurer's obligation of performance.

*389.* There is also the question of prolongation of the insurance contract term, either by the provisions of the contract itself or by the general terms and conditions of the insurer. By the general terms on the insurance of property, if only the start of the insurance contract is stipulated in the contract, the insurance is prolonged each year for the following year if the contracting side does not cancel the contract at least three months before the current year.[418] This is considered a tacit prolongation of the insurance contract that is allowed by the LO, since there is no corrective norm of this law that would exclude this option.

## §3. Termination of an Insurance Contract in the Event of Cancellation

*390.* Cancellation of the insurance contract is more commonly used in cases where there is no term of insurance defined in the contract. The LO contains mandatory provisions regarding the cancellation of the contract. In the event that the insurance time limit is not provided by the contract, each party is entitled to a rescission of the contract, which will become effective on the day of the maturity of the insurance premium after notifying the other party accordingly in writing three months before the maturity of the premium at the latest. If the insurance is stipulated for a period exceeding five years, each party is entitled, after the expiration of

416. *See*: Appellate Court of Montenegro, Pž. No. 894/12.
417. Predrag Šulejić, *supra*, p. 254.
418. *See*: Opšti uslovi osiguranja imovine (General Terms of Property Insurance), Lovćen osiguranja, No. US-PR-OUI/10-12-cg, Art. 25, para. 2. Opšti uslovi osiguranja imovine, Sava osiguranja, No. OU-IM-06/21, Art. 25, para. 2. Opšti uslovi osiguranja imovine, Generali osiguranja, of 27 Feb. 2008, Art. 25, para. 2.

that time limit, to notify the other party by letter of their intent to rescind the contract, honouring a six-month period of notice.[419] In these two cases, the norms of the LO are mandatory, and the right to cancel the contract may not be a matter of stipulation by the parties or is it better to say that the LO, in this case, provides additional protection towards the insurance contractor in relation to the insurer, who is in a position to dictate the terms of the contract. The general terms and conditions of property insurance contain additional rules with regard to the obligations of the insurance contractor. So, in the general terms and conditions, it is stated that if the insurance contractor terminates a contract that has been concluded for a term longer than five years, the contractor is obliged to pay the premium difference in the amount of the discount approved on the basis of the multi-year term of the insurance.[420]

*391.* The cancellation of the contract means that the effects of the contract are terminated *pro-futuro*, so all the effects of the contract in the past are invalid, and there is an obligation of the insurer to cover the risk until the moment of contract termination, and there is an obligation of the insurance contractor to pay the premium for that year. But we must again point out that these rules on contract termination, that is, according to the LO, possible only in cases where there is no term in the contract or the contract is concluded for a period longer than five years, are applicable only in the cases of non-life insurance, since the insurance contractor of life insurance contracts always has the option of cancelling the contract.

## §4. Termination of an Insurance Contract Because of Nullity

*392.* Nullity of a contract is one of the areas where the general rules for all contracts apply and where there are special provisions in the area of the LO pertaining to the insurance contract. In the general part of the LO, there is a differentiation between absolutely and relatively null contracts. Absolutely null contracts are ones that are contrary to the mandatory legislation or the morals of society, unless the purpose of the rule violated refers to another sanction or unless the law provides for something else in the specific case.[421] Relatively null contracts (voidable contracts) are those concluded by a party having a limited business capacity, should there be any defects in respect of the will (intention) of the parties, or when so provided by the present law or special legislation.[422] In both cases, the reason for termination must have been present at the time the contract was concluded, but the difference still exists between the court decisions determining termination of a contract for the reason of nullity. In the case of absolutely null contracts, the decision only establishes the nullity, and in the case of relatively null contracts, the contract is annulled

419. *See*: Article 1019, paras 2,3 and 4, LO.

420. *See*: Opšti uslovi osiguranja imovine (General Terms of Property Insurance), Lovćen osiguranja, No. US-PR-OUI/10-12-cg, Art. 25, para. 4. Opšti uslovi osiguranja imovine, Sava osiguranja, No. OU-IM-06/21, Art. 25, para. 4. Opšti uslovi osiguranja imovine, Generali osiguranja, of 27 Feb. 2008, Art. 25, para. 3.

421. *See*: Article 101, para. 1, LO.

422. *See*: Article 109, para. 1, LO.

by the decision. The LO contains the rules on the nullity of a specific provision of the contract, stating that the nullity of a contractual provision will not imply the nullity of the contract itself if it can stand without the null provision and should such provision be neither a requirement for the contract nor a motive decisive for making it.[423] But in this case, the contract itself is not null and terminated, so this provision is not especially relevant for insurance contracts.

*393.* Absolute nullity of an insurance contract is established as the sanction in a large number of particular cases:

- if, at the moment of its conclusion of that contract, the insurance case has already materialised or is at the point of occurring, or if it is certain that it is going to occur, or if, even at that time, there was no possibility of its occurring (in this case, the question of uncertainty of the insured event occurring is eliminated, so there is no aleatory element in the insurance contract);[424]
- if it was stipulated that the insurance shall encompass a specified period of time preceding the conclusion of the contract, only if, at the moment of its conclusion, the interested party was aware that the case covered by the insurance had already taken place or that even then the possibility of it taking place had ceased to exist;[425]
- at the moment of the conclusion of the life insurance contract, the age of the insured person is incorrectly stated and their real age exceeds the limit up to which the insurer, by their terms and tariffs, normally enters into life insurance transactions;[426]
- if the insurance relates to the death of a third party, the validity of the contract is dependent on his written consent, indicated on the face of the insurance policy or in a separate letter at the moment of signing the insurance policy, with an indication of the insured amount;[427]
- if the insurance relates to the death of a third party older than 14, the validity of the contract is dependent on the written consent of that person's legal representative and the written consent of the insured person themself;[428]
- if the insurance relates to the death of a third party younger than 14 or to a person completely deprived of business capacity.[429]

*394.* Relative nullity of the insurance contract usually pertains to a breach of the individual interest of the contracting party, and the determination of insurance contract voidability is established in the following cases:

- if the insurance contractor deliberately files an incorrect application or intentionally suppresses circumstances of a nature that would induce the insurer, if they

423. *See*: Article 103, para. 1, LO.
424. *See*: Article 995, para. 2, LO.
425. *See*: Article 995, para. 3, LO.
426. *See*: Article 1041, para. 1, item 1, LO.
427. *See*: Article 1043, para. 3, LO.
428. *See*: Article 1044, para. 2, LO.
429. *See*: Article 1044, para. 1, LO.

knew the real situation, not to enter into a contract (the case of deliberate non-performance of the duty to inform the insurer about the facts relevant for the assessment of risk at the time of conclusion of the insurance contract);[430]
- if the insurance contractor, at the conclusion of the contract, deceived the other contracting party, stipulating an amount of insurance that is higher than the real value of the insured object (the case of deliberate over-insurance);[431]
- if the insurance contractor insures the same object with two or more insurers against the same risk, for the same interest, and for the same period of time, so that the sum of the insured amounts exceeds the value of such objects (the case of deliberate double insurance).[432]

*395.* The establishment of nullity, in cases of absolute nullity, or avoidance of the contract, in cases of relative nullity, brings the same legal consequences. It shall be deemed that that insurance had never existed, and the parties have to return whatever they have received based on that contract. But, in cases where one of the parties has acted in bad faith, their rights may be deprived of the right to seek damages, so that only the party that acted in good faith may ask for damages. In insurance contracts, this would mean that if the deliberate actions of the insurance contractor are ones that are established as the reasons for nullity, the insurer will have the right to keep the premium already paid by the insurance contractor or, in the case where none of the premiums are paid, to seek the premiums up until the time of their awareness of the reasons of nullity.

## §5. Termination of an Insurance Contract in the Event of Rescission

*396.* Contracts that are effectively concluded may terminate in the case of rescission, which may be a compromise between the parties or unilateral. The general rules of the LO allow the termination of contracts by means of rescission; since the contract is concluded as to the autonomous will of the contracting parties, it is natural that the same contract could be rescinded by the autonomous will of the parties also. The general reasons for the unilateral rescission of the contracts pertain to the non-performance of the insurance contract obligations[433] or the changed circumstances.[434] Special provisions on insurance contracts also contain some additional reasons for unilateral rescission of the contract.

*397.* All the cases of non-performance of the insurance contract obligations are connected to the obligation of reporting the relevant risks in the procedure of contract conclusion, reporting changes in the risks during the lifetime of the insurance contract, and regarding the duty of premium payment, and they were deliberated previously in the chapters pertaining to the risk and premium. Usually, in these

430. *See*: Article 1005, para. 1, LO.
431. *See*: Article 1029, para. 1, LO.
432. *See*: Article 1031, para. 2, LO.
433. *See*: Articles 119–127, LO.
434. *See*: Articles 128–132, LO.

cases, the insurer is the contracting party who may invoke a rescission of the contract, since the obligations of the insurance contractor are ones that are unconditional. But in the case of a lowering of the risk, after the insurance contractor notifies the insurer in that circumstance, in the case where the insurer does not agree to a reduction of the premium, the insurance contractor is the one who has the right to rescission of the insurance contract.[435]

*398.* The transfer of ownership of an insured object gives the insurer and the third party who is acquiring the object the right to seek a rescission of the contract due to that change in ownership. The insurer and the acquirer of the insured object may withdraw from the insurance, honouring a fifteen-day period of notice, on the condition that their notice is submitted within thirty days of becoming aware of the transfer.[436] But the contract of insurance may not be rescinded should the insurance policy be issued to the bearer or on order.[437]

## §6. Termination of an Insurance Contract Due to the Initiation of Insolvency Proceedings

*399.* Initiation of insolvency proceedings, as one of the ways of winding up the business of an insurance company or any other company that is an insurance contractor, has certain effects on an insurance contract. Since this is a contract, we must ascertain the consequences of the insolvency proceedings of the insurer, as well as the insurance contractor, if the latter has the status of a legal entity.

*400.* If the insurer's bankruptcy is in question, then, under the provisions of the LO, the insurance contract shall be terminated thirty days after the institution of bankruptcy proceedings.[438] A similar provision is contained within the Law on Liquidation and Bankruptcy of the Insurance Companies (LOLBIC), stating that insurance contracts shall cease to be valid on the thirtieth day as of the publication of an advertisement on the opening of the bankruptcy proceedings in the Official Journal of Montenegro (OJM).[439] So, the thirty-day period is determined by both legal texts as relevant for the contract termination. In this time period, the obligation of the insurer will exist so that in the event of the insured event occurring, the insurance contractor may be one of the claimants in the bankruptcy proceedings. Also, the insurance contractor has the obligation to pay the premium for this period, and in the case that the contractor has paid the premium in advance, they will again have the right to be a claimant for part of the premium in the bankruptcy proceedings. Upon the termination of the deadline, the object will be deemed uninsured. But these are the general rules of the LO and LOLBIC, and other laws can establish different rules.

---

435. *See*: Article 1013, LO.
436. *See*: Article 1034, para. 5, LO.
437. *See*: Article 1034, para. 6, LO.
438. *See*: Article 1020, para. 2, LO.
439. *See*: Article 38, para. 1, LOLBIC.

*401.* In the case of the LMIT, if an insurance company with which the compulsory insurance contract is concluded is subject to the initiation of a liquidation procedure or bankruptcy procedure, the owner of the means of transport must, within fifteen days of the day of publication of the decision on the initiation of liquidation or bankruptcy, conclude a compulsory insurance contract with another insurance company for the period until the insurance coverage or registration validity expires.[440] Failure to comply with this obligation sanctions only the owner of the vehicle, since, upon the termination of the deadline, the means of transport will be deemed to be uninsured.[441] So, in the case of mandatory transport insurance, the deadline for contract termination is shorter than the deadlines in the LO and LOLBIC. Additionally, the question of the obligation of the owner of the means of transport to conclude the insurance against liability is stipulated again with defined terms. In cases where the insurance contractor has paid the insurance premium in advance, the contractor is entitled to pursue claims for the unused portion of the paid insurance premium from the liquidation or bankruptcy estate of the insurance company under liquidation or bankruptcy.[442] One of the major differences in the treatment of the insured under the provisions of LMIT is that the claim for the insured sum, or the claim of the injured person, will be paid out from the Guarantee Fund,[443] which in this case will have the right of recourse from the bankruptcy estate of the company, which is subject to the initiation of a bankruptcy procedure, according to the order of settlement prescribed by a special law.[444]

*402.* The LOLBIC constitutes the seniority classes for a settlement from the bankruptcy estate of the insurance company. In the first place are the secured claims up to the value of the security instrument thereof, less the reasonable sale costs, followed by the remuneration for the bankruptcy administrator or liquidator and costs arising in relation to the pursuit of such activities in the second. In third place are the receivables and claims of creditors arising from life insurance contracts and other contracts for which a mathematical reserve is established, which were not able to be paid from the mathematical reserve funds, and so up to the amount of liabilities stated in the mathematical reserve funds. The receivables and claims of creditors arising from other insurance classes are in fourth place, just before claims from the Guarantee Fund. All other creditors' claims are higher in seniority than those from the company's shareholders.[445]

*403.* Creditors from life insurance contracts and other multi-year insurances where probability tables and calculations are used for life insurance are entitled to a separate settlement from the assets for coverage of the mathematical reserve or from funds collected by converting assets for coverage of the mathematical reserve into cash. Assets for coverage of the mathematical reserve are not included in the

440. *See*: Article 8, para. 1, LMIT.
441. *See*: Article 8, para. 2, LMIT.
442. *See*: Article 8, para. 3, LMIT.
443. *See*: Article 57, para. 1, item 3, LMIT.
444. *See*: Article 58, para. 3, LMIT.
445. *See*: Article 37, LOLBIC.

bankruptcy estate.[446] The right of the settlement from the assets for coverage of the mathematical reserve is regulated in detail by the LOLBIC.[447]

*404.* In the case of bankruptcy of the insurance contractor, the insurance will continue, but each party will be entitled to rescind the contract of insurance within a three-month time limit from the institution of bankruptcy proceedings, in which case the negotiator's estate in the bankruptcy shall be increased by the part of the paid insurance premium corresponding to the remaining time of the insurance.[448] If the parties rescind the contract, part of the premiums for the remaining period of the contract will become part of the estate of the insurance contractor. In the event of the insured event occurring before the contract is rescinded, the insurer will have the obligation of performance, and the estate of the insurer is the creditor in the case where the insurance contractor did not designate a third party as the beneficiary of the contract. The designation of the beneficiary creates the option that the amount of insurance will not become the estate of the insurance contractor.

## §7. Cancellation of a Contract Due to the Statute of Limitations

*405.* Termination of the effects of an insurance contract may occur in cases of unenforceability due to the statute of limitations. As a general law in the field of contract law, the LO contains general provisions on the statute of limitations and special provisions regarding insurance contracts. The statute of limitations is defined as the termination of the right to claim performance of an obligation that takes place before the expiration of the period specified by the statute during which the creditor was entitled to claim performance of the obligation. The courts may account for the statute of limitations only if the debtor invokes it.[449] The period for expiration due to the statute of limitations shall begin to run on the first day following the day the creditor was entitled to claim performance of the obligation, unless something else is provided by the statute for specific cases. If an obligation consists of refraining from action, omission or tolerating something, the period for expiration due to the statute of limitations shall begin to run on the first day following the day the debtor acts contrary to their obligation.[450] Expiry due to the statute of limitations is effective after the lapse of the last day of the period specified by the statute. After the expiration of a principal claim due to the statute of limitations, accessory claims also expire, such as claims relating to interest, income, expenses, and liquidated damages. The LO prohibits the possibility of altering the time for expiry due to the statute of limitations or the possibility of suspension of the expiry period by way of legal transaction. Waiving the expiry due to the statute of limitations prior to the expiration of the time provided for such an expiration is not

446. *See*: Article 41, LOLBIC.
447. *See*: Article 42, LOLBIC.
448. *See*: Article 1020, para. 1, LO.
449. *See*: Article 369, LO.
450. *See*: Article 370, LO.

allowed. Written acknowledgment of an obligation that has expired due to the statute of limitations or the provisions of providing a pledge or other kind of security to cover a claim that has expired due to the statute of limitations is construed as renouncing unenforceability. Fulfilment of an expired obligation is the performance of the obligation, and a debtor is not entitled to claim restitution, even if the debtor was ignorant of the expiry of the obligation, due to the statute of limitations. A claim secured by a pledge or mortgage is enforceable only by the rules of the security, but claims of interest and other periodical dues are not enforceable.[451]

*406.* By the general rules on the statute of limitations, claims shall expire after a ten-year period, unless some other expiry time limit is provided by the statute.[452] For commercial law contracts, a general rule is that mutual claims of legal persons from contracts entered into in exercising their business activities, as well as claims relating to reimbursement of expenses made in connection to such contracts, shall expire due to the statute of limitations after a three-year period.[453] But for insurance contracts, the special provisions on time are relevant. So, the claims of an insurance contractor or of a third party designated in a life insurance contract shall expire after five years, while those from remaining insurance contracts shall expire after three years, calculated from the first day following the calendar year of the origination of the claim. In the event that the interested person is successful in proving that, until the day specified above, they were not aware of the occurrence of the insured event, the expiration period shall begin to run from the day of their becoming aware thereof, while in any event, the claim shall expire, in the case of life insurance, after ten years and, in the case of the remaining insurance contracts, after five years, beginning from the day specified above. Claims of an insurer on the grounds of an insurance contract shall expire due to the statute of limitations after three years. Should, in the event of third-party liability insurance, a person sustaining damage demand compensation from the insured, or should the person obtain it from the insured, the expiration period for the insured person's claim against the insurer shall begin to run on the day the person sustaining the damage requested compensation through the court from the insured, or on the day of their being compensated by the insured. A direct demand by a third party sustaining injury or loss from the insurer shall expire due to the statute of limitations after a period otherwise applicable to the expiration of their claim against the insured person liable for damage. The limitation period of an insurer's claim against a third party liable for the occurrence of the insured event shall begin to run at the time otherwise applicable to the limitation period for the claims of the insured against such a person and shall be completed within the same time limit.[454]

451. *See*: Articles 371–379, LO.
452. *See*: Article 380, LO.
453. *See*: Article 383, para. 1, LO.
454. *See*: Article 390, LO.

# Part III. Property and Liability Insurance

## Chapter 1. Fire Insurance

*407.* The risk of fire is considered one of the basic risks in property insurance and is one of the oldest property risks covered by insurance. This is a basic risk because the conclusion of insurance for many other risks is conditional on insuring the property from the risk of fire first. In the case of risk selection by the insurance contractor, this risk is almost always contracted since the consequences of its realisation are extremely high.[455]

*408.* In Montenegro, the risk of fire is usually connected with several other risks, so a package deal of insurance against several risks is offered to the insurance contractor. Some of them are: naming the package deals with appropriate names; trying to present to the consumers the risks in such a way that they can understand the offer better; and some of them have traditional terms and conditions, such as special conditions of insurance against the risk of fire and additional risks. Either way, the risk of fire is almost never contracted as a sole risk, and if something is not regulated within the special terms and conditions of fire insurance, the general terms and conditions of property insurance apply.

*409.* Fire, in the sense of the terms and conditions of insurers in Montenegro, is considered to be a fire that has started outside a certain fireplace or a fire that has left this place and is capable of spreading further under its own power. The resulting fire is not considered, and the insurer is not obliged to compensate for the damage: if the insured object is destroyed due to exposure to fire or heat for processing or other purposes (e.g., during ironing, drying, frying, etc.) or due to it falling or being thrown into the fireplace (stove); if the insured object is damaged by burning, frying, or burning with cigarettes, ashes, lighting devices, electric heaters, embers, etc.; if damage occurs to the insured object due to self-ignition, boiling or heating, cooking, smoking, etc.; on chimneys caused by their use.

*410.* When determining the object of the insurance, insurers in Montenegro usually define the separate buildings, parts of the construction, and movable property that fall under the contract. When insuring separate buildings, the coverage includes all parts of the building, the foundation and basement walls, built-in installations,

455. Zdravko Petrović, Dragan Mrkšić & Katarina Ivančević, *Neživotna osiguranja (Non-life Insurance)*, Intermex, Beograd, 2007, p. 103.

and built-in equipment (elevator, central heating with fuel tank, boilers, central air-conditioning system, water pumps, and others), and some of them specify that the roof and other combustible parts of the building may not be insured separately. When insuring the physical parts of construction facilities – apartments and business premises – the insurance includes installations and equipment installed in the apartment or business premises. The insurance does not cover the common property of the components of the construction object that make up a common property (rooms for common use, stairs, elevators, roofs, etc.), unless otherwise agreed. In the case of movable property insurance, if, in the insurance document, the items are not listed individually but are indicated as a group, it is considered that all things that are located at the place of insurance and belong to the insured group are insured, as well as those that existed at the time of the conclusion of the insurance contract, as well as those that are included in that set during the duration of the insurance contract. When insuring the movable property of natural persons, only those things that are the property of the insured and persons who live with the insured in a joint household are insured.

*411.* According to the terms and conditions of fire insurance, the value of the insured objects is calculated. The terms are not uniform in this part. Some of them define the options for the deductible franchise and the limit per insured event. In one case before the Supreme Court of Montenegro, there was a question of calculation of the material damage on the basis of fire insurance. Based on the insurance contract for car parts that were destroyed in the fire, it was decided that the plaintiff was entitled to compensation in the amount of the costs of purchasing the destroyed car parts, which amount must be within the sum insured and not in the amount that the plaintiff would have gained by selling them.[456] In another case, it was pointed out that if the insured's building is completely destroyed in a fire, the insurer is obliged to compensate the insured for damages in the amount of the construction price of a new building of the same type, size and construction method at the prices in the place where the building is located. The agreed insurance sum, i.e., the coverage limit, is not important for determining the actual extent of damage suffered as a result of the destruction of things but represents the amount beyond which the damage could not be paid.[457]

*412.* Other risks that are usually covered by insurance against fire are: earthquakes, explosions, thunderstorms, hail, aircraft crashes, the impact of one's own motor vehicle and one's own mobile work machine into an insured building, public events and demonstrations, floods, torrents and high water, water spilling from installations, landslides, ground subsidence, leakage, etc.

456. *See*: Supreme Court of Montenegro, Rev. No. 783/14.
457. *See*: Supreme Court of Montenegro, Rev. No. 180/21.

## Chapter 2. Loss of Benefits Insurance

*413.* The general terms and conditions of property insurance provide for insurance of actual loss of value, meaning loss of real property. But, there is an option for a legal person to contract this type of insurance for fixed assets and non-monetary assets (stocks) against fire and some other dangers. This risk may be insured at the time of the conclusion of fire insurance, or it may be contracted at a later time. The insured may be any legal entity that performs economic activity and generates total income based on it.

*414.* The insured events are the same as in fire insurance, starting with the risk of fire, explosion, thunderstorm, lightning strikes, hail, etc. Almost all insurers give a basic list of the risks covered, but they all allow the addition of supplementary risks to a specific contract.[458]

*415.* The object of this insurance may be profit, income or certain business expenses. Income means only that income which is realised by performing a registered economic activity, as well as income related to that activity. The expenses are only those that are of a fixed nature and arise regardless of whether or not the economic activity takes place and which the insured must bear. Those that are directly related to the performance of an economic activity, such as the costs of raw materials, consumed energy, etc., are not considered expenses.[459]

*416.* The insurance sum is contracted in a fixed amount on the policy and its attachments and may not be less than the annual gross profit or annual fixed costs and net profit. In the event that the maximum compensation period is longer than twelve months, the gross profit or the specified fixed costs will be proportionally increased for that period. After the payment of any compensation from the insurance in accordance with this section, the insurance sum is not exhausted, and it is automatically renewed.

*417.* Damages caused by the suspension of business activities are the amount of income that the insured could not earn during the period of downtime due to the interruption of work, and the uncovered amount of insured expenses realised or incurred during that period are considered to be damages from the interruption of work. The insurer is liable for damages that would arise from the interruption of work for a contracted duration of at least three months, calculated from the day when the insured event occurred. The warranty period may be agreed upon for a longer period. The length of the agreed guarantee period, for the duration of the insurance, is reduced successively for the corresponding period for which the compensation was calculated. In the event of a subsequent interruption of work, the insurer is only liable for the unused period of the warranty period.

---

458. Zdravko Petrović, Dragan Mrkšić & Katarina Ivančević, *supra*, p. 149.
459. *Ibid.*, *supra*, p. 148.

*418.* The obligation to compensate for damage in this case is valid only if there is an obligation to compensate for material damage based on insurance against the risk of fire and some other risks. So, this risk is connected to fire insurance, and in the case of an invalid contract on fire insurance, there is no valid obligation of insurance on the loss of benefits.

*419.* Insurers in Montenegro that offer this insurance almost always contract the deductible franchise, but others insist on it, so this type of insurance may not be concluded without the insured's participation in the damage, that is, a 10% participation in the damage.

## Chapter 3. Transport Insurance

*420.* Transport insurance can be divided into categories based on different grounds of division. On the basis of the area of transport, it can be divided into marine, air, road and rail transport. On the basis of the object of insurance, it can be divided into Casco and cargo insurance. Cargo and Casco insurance may be concluded in all areas of transport. Montenegrin insurers offer goods insurance that covers physical damage or loss of goods while in transit by land, water or air. But we must again emphasise one of the characteristics of the LO: that the provisions of this law do not relate to marine insurance. Also, the relevant legal source in the area of air transport is the LOBORAT. Also, the provisions of the LMIT are relevant since this law provides for mandatory insurance in transport and pertains to damages to third parties, including passengers, their luggage and their cargo. So, Montenegro, as a state, has opted for regulating transport insurance according to special laws and, in the area of marine insurance, by the marine law, as opposed to the approach of some states that regulate these types of contracts by general laws that regulate insurance contracts.[460]

*421.* The LI also provides one relevant provision for transport insurance. Namely, by the provisions of this law, property and persons in Montenegro may be insured only by an insurance company established under this law, and with one exception, they may be insured by a foreign insurance company in air and sea transport above the mandatory traffic insurance.[461] In this part, we will present the relevant rules of marine and land transport insurances, while air traffic insurance will be covered in the part on aviation and space insurance.

### §1. Marine Transport Insurance

*422.* The LMIN is the most relevant law for insurance in marine transport, containing more than sixty articles on insurance. In the general part of the LI, there are more than forty articles that are applied to all insurance contracts that may be concluded under this law, and in addition, there are special rules regarding ship insurance contracts, insurance contracts of goods carried by ship, freight insurance contracts, insurance contracts against ship owner liability, and others.

*423.* The general part is the provision on application of the rules of this law on: the insurance contractor, the insured, and material interest for the insurance; insurance on a third party's behalf; description of risks and consequences of the failure of this obligation; the insurance policy and its transferability; the value of the insured object; over-insurance, under-insurance and double insurance; obligations of the insurance contractor and insurer; insurance-covered damages; putative risk coverage; intentional causation of the insured event; loss of the insured object; rules

460. Borislav Ivošević, *Transporno osiguranje (Transport Insurance),* Pravni fakultet Univerziteta Union u Beogradu, 2009, p. 51.
461. *See*: Article 6, LI.

on consecutive damages; making of a claim by the insured; and the statute of limitations in marine insurance contracts. These provisions are too detailed for all these details to be described.

*424.* Ship insurance includes the ship's hull, its machinery, devices and equipment, regular supplies of fuel, lubricants and other ship materials, as well as supplies of food and drinks needed by the ship's crew. Extraordinary stocks of fuel, lubricants and other materials, stocks of food and drinks that do not serve the regular needs of the ship's crew, as well as the costs of equipping and insuring the ship, are included in the ship's insurance only if it is expressly agreed.[462] The insurance costs, freight charges, customs and other costs related to the transportation and delivery of goods, as well as the expected profit, may be insured with one agreed value and, if the value is not agreed, with one insured amount, in addition to the value of the goods at the point of departure, whereby it is not necessary to explicitly state in the contract all these costs and expected profit, which are covered by the same insurance contract.[463] Freight insurance covers the gross amount of freight, unless otherwise agreed.[464] In the case of liability insurance for damages caused to third parties, the amounts that the insured is obliged to pay to these persons in connection with his liability covered by the insurance, as well as the costs necessary to determine the amount of his liability, are reimbursed from the insurance.[465] We have presented only the definitions of the contracts regulated by the LMIN, since there are too many regulations to present them all.

*425.* Insurers in Montenegro offer marine transport insurance of goods against loss of goods or their damage as individual insurance products. Goods may be insured against 'basic risks' or 'all risks' that can endanger goods in transport by sea. As individual coverage, the risk of complete loss of goods may be insured as a sole risk in the contract. The insurers offer lists of risks, but they present the opportunity to the insurance contractor to seek insurance against the risks not covered by the standard terms of any object that can be transported. Goods may be insured based on their actual or invoiced value. In addition to the invoice value, costs related to the transport of goods, such as transport costs, customs, insurance, costs of freight, etc., may be insured. In addition to these costs, the expected profit may be insured for up to 20% of the value of the goods. If nothing is specified in the contract about the value of goods, it is considered that the goods are insured based on their actual value. The payment of the premium is not connected to the beginning of the insurer's obligation to cover the risk, but in the event that the premium is not paid within the contracted term, there is a possibility that the insurer may reject the claim of the insured. The terms of marine transport insurance cover the question of the way of determining the damages and the way of claiming the damages with a list of appropriate annexes to the claim.[466]

462. *See*: Article 769, LMIN.
463. *See*: Article 775, LMIN.
464. *See*: Article 783, LMIN.
465. *See*: Article 787, LMIN.
466. General Terms on Goods Insurance in Marine Transport, Generali Insurance, of 27 Feb. 2008.

## §2. Land Transport Insurance

*426.* Although there are no special provisions of the laws of Montenegro that govern land transport, this is one of the most important areas of transport, and Montenegrin insurers offer insurance in this area based on the rules of the general terms of land transport and special terms on road transport. So, what follows will be an elaboration of those rules. Insurers offer insurance of the carrier of goods against liability under the CMR convention[467] and additional insurance of the goods not covered by the proven subjective carriers' liability. Damage caused by physical loss or damage to goods in international or domestic transport by any type of vehicle, from warehouse to warehouse, is offered by the insurers, offering coverage of the basic risks or comprehensive coverage of all risks. Within this type of insurance, there are two possibilities of concluding a single policy, which is contracted for each transportation in general, which includes all shipments by means of transport within the contracted period of time. As in the case of marine transport, goods may be insured based on their actual or invoiced value. In addition to the invoice value, costs related to the transport of goods, such as transport costs, customs, insurance, costs of freight, etc., may be insured. In addition to these costs, the expected profit may be insured for up to 20% of the value of the goods. If nothing is specified in the contract on the value of goods, it is considered that the goods are insured based on their actual value. But, unlike with marine transport insurance, the payment of the premium is connected to the beginning of the insurer's obligation to cover the risk, so in the event that the premium is not paid within the contracted term by the insurance contractor or by a third interested party, there is no obligation on the insurer, and they will reject the claim of the insured. The general terms of road transport insurance cover the question of the way of determining damages and the way of claiming the damage.[468]

The Supreme Court of Montenegro deliberated one interesting case in which it was determined that, in the case of an insurance contract on the transport of goods, the insurance starts from the moment when the goods are loaded onto the means of transport in the place specified in the insurance policy as the place of dispatch and lasts until the goods are unloaded from the means of transport to the place specified in the policy as the place of destination. The lower courts mistakenly took that, in this case, by the transfer of all risks by the CXW Incoterms clause, the risk was transferred to the buyer and that, at that time, the insurance contract was concluded by the seller. They misconstrued the rules and took the stand that the insurance contract was terminated. But in that contract, it was clearly stated that it should cover the transport risks on the specified route. This is why the Supreme Court of Montenegro gave its reasoning in its decision, granting the right of compensation to the buyer of the goods for the damages incurred during transport.[469]

---

467. Convention on the Contract for the International Carriage of Goods by Road, United Nations, 1956. *See*: Conditions for insurance from the liability of the road carrier for damage to the consignment of goods received for transport in road transport, Generali Insurance, 2016.
468. *See*: General terms on goods insurance in road transport, Generali Insurance, of 27 Feb. 2008.
469. *See*: Decision of the Supreme Court of Montenegro, Rev. No. 68/12.

## Chapter 4. Liability Insurance

*427.* Liability insurance is one of the types of insurance regulated by the LO. But there are only two articles of the LO dedicated directly to liability insurance, regulating the liability of the insurer and the personal rights of the person sustaining damage and their direct action. Additionally, the general rules for all insurance contracts apply in the case of liability insurance. In the case of liability insurance, the insurer is liable for damage caused by the insured event only if the third party sustaining the damage requests compensation, and he will bear, within the limits of the amount of insurance, the expenses of litigation over the liability of the insured person.[470] A direct claim of the person sustaining damage may be made in cases where the damage was sustained due to an event falling within the sphere of liability of the insured person and up to the amount of the insurer's obligation. The direct claim is the right of the person that sustained the damage from the day of occurrence of the insured event, so any subsequent change in the insured person's rights against the insurer has no effect on the right to compensation of a person sustaining damage.[471]

*428.* We can differentiate between four distinctive groups of liability insurance contracts. The first would be compulsory insurance of owners against damages caused to third parties by the use of motor vehicles, boats or aircraft. The second group can be identified as contracts of commercial entities against liability for the damage caused to third parties in conducting business activities. Similar to the second group is the insurance of certain free professions, such as lawyers, notaries, public bailiffs, accountants, auditors, etc. But, in the case of the third group, the insured is not a commercial entity but rather a person conducting a business activity. We can incorporate into the fourth group general liability contracts that do not fall within the scope of professional and business operations.

*429.* In the practice of Montenegrin insurers, several types of insurance against liability are advertised: insurance against general liability; insurance against employer liability; insurance against the professional liability of directors and members of the management board; insurance against the professional liability of insurance intermediaries; insurance against the professional liability of accountants and auditors; and insurance against the professional liability of designers, consultants and persons performing supervision. All these types of liability insurance are offered to the legal person or persons performing their work or their business activity.

### §1. Professional Liability

*430.* Insurers in Montenegro have general rules on liability insurance and special rules regarding additional types of insurance for certain risks or professions.

---

470. *See*: Article 1037, LO.
471. *See*: Article 1038, LO.

The subject of insurance, according to these general terms and conditions on liability insurance, is the civil legal liability of the insured for the damage caused as a result of death, injury to body or health, damage or destruction of the property of third parties, caused by a sudden and unexpected harmful event. This insurance covers liability for damage caused by the activity, from the possession of objects, or from the property as a source of danger that is indicated in the insurance policy. The insurance coverage may also be extended to liability from new sources of danger, which appear after the conclusion of the insurance contract, if it was specially stipulated in the contract and if the new source of danger is not covered by the existing insurance. After a new danger appears, the insured must inform the insurer, who has eight days to decide if they are going to cover the new source of danger, and if they do not decline in writing, then the new danger is considered to be covered by the existing insurance if it is in accordance with the terms and conditions of the insurance. The terms and conditions list the supplementary provisions for certain sources of danger in specific areas of business, such as: hospitals, spas, sanatoriums, dispensaries, construction, assembly, and similar activities; swimming pools; ports and public warehouses; schools; institutions for upbringing and education; etc. In that regard, the terms and conditions contain a list of special clauses that may be added to the insurance policy.[472]

*431.* In the case of insurance liability of employers, the subject of the insurance is the civil legal liability of the insured for the damage caused, as a result of death, injury to body or health, damage or destruction of property of employees, caused by a sudden and unexpected harmful event. The remaining provisions are almost the same as in the case of general liability insurance.[473]

*432.* According to the conditions for ensuring the professional liability of the director and members of the Management Board, the insurance covers liability for purely financial damages, i.e., damages that were not caused either by injury to the body or health of a person or by damage or destruction of the belongings of third parties. So, the subject of the insurance is defined as the purely financial damages caused to third parties, which occurred as a result of a future, unexpected and adverse event beyond the insured's control. This insurance covers the liability for damage caused by a violation of the obligation of a proper business assessment in the best interest of the company. Upon the occurrence of the insured event, the insurer is obliged to: undertake a defence together with the insured against unfounded or excessive claims for damages, comply with established requests for insurance compensation, and reimburse the costs of the court proceedings.[474]

*433.* The professional liability of insurance intermediaries may be insured separately. The subject of insurance is the civil liability of the insured for damages resulting from the death, injury to the body, or health of third parties, or destruction

472. *See*: Conditions for General Liability Insurance, Generali Insurance, of 27 Feb. 2008.
473. *See*: Conditions for Employer's Liability Insurance, Generali Insurance, of 27 Feb. 2008.
474. *See*: Conditions for Ensuring the Professional Liability of the Director and Members of the Management Board, Generali Insurance, of 27 Feb. 2008.

or damage to property of third parties, as well as purely financial damage caused to third parties that occurred as a result of a sudden, unexpected and adverse event independent of the will of the insured. This insurance covers liability from professional activity if the activity is performed in accordance with the LI or from the possession of items. The conditions for ensuring the professional liability of accountants and auditors cover the same subject of insurance and the same conditions for insurance as in the case of insurance for insurance intermediaries, but they limit the liability in the area of their work in the field of accounting and auditing. The same is true in the case of insurance of the professional liability of designers, consultants and persons performing supervision.[475]

## §2. Product Liability

*434.* Product liability is regulated by the LO in Montenegro, and insurers offer the possibility of insurance against product liability. The subject of insurance is the insured's civil liability for product damage after product delivery due to defects that the insured did not know existed. Damages may be the result of: bodily injury, illness or death of a third party; or the destruction, damage or loss of property of third parties. A product defect is understood to mean an error in the design, construction, material or manufacturing, as well as defects in the instructions for the correct use of the product, which can cause bodily injury, illness or death of a third party, as well as damage, destruction or disappearance of things owned by third parties. A defect exists if the product does not provide the safety that is rightly expected considering all the circumstances, including advertisement, the purpose for which it is intended, and the time it was put on the market. A product is not considered to have a defect just because a better-quality product was put on the market later. The subject of the insurance is also the insured's liability due to damage caused by components of the product and other elements that were ordered and procured by other persons and which the insured incorporates into the products under their own name or logo. If separately stipulated, the insurance will cover damages to third parties caused by the final product that was created by installing, connecting or mixing the insured's product with other products without defects. Some insurers also offer coverage of the damages in the case of salmonella poisoning, but at most, up to 20% of the sum insured, which is indicated on the policy. The terms and conditions of the insurance against product liability also list the insurance exclusions, which are numerous (up to twenty-seven cases of exclusion). The insurance covers cases occurring on the territory of Montenegro and geographical areas of Europe, which are separately defined.

475. *See*: Conditions for Ensuring Professional Liability of Insurance Intermediaries, Generali Insurance, 2008; Conditions for Ensuring Professional Liability of Insurance Intermediaries, Generali Insurance, 2008; Conditions for Ensuring the Professional Liability of Accountants and Auditors, Generali Insurance, 2008. Date accessed: 5 Jan. 2023, available at: https://www.generali.me.

*435.* The amount of the insurer's obligation is regulated by the insured sum per individual event and by the total annual sum of insurance. The insurance sum is contracted in a fixed monetary amount and represents the maximum obligation of the insurer per single insured event, regardless of the number of injured persons and persons whose liability is covered by the insurance. This insurance sum refers to cases of death, injury to body or health, and damage or destruction of the belongings of third parties. According to the terms and conditions, the total annual sum of insurance represents the total obligation of the insurer for all insured cases arising in one year of insurance – it may not exceed the amount of seven contracted sums of insurance. The total annual sum of insurance is reduced by the payment of individual compensation. After the total annual insurance sum has been exhausted, the insurance ceases to be valid.[476]

476. *See*: Conditions for Product Liability Insurance, Generali Insurance, of 27 Feb. 2008.

## Chapter 5. Legal Aid Insurance

*436.* The subject of legal aid insurance is the cost incurred in providing legal assistance to the insured. Since this is a type of property insurance, all the general rules of the LO on property insurance apply in the case of legal aid insurance.

*437.* Legal aid insurance is not found as a separate insurance that can be contracted as such. It is usually offered as an ancillary risk in the event of the conclusion of other liability insurances. Usually, the terms and conditions of liability insurance prescribe the obligations of the insurer upon the occurrence of the insured event: to undertake a defence together with the insured against unfounded or excessive claims for damages (legal protection); to comply with established requests for insurance compensation (insurance compensation); and to reimburse the costs of the court proceedings.[477] For us, the obligation to undertake a defence together with the insured against unfounded or excessive claims for damages and to reimburse the costs of the court proceedings is significant.

*438.* The insurer's obligation to provide legal protection includes: examination of the liability of the insured for the resulting damage; managing the dispute on behalf of the insured if the injured party realises the right to compensation for damages in civil proceedings; and giving all statements on behalf of the insured that the insured considers expedient for satisfaction or defence against unfounded or excessive demand for damages. The conduct of the dispute may be entrusted to the insured with the consent of the insurer, and the insured must comply with the instructions and orders of the insurer regarding the conducting of proceedings in litigation. The right of the insurer to intervene in the proceedings or to take over the litigation is set by the terms and conditions, as is the right of the insurer to refuse to handle the dispute or to leave handling of the dispute to the insured if the insurer deems that there is no place to provide legal protection, considering the ratio between the claims for compensation for damages and the amount of the insurance sum. There is no obligation on the insurer to provide legal protection if the insured pays the insurance amount in the name of insurance compensation before initiating a dispute.[478]

*439.* The insurer reimburses all costs of the civil proceedings if they handled the dispute themselves or gave their consent to the insured's management of the dispute. This obligation exists in all cases, even when the request for compensation was not founded. The knowledge and consent of the insurer are significant for the limit of their obligation, so if they were not aware of the proceedings, the insurance will cover only the costs within the limits of the sums of insurance if the dispute was well founded and the expenses are justified. The expenses of the criminal proceedings initiated against the insured due to an event that could result in a request for compensation from insurance based on liability insurance will be covered by the insurer only exceptionally if they are familiar with the testimony of the defence

477. *See*: Article 12, Conditions for Product Liability Insurance, Generali Insurance, of 27 Feb. 2008.
478. *See*: Article 13, Conditions for Product Liability Insurance, Generali Insurance, of 27 Feb. 2008.

counsel and accept to bear the costs. In all other cases, the costs of criminal proceedings, as well as the costs of representing the injured party, will not be reimbursed by the insurer. After the insurer has fulfilled their obligation by paying the insurance sum and corresponding part of the costs, they will be released from the obligation of further payments in the name of cost compensation per insured case.[479]

*440.* Almost identical provisions can be found in all the terms and conditions on liability insurance of the same insurer that offers this type of insurance in Montenegro.

479. *See*: Article 15, Conditions for Product Liability Insurance, Generali Insurance, of 27 Feb. 2008.

## Chapter 6. Aviation and Space Insurance

*441.* Aviation insurance in Montenegro is developed by the provisions of the LOBORAT and the LMIT, as well as the accompanying terms and conditions of insurers offering insurance in this field. Space insurance is not present in the Montenegrin insurance legislature or the practice of insurance companies, so the following discussion will be on the regulation of insurance in air traffic.

*442.* According to the provisions of the LOBORAT, the object of insurance in air traffic may be: aircraft and its equipment; cargo and baggage transported by aircraft; passengers against the risk of an accident; freight and other fees for transportation; insurance costs; expected profit; lien and other rights and the benefits that exist or can reasonably be expected in connection with air transport, and may be estimate in money; and liability for damage caused to third parties by using the aircraft. The third parties referred to above are persons who are not the subjects of the contract insurance.[480] The provisions of LOBORAT relate to insurance and apply to reinsurance of the objects of the insurance referred to above, if it is concluded under the conditions usual for air transport insurance.[481]

*443.* This law contains provisions on the beginning of aircraft insurance for a specific trip, so an air transport insurance contract is concluded for a specific period of time and may be concluded for a specific trip. Aircraft insurance for a specific trip starts from the moment the aircraft is set in motion to perform the insured trip at the place of departure specified in the insurance contract until the aircraft stops immediately after landing at the destination specified in the insurance contract.[482] The LOBORAT also lists the exemptions from aircraft insurance. Damages caused directly or indirectly as a result of defects or incapacity of the aircraft for safe air traffic are excluded from aircraft insurance if the insured knew about them or should have known about them and did not prevent the damage even though they could have. So, cases where the insurer knew about the defects by way of information from the insurance contractor or learned about them in another way do not excuse the insurer from the obligation of performance. The law also defines the unfitness of an aircraft for safe air traffic as unfitness due to technical defects or insufficient equipment of the aircraft, inadequate crew, and improper loading of the aircraft.[483] Damages caused directly or indirectly as a result of risks incurred outside the area of air traffic stipulated in the insurance contract are excluded, unless the limits of the area of air traffic were exceeded due to force majeure, an error in managing the aircraft, saving property and life, or providing medical assistance, as well as in the case of minor excesses that did not significantly affect the occurrence or extent of damage.[484] By the provisions of the law, aircraft insurance for a fixed period is extended for the duration of urgent repairs of damages covered by the insurance that

480. *See*: Article 123, LOBORAT.
481. *See*: Article 124, LOBORAT.
482. *See*: Article 125, LOBORAT.
483. *See*: Article 126, LOBORAT.
484. *See*: Article 127, LOBORAT.

began during the insurance period and are carried out without unjustified delay for a maximum of fifteen days from the date of expiry of the contracted insurance period, if during that time the aircraft cannot be used for safe air traffic. The obligation of the insured to promptly inform the insurance company of these circumstances is especially elaborated.[485]

*444.* The principle of the actual cost of the repair is implemented in aircraft repairs. So, in the event that the damaged aircraft is repaired or the lost or destroyed parts of the aircraft's equipment are replaced, only the damage in the amount of the actual costs necessary for the repair of the aircraft and the replacement of parts is compensated from the insurance, not the damage caused by the loss of the value of the aircraft, which came about despite the repair and replacement of parts. The question of whether the value of the aircraft increased by repairing it and replacing parts is irrelevant, so in all cases where repairs are needed, compensation for the damages will be made.[486]

*445.* The LOBORAT also contains a provision on the disappearance of aircraft so that in the case of an insurance contract, the aircraft is considered to have disappeared on the day when all communication between the aircraft and the competent air traffic control is interrupted, that is, on the day to which the last reliable news about the aircraft refers.[487]

*446.* Also relevant is the provision of the LOBORAT on the statute of limitations, which states that all claims from insurance contracts expire in five years.

*447.* Insurance against damages caused to the parties and passengers is mandatory under the provisions of the LMIT. Aircraft owners or users must enter into a liability insurance contract against damage caused to third parties and passengers by using an aircraft. This insurance contract covers damages to cargo and luggage as well, except for aircraft not used for commercial purposes. This insurance contract also covers damages caused by the risk of war and terrorism, except for aircraft with a Maximum Take-Off Mass (MTOM) of less than 500 kg.[488] The liability of an insurance company is limited to the sum insured applicable as of the loss on the date of the event, unless the insurance contract stipulates a higher sum insured. The minimum sums insured for an insurance contract are given for: the damage caused to third parties for aircraft with MTOM, for an individual passenger, for registered luggage per passenger, and for cargo transported per kg, all expressed in Special drawing rights (SDR). The amounts of SDR are given in exact numbers: for individual passengers – 250,000 SDR; for registered luggage per passenger – 1,288 SDR; and for cargo transported per kg – 22 SDR. In the case of damage caused to third parties by aircraft with MTOM, an extensive list of MTOM masses in kilograms is presented with the appropriate limit in the SDR amount of the insurer's minimal

485. *See*: Article 128, LOBORAT.
486. *See*: Article 129, LOBORAT.
487. *See*: Article 130, LOBORAT.
488. *See*: Article 42, LMIT.

liability that may be concluded. The decision regarding the increase in the sum insured may be passed by the government at the proposal of the regulatory authority.[489]

*448.* The provisions of the LMIT that refer to the compensation of damage caused to third parties and passengers by the use of a vehicle and the provisions of the law governing contracts and property/legal relations in air traffic shall be applied accordingly to the liability of owners or authorised users of aircraft for damage caused to third parties, unless otherwise regulated by the relevant provisions of the LMIT.[490]

*449.* Montenegrin insurers offer two types of coverage in aviation insurance: mandatory liability insurance for the use of aircraft; and Casco insurance for the aircraft. Mandatory insurance is contracted by the provisions of the LMIT and by the terms and conditions of the insurers. Casco insurance covers physical loss or damage to the insured aircraft that occurs during flight or on the ground, as well as the cost of transporting the damaged aircraft to a place of repair. Also, under the terms and conditions of the insurers, all owners, operators or service providers at airports, airfields, runways or hangars may be insured against liability in connection with the performance of their activities.

*450.* In accordance with the Rulebook on the conditions for the use of unmanned aircraft systems and aircraft models,[491] the owner or operator of the unmanned aircraft must have a liability insurance policy against damages caused to third parties.

489. *See*: Article 43, LMIT.
490. *See*: Article 44, LMIT.
491. OJM, No. 11/16.

## Chapter 7. Theft and Embezzlement Insurance

*451.* Theft insurance is property insurance, so the general rules of property insurance apply. In Montenegrin insurance practice, this type of insurance is better known as burglary and robbery insurance, and it is offered to natural persons as an ancillary risk in fire insurance so that the theft of the object may be insured with a fire insurance contract or it can be the subject of a separate contract, which provides a more comprehensive list of covered risks. Burglary and robbery are equally defined in both.

*452.* According to the conditions for insurance against burglary and robbery, the subject of insurance against the risks may be movable property, except for: objects exhibited at fairs, motor vehicles, watercraft, trailers, self-propelled machines, and aircraft. But even these objects may be the subject of the insurance contract while they are being stored as stocks in trade and customs warehouses or while they are being repaired in workshops. The belongings of the insured and persons living in a joint household with them are insured. By a special agreement noted in the insurance policy, the belongings of workers at the place of insurance, the belongings of third parties received for repair, processing, processing, sale, rent, for keeping, in pledge, in service, and similar are insured. According to the conditions, the insurance provides insurance protection against the risk of committing or attempting a burglary or robbery, as well as vandalism during the commission of a burglary. Burglary and robbery are defined by the conditions of insurance. Damages from fraud and embezzlement are not covered by this type of insurance, nor are the risks of ordinary theft, indirect losses and shortfalls determined by the inventory. Ordinary theft may be the subject of a separate insurance contract. By the decision of the Supreme Court of Montenegro, the theft of the insured property by the lessee of the insured, who is considered a member of the insured, excludes the insurer's obligation to compensate the insured for damages. The Supreme Court was interpreting the general conditions for insurance against the risk of burglary and robbery, by which the insurance does not cover the damage if the burglary or robbery, or attempted burglary or robbery, was committed or participated in as a participant or instigator by a member of the insured. Members are considered to be persons living with the insured or in a lease relationship with them (subtenants, etc.), as well as the insured's employees who perform their work at the place where the insured items are located.[492]

*453.* The insurance covers damage from the removal, destruction or damage of insured items, as well as damage to the building parts of premises, installations and equipment in which the insured items are located during the execution of or attempts to commit burglary or robbery, in the amount of repair costs at a certain percentage of the insurance sum. The amount of compensation is determined according to the value of the insured item at the time of the occurrence of the insured event, less the value of the remnants, average manipulative costs, and

492. *See*: Supreme Court of Montenegro, Rev. No. 742/21.

approved breakage, breakage, and damage in the case of the removal or destruction of items. In the event that insured objects are damaged, the amount of the repair cost at the time of the occurrence of the insured event, reduced by the amount of estimated use and the value of the remnants, will be paid, but if the costs of repair are greater than the value of the object, it will be treated as destroyed, and compensation will be paid accordingly. Under the conditions, deductible franchise is prescribed, but it can be waived by the insurer upon agreement with the insured. If the perpetrators are found and it is established without a doubt that the insurer has paid a higher amount than they should, the insured will be obliged to return the difference. In the case the insurer has paid a lower amount, the insurer will have the obligation to pay the difference.[493]

*454.* In Montenegrin insurance practice, there are no terms and conditions available offering insurance in the case of embezzlement, although there is a notation in the legal texts or the accompanying regulation that would prohibit the conclusion of such a contract.

493. *See*: Conditions for Insurance against Burglary and Robbery, Generali Insurance, of 27 Feb. 2008.

## Chapter 8. Agricultural Insurance, Hail Insurance, Livestock Insurance

*455.* The development of the agricultural insurance market in Montenegro is still in progress. Out of five non-life insurance companies that operate in the insurance market in Montenegro, only one company deals with agricultural insurance, and it entered into this business after it had concluded a contract with the Ministry of Agriculture on providing part of the premium for registered agricultural estates in Montenegro. But within five years from the initiative of the ministry in 2021, less than 300 agricultural estates in Montenegro will have been insured.

*456.* The subjects of crop and fruit insurance are: plantings of plants in fields and gardens, lawns, vineyards and orchards, such as cereals, fodder, industrial plants, fruit and vineyards, fruit and vegetables in greenhouses and greenhouses, as well as grapevines, forests and planting material. Insured risks that may be contracted for crop insurance are: basic risks, hail, fire and lightning, while supplementary risks that must be contracted additionally are spring frost, storms and floods. Insurance contracts start from the twenty-fourth hour of the day on which they are contracted and last until the harvest for every individual plant, in accordance with optimal agrotechnical terms. The subject of the insurance is the expected annual yield of the insured crops. The insurance covers the loss of the amount of yield due to the occurrence of the insured event. In addition to a loss of yield for all types of fruit and grapes, insurance against a loss of yield quality and insurance against a loss of seed quality may also be contracted for crops for the production of seed material.[494]

*457.* In regard to livestock insurance, two insurance companies in Montenegro offer this type of insurance, again in cooperation with the Ministry of Agriculture, which pays part of the insurance premium. Livestock insurance covers the potential damages caused by the death of an animal from disease or an accident or the forced (emergency) slaughter of an animal due to illness or accident. An insurance contractor may insure domestic animals, i.e., ungulates, cattle, pigs and small livestock. The condition for insurance is that the animals are healthy and fit for a specific purpose, as well as that they are marked and registered in accordance with legal regulations. As additional risks, loss of calves and/or foals at birth, loss of reproductive capacity of cows and heifers, loss of reproductive capacity of bulls and stallions, medical expenses, liability of animal owners, and the disappearance and theft of animals may be the subject of the insurance as well. Special livestock insurances are possible, and they refer to quarantine insurance, insurance at exhibitions and competitions against risky castration and ovariotomy operations, and equine insurance at shows. In the provisions of the terms and conditions of livestock insurance, a list of the risks excluded from livestock insurance is provided.

494. Two companies offer this type of insurance, Sava Insurance and Lovcen Insurance, with similar risk coverage.

*458.* The penetration of agricultural insurance is still very low in Montenegro, which is the result of farmers' opinions that the insurance premiums are too high but also the belief that 'it won't happen to them', and also the overall opinion that the payment of an insurance premium is seen solely as an expense that does not contribute to the overall return.

*459.* Agriculture and livestock insurance fall into the category of property insurance, so the provisions of the general terms and conditions of property apply to all situations that are not specifically regulated by the special terms and conditions of these types of insurance. Also, the statutory provisions of the LO and LI pertaining to the insurance of property are applicable in this case.

# Chapter 9. Catastrophe Insurance

## §1. General

*460.* Catastrophe insurance protects the person who is insured against low-probability, high-cost events from natural disasters, such as earthquakes, floods and storms, and against human-made disasters, such as those caused during public events or demonstrations and civil disobedience. Insurers in Montenegro offer insurance against these risks as basic or supplementary risks in fire insurance that is usually linked with some other dangers that are offered to be insured against. Insurance provides protection against the following basic risks: fire and lightning strikes, explosions, storms, hail, an impact from one's own motor vehicle, one's own mobile work machine into an insured construction facility, a falling aircraft, public event and demonstration. As an additional risk that must be contracted separately with an additional premium paid, the insurers offer to cover one or more additional risks, such as: floods, torrents and high water, landslides and earthfall, ground subsidence, snow avalanches, leakages, pouring water from installations, self-ignition of supplies, leaking of a heated liquid molten mass, collision of an unknown motor vehicle with an insured building, earthquake, snow and ice pressure, smoke, breaking the sound barrier, the fall of a foreign body, vandalism, civil unrest, strike, dismissal of employees from work by an employer.

## §2. Nuclear Risks

*461.* Nuclear insurance may not be found in the insurance terms and conditions of the insurance companies in Montenegro. This is the case because there is no active nuclear power plant in Montenegro, nor has there ever been any nuclear power plant on its territory. In the general terms and conditions of property insurance of some insurers in Montenegro, the risk of a nuclear reaction, nuclear radiation and radioactive contamination is excluded as a potential cause of damage, so damages from this risk may not be covered by insurance. Regulations on nuclear ships exist in the LMIN in regard to the obligation of the owner of a commercial nuclear ship when entering a Montenegrin port and the rules on the limitation of its responsibility per insured event, but these regulations are rarely in use.

## §3. Natural Catastrophes

*462.* Natural catastrophes are insured either as a basic or as an additional risk. The insurers do not cover all natural disasters as basic risks and there can be differences in the offer of individual insurers regarding basic coverage. Usually, the risk of fire (natural or human-made), lightning strikes, storms and hail are the basic risks. Other risks are considered to be excluded from the basic plan and may be contracted as additional risks in the cases of the risks listed above.

## Chapter 10. Credit and Caution Insurance

*463.* Credit insurance is a type of claim insurance, and according to the articles of the LO, the provisions of this law do not pertain to the insurance of claims. Credit insurance is primarily regulated by autonomous regulation of the insurers and by their terms and conditions on credit insurance. In legal theory, two distinct categories of credit insurance are recognised: *del credere* credit insurance and caution credit insurance.[495]

*464.* First, *del credere* credit insurance is the insurance of the risk of an inability to claim the pecuniary obligation. This contract is concluded by a creditor who has the obligation to pay a premium and the insured who has the right to seek payment of the insured sum in the event that the debtor is unable to pay the pecuniary obligation. The debtor is usually unaware of the existence of the insurance. The creditor is the one seeking to insure themself against the risk of the debtor's inability to pay the pecuniary obligation, and this is his arrangement with the insurer.[496]

*465.* In the case of caution credit insurance, the roles are somewhat different since the insurance of the pecuniary obligation of the debtor is still the subject of the insurance contract. In this contract, the debtor is the one securing their obligation of payment, so the insurer will have the obligation of payment in the event that the debtor is unable to pay. The insurer is a warrantor to the creditor, meaning that the insurer will be the one to fulfil the pecuniary obligation of the debtor in the event that he is unable. This is one of the securities that the creditor warrants from the debtor for the realisation of the credit arrangement, since the inability to pay, especially in the case of long-term loans, carries additional risks. Creditors in Montenegro offer this type of insurance as part of the credit arrangement, and in some cases, insurance of the debtor is a requirement for approval of the credit arrangement by the bank. Several risks are offered to the general public: the risk of death, the risk of death due to an accident and permanent disability as a result of an accident, and the risk of unemployment. It is interesting that in one case, a bank which had caution credit insurance covering the risk of death sued the heirs of the deceased client and did not ask for payment from the insurer. The credit was refinanced by the same bank and the client has kept paying the premiums on caution insurance since this remained the method of security for the approved loan. All the courts deliberating this case took the position that the insurer had the obligation to pay the remainder of the debt and that the bank had the right to directly present the claim to the insurer.[497]

*466.* Insurance against the risk of death is mandatory for the credit arrangements of senior citizens, users of old-age, disability or family pensions who are applying for bank loans. This insurance is contracted by the bank to secure its

495. Zdravko Petrović, Dragan Mrkšić & Katarina Ivančević, *supra,* p. 145.
496. *Ibid.,* p. 146.
497. *See*: Supreme Court of Montenegro, Rev. No. 224/19.

claims in the event of the inability to repay the loan due to the death of the beneficiary. The insurance contractor is the creditor, and the debtor is the beneficiary. In the case of the occurrence of the insured event, the creditor receives the amount of the debtor's outstanding debt, which also represents the insured amount. This insurance is contracted by the bank without the individual assessment of the beneficiary, without medical examinations, and without the determination of the individual risk of the beneficiary.[498] One of the limits of this insurance is the maximum age of the beneficiary, which may not exceed the age of 75 at the moment of the application for the credit. In recent years, this type of securing of the claims of senior citizens has become a regular practice by the banks offering credit arrangements to them. Similar products are available for other applicants for banking loans, but the age limit in these cases is somewhat lower and is set at the age of 70, with the exception of seafarers, with the limit set at the age of 60.

*467.* In some cases, credit insurance is offered as a contract linked to the credit arrangement with the bank. This insurance represents additional security for the bank, but it is contracted by the debtor. This is offered as a possibility, and usually, if the insurance contract is concluded, the banks offer lower interest rates due to the lowering of the risk of the entire credit arrangement. The banks advertise this insurance as a chance to get a loan faster and easier and that the family of the debtor will be secure in the event of the occurrence of the insured events. In the event that the insured event occurs, the insurer has the obligation to take over the payments of the monthly annuities or the entire loan, depending on the insured event. Since unemployment is one of the risks, one of the conditions for concluding this type of insurance is that the person is employed before the conclusion of the contract and has been employed continuously for a period no shorter than six months. If the risk of unemployment for the contractor occurs, the insurer then takes over the obligation to pay the monthly annuities, not the entire loan. Only in the event of permanent disability or death due to an accident will the insurer have the obligation to pay the entire loan.[499] The premiums are dependent on the total amount of the loan and its maturity, as are the obligations of the insurer in the event of unemployment, since in this event, there is no obligation to cover the entire loan. Depending on the period

498. In one case, right direct claim of the bank was disputed by the insurer because the insured, a client of the bank, deliberately did not report facts relevant for the risk assessment. The courts argued that this contract was a contract benefitting a third party, the bank in this case, and that the beneficiary did not know or did not have to know that the insurance contractor had falsely represented the facts about their medical condition. The courts argued that it is the responsibility of the insurer to verify the accuracy of these data by requesting that the insured perform a medical examination or by requesting that a health record be submitted to the insurer, as stated in the statement signed by the defendant and the insured, regardless of whether it is expressly prescribed as an obligation in accordance with its acts, because the defendant is an insurance company that had to act with increased care when concluding the insurance contract. *See*: Appellate Court of Montenegro, Pž. No. 16/23; Appellate Court of Montenegro, Pž. No. 736/19.

499. Some older special conditions for life insurance in the case of the death of the loan beneficiary stipulate that the insurer's obligation will be to pay 50% of the insured sum if the death of the insured occurred within the first six months from the beginning of the insurance. The case was argued before the Supreme Court due to the wrong application of substantive law and errors in determining the factual situation. *See*: the Supreme Court of Montenegro, Rev. No. 819/09.

of credit arrangements, the obligation of the insurer differs. In the case of a credit contract of up to thirty-six months, the insurer usually covers the risk of unemployment with a maximum of six monthly annuities per adverse event, with a maximum of nine annuities for the entire duration of the loan. In the case of a credit contract lasting longer than thirty-six months, the insurer usually covers the risk of unemployment with a maximum of twelve monthly annuities per adverse event, with a maximum of eighteen annuities for the entire duration of the loan. In addition to the rule on the duration of the precontract employment of an insurance contractor, they must be a citizen of Montenegro, employed by an employer based in Montenegro, which is not in bankruptcy or liquidation proceedings and is not within the notice period from the employment agreement. The risk of unemployment is offered after the expiration of a sixty-day period after the conclusion of the contract.[500]

500. *See*: General Conditions for Insurance for Unemployment Loan Beneficiaries (US-bni/16-05-cg) and Conditions for Accident Insurance of Loan Beneficiaries in the Event of Death due to an Accident and Permanent Disability as a Result of an Accident (US-bni-nsi/16-09-cg), Lovćen Osiguranje.

## Chapter 11. Technical Insurance

*468.* Production plants, construction projects and businesses are exposed to many risks. Damages due to machine breakdowns, work interruptions, damage to electronic equipment and accidents represent large financial expenses for the owners, so they seek to insure themselves against relevant risks. Insurers in Montenegro offer insurance for movable technical apparatus used by the insured. This type of insurance is property insurance, so the general legal provisions and general terms and conditions of the insurers apply here as well. But, since insurers offer different varieties of insurance for each type of insurance, special terms and conditions apply as well. So, besides the General Conditions of Property Insurance, there are: Conditions for Property and Business Interruption Insurance against All Risks; Conditions for Insurance against the Risk of Interruption of Work due to Fire and Some Other Risks; Conditions for Insuring Interruption of Work due to Machine Breakdown and Some Other Hazards; Conditions for Combined Insurance of Devices, Apparatus and Instruments (Mobile Equipment); Conditions for Insurance of Construction Equipment and Machinery; Conditions for Combined Insurance of Electronic Computers, Processors and Similar Devices; and Conditions for Insuring Machinery against Breakage and Other Hazards. Some insurance companies offer the insurance of equipment for work, hobbies and other uses, such as appliances, electronic equipment, computers, musical instruments, electroacoustic devices and machines, against certain risks, meaning that this type of insurance is offered to natural persons who can insure the most valuable movable devices.

*469.* The subject of the insurance is determined depending on the specific insurance products. In the case of the insurance of machines against breakage and interruption of operation, the machines are insured against damage caused by an accident in operation, clumsiness, negligence or malicious intent of a worker or other person. If the insurance against interruption of work due to machine breakdown was contracted as a separate product, the insured may be compensated for the loss of gross profit due to a decrease in business income and an increase in business expenses during the contracted period. As a separate insurance, the insurance of electronic computers and mobile technology is possible, since nowadays we cannot imagine working without computers and computer equipment. This type of insurance provides for the insurance of electronic devices and apparatus for field tests that are exposed to various external influences, so coverage against a wide range of risks is possible: fire, lightning, explosions, storms, hail, water and steam, machine breakdown, burglary, robbery and many others. Construction equipment and machinery are exposed to a large number of risks. As a separate type of insurance, the insurance contractor may contract this insurance regardless of his ownership of the equipment. This insurance is available for the owners of the equipment, the buyers of the equipment, or a leasing user. The equipment may be insured against physical damage or destruction caused by any sudden and unforeseen event, according to the agreed-upon insurance terms.

## Chapter 12. Miscellaneous Types of Insurance

*470.* Various other types of insurance are available in Montenegro. The insurers often offer a package of risks to the interested public, often combining risks from different types of insurance. Some of them will be presented as illustrative examples.

*471.* In that regard, besides the homeowner's insurance, there is the possibility of insurance of immovable property in the tourist sector, offered to small business owners in tourism, providing insurance of the risks not only of property – tourist apartments, immovable and movable property – but also against the liability of the property owner to tourists. This is property-based insurance covering property loss and liability for the owner.

*472.* New developments in micro-mobility in urban centres have presented an opportunity for insurers to offer new insurance products, since there are no regulations on the liability of micro-vehicle owners, such as bicycles, electric bicycles, electric scooters, Segways and other motor-driven micro-vehicles. The insurer's liability is limited only to products with a design speed of up to 25 km/h in the case of damage to third parties caused by the owning and use of the vehicle causing the accident, as well as the supplementary risk included in the Casco insurance of the vehicle itself. The limit of the insurer's liability for damages to third parties due to the possession and use of a micro means of transport is set at EUR 50,000, with the appropriate deductible franchise. Natural persons on the territory of Montenegro may be protected in the case of an accident, if they are between the ages of 14 and 75, from accidental death, serious injuries, comas, dislocations, burns and soft-tissue injuries, in the event that these accidents and injuries occurred to the insured while driving and operating a micro transport vehicle. Extension of the territorial coverage outside of Montenegrin territory is possible, but it has to be contracted separately for an additional premium. The insurers offer Casco insurance for these vehicles that covers damage due to the loss, damage or destruction of the insured micro transport vehicle due to a traffic accident (as a result of a sudden event), fire, lightning strikes, explosions, storm, hail, aircraft crashes, public events and demonstrations, burglary, robbery and earthquakes. Again, in this case, an appropriate deductible franchise is envisaged by the terms of the insurance.

# Part IV. Motor Vehicle Insurance

## §1. General

*473.* Motor vehicle insurance is one of the most developed insurance types in Montenegro. This is because motor vehicle insurance is one of the compulsory types of insurance in traffic, so every owner of a motor vehicle has to be insured against damages caused to third parties. Sadly, after the economic crises in the former Yugoslavia and the general level of the economy nowadays, Montenegrin citizens and companies often conclude only compulsory forms of insurance, since other types of insurance are often regarded as too expensive for the average person.

*474.* This type of insurance is regulated by the LMIT and by the conditions for compulsory insurance of the vehicle owner and user against liability for damage caused to third parties by each individual insurer offering this type of insurance. After the enactment of the LMIT in 2012, a transitional five-year period was established for the obligation of insurers to provide their conditions for compulsory insurance of vehicle owners and users against liability for damage caused to third parties for the purpose of verification of their compliance with the law, actuarial principles and professional rules by the regulatory authority. In this transitional period, it was the association of insurers that established the joint proposal of the conditions for motor vehicle insurance. Today, all insurers have their own conditions for this type of insurance that fall under the control of the regulatory authority.[501]

*475.* The obligation to have an insurance contract with the operator of a means of transport is established by the provisions of the LMIT. The contract has to be concluded prior to the vehicle entering traffic and must be presented at the request of the authorised person. Also, the owner or user of the means of transport has the obligation to inform the insurance company of the realisation of the insured event within seven days of its occurrence.[502] Regular renewal of an insurance contract is

501. *See*: Article 10, LMIT.
502. *See*: Article 6, LMIT. In one case before the Supreme Court of Montenegro, there was a dispute between the parties about whether an unregistered motorcyclist can receive compensation of damages from an unregistered vehicle owner. The lower courts determined that because the latter was unregistered, they lost the right to claim damages from the first defendant. However, this reasoning was not accepted by the Supreme Court, because the obligation of the owner of a motor vehicle to register a motorcycle entails the sanctions (penalties) prescribed in the Law on Road Traffic Safety, but not the loss of the right to compensation for damages from the first defendant who is obliged by law to compensate damage caused by an uninsured vehicle. Also, Supreme Court did not accept

the obligation of the owner or the user of the means of transport, as long as it is in use in traffic, which will be certified by the issuance of a traffic permit by the registration's authority upon the submission of a copy of the insurance agreement. The insurance contract is concluded on the basis of the law, the insurance terms and conditions and the premium tariffs. The insurance conditions are the part of the insurance contract that must be delivered to the insured at the moment of the contract's conclusion, at the latest. The insurer may not decline the offer of the owner or the user of the means of transport if he agrees to the conditions under which the insurer is providing this mandatory insurance. The liability of the insurance company under the insurance contract begins upon the expiry of the twenty-fourth hour of the day specified in the insurance document as the date of the commencement of the insurance and ceases upon the expiry of the twenty-fourth hour of the day specified as the expiry date in the insurance document, unless otherwise contracted.[503] So, there is room for stipulating something different in the insurance contract, but this provision is here to protect the insurer from possible fraudulent claims of the contracting party for damages that were incurred prior to the conclusion of the insurance contract. The insurance sum, which represents the maximum liability of the insurer, may not be lower than the one specified in the law and is determined by the contract.[504] The insurance company is the one determining the premium for each class of the premium system based on the relevant data. The bonus-malus system in compulsory insurance is an obligatory part of the premium system. The regulatory authority ensures the proper application of the premium system.[505]

*476.* This law has brought one major novelty: the introduction of the bonus-malus system of mandatory insurance policy premium calculations. Before this law, the system of mandatory traffic insurance did not use this type of premium calculation and all the premiums were the same. The new system was introduced as a way to calculate the previous behaviour of the insured into the insurance premium and a way of stimulating the insured to be particularly cautious. The bonus-malus system has gone through some changes over the years, and it was first developed by the rules of the Association of the Insurers, by the system of tariffs on premiums in motor insurance.[506] Some problematic aspects of the system of tariffs established by the Association of Insurers were discussed in legal theory since the rules established the inheritability of the obligation of the bonus-malus, an obligation that should not have been inheritable.[507] The insurers share data on the behaviour of the insured, so the new policies take into account the previous behaviour of the insured.

---

the reasoning of the lower courts that this fact was his share in the damage, nor that the damage could be lowered on that basis. *See*: Decision of the Supreme Court of Montenegro, Rev. No. 317/ 17.

503. *See*: Article 7, LMIT.
504. *See*: Article 9, LMIT.
505. *See*: Article 11, LMIT.
506. Nikola Dožić, Bonus-malus sistem u osiguranju od autoodgovornosti u Crnoj Gori, *Bezbjednost saobraćaja, osiguranje i naknada štete – XVIII Međunarodni naučni skup – Udruženje za odštetno pravo*, Beograd, 2015, pp. 59–70.
507. Nikola Dožić, Nasledivost prava i obaveza iz ugovora o osiguranju od autoodgovornosti u pravu Crne Gore, *XXII Međunarodni naučni skup – Udruženje za odštetno pravo*, Beograd, 2019, pp. 403–417.

This system is usually perceived by the Montenegrins as a solution by the legislator that was instituted to benefit only insurers, but its benefits for the insured who have benefited from the bonuses they have received are beginning to change the opinion of the general public.

## §2. Settlement of Claims

*477.* The procedure for decision-making and the settlement of insurance claims in compulsory insurance is uniformly regulated for all cases of compulsory insurance. Some specificities regarding claims in motor vehicle insurance are part of the special chapter of the LMIT dedicated to motor vehicle insurance.

*478.* The claim of a person suffering damage may be directed to the insurance company or to the Insurance Association in cases of damages caused by an uninsured or unknown means of transport or a means of transport insured by a company whose licence has been revoked or which has been subject to the initiation of liquidation or bankruptcy proceedings. The right to file a lawsuit is suspended for a period of sixty days, during which the insurance company must present an offer for settlement of the claim in the event that the liability for compensation and the amount of the claim are not disputable or it must present a detailed response if the liability for compensation or the amount of the claim is disputable.[508] If the insurance company cannot determine the amount of compensation within the sixty-day period, it must offer and pay to the claimant the undisputable portion of its liability as an advance payment.[509] The criteria for determining the amount of compensation were set by the LMIT, but the article was repealed by later changes to the law in 2021. The insurance company is obliged to pay the full amount of compensation within eight days of the day of the decision-making or of the day of the conclusion of the compensation agreement, unless otherwise specified by the agreement. Failure to make payment within the deadline creates the obligation to pay at the default interest rate.[510]

*479.* In response to the claim of the party suffering damage, the insurance company may not present appeals in the same way as it may to the insured person due to the latter's failure to adhere to the law or contract based on the law or insurance contract. The insurance company that indemnifies the claimant has the right of recourse against the person liable for the damage in respect of the amount of compensation paid, interest on the amount of compensation paid, and loss adjustment expenses if the liability of the company has not been incurred pursuant to the terms and conditions of the compulsory traffic insurance contract.[511] The insurance company or insurance association establishes the rules for the procedure of settling

508. *See*: Article 12, LMIT.
509. *See*: Article 13, LMIT.
510. *See*: Article 15, LMIT.
511. *See*: Article 16, LMIT.

claims in order to ensure timely and appropriate payment of compensation to claimants, but the LMIT gives the minimum rules that must be regulated by this procedure.[512]

*480.* The LMIT regulates the obligation of the insurance company towards the social funds carrying out activities of health, pension and disability insurance, but only for the actual loss within the limits of liabilities assumed under the insurance contract. Actual losses are medical treatment expenses and other expenses incurred in accordance with the regulations on healthcare insurance, as well as the proportionate amount of the pension of the claimant or members of their family. These funds have a right of recourse towards the insurance company, but all these requests are paid out after the payment of the obligations in respect of all claims of claimants under the same loss event submitted to the insurance company.[513]

## §3. Conclusion of the Insurance Contract

*481.* The subject of compulsory liability insurance for the damage caused to third parties by using a vehicle is the civil obligation of natural persons and legal entities for damages affecting persons or property caused to third parties by using vehicles. A lessee who is an insurance policyholder and user of a vehicle and is not responsible for a traffic accident in which they suffered damage by a vehicle of the same lessor is also considered to be a third party.[514] The provision on the lessee was added in 2021 after an increase in the number of accidents where vehicles of the same owner were involved in an accident but were under lease. So, now there is no doubt that the lessee will be considered a third party. The insurance company has the obligation to keep records of the claims submitted with respect to individual vehicles, but only the person entering into the motor insurance contract has the right to access this information.

*482.* The obligation of signing a compulsory insurance contract that will cover damages caused to third parties due to the use of a motor vehicle as a result of death, bodily injury, impaired health, material damage or destruction, except for damage to things that it was agreed would be transported, is on the owner or the user of the vehicle. Damage to the objects transported will be covered only if they are the personal belongings of the persons that were present in the vehicle at the moment of the accident. Damage to a third party may occur in the accident or due to things falling off a motor vehicle in motion. Any kind of franchise is strictly forbidden by the LMIT, so the insured person may not be obliged to participate in compensation for damage under the vehicle insurance. Motor insurance covers damages incurred in the territory of the Member States of the EU and the territory of the Member States

512. *See*: Article 17, LMIT.
513. *See*: Article 18, LMIT.
514. *See*: Article 25, paras 1 and 2, LMIT.

of the Green Card System or countries whose national insurance bureau is a signatory to the Multilateral Agreement without paying an additional insurance premium.[515]

*483.* According to the LMIT, the insurance contract/insurance policy is uniform for the territory of Montenegro and is determined by the Regulatory Authority at the proposal of the Association.[516] In addition to the motor liability insurance policy, the insurance company must hand over a copy of the European Accident Report to the insured person, which the insured must keep in the vehicle and present to an authorised person upon request. This report may be used as a claim against the relevant insurance company for accidents where no one was injured, and there was only damage to the vehicles, which are still able to move properly, and when the participants have agreed on the circumstances under which the accident occurred.[517] The LMIT also deals with the registrations of vehicles, which may be extended or temporary plates issued only upon the presentation of evidence of a concluded motor liability insurance contract to the authority competent for registration. If there is no obligation to register the vehicle annually, the owner must sign a motor liability insurance contract prior to obtaining the operating licence and renew the contract on a regular basis.[518]

## §4. Persons Entitled to Claim Damages

*484.* By the general provisions of the LMIT, motor insurance is intended to cover damages suffered by third parties. After a brief description of the third parties and clarifications on the rights of the lessee to be considered a third party, the provisions on entitled persons are focused on determining who the persons are who will not be entitled to claim damages. First, an owner, co-owner, or any other user of a motor vehicle causing damage in the case of material damage to objects, irrespective of whether they were operating the vehicle at the moment the damage was incurred, will not be entitled. Second, the driver of the motor vehicle who caused the accident and their legal successors in case of bodily injury, impaired health or death of the driver will not be entitled to seek these damages. Third, a person who has performed or participated in illegally coming into possession of a motor vehicle, use of which has caused damage, regardless of whether that person was operating the vehicle at the time of the damage occurrence, will not be entitled. Fourth, a person who has suffered damage – due to the use of a motor vehicle at car and kart racing competitions and parts of such competitions at closed tracks, intended for achievement of the maximum speed, as well as on test drives (practising) for such events, which are officially approved by a competent authority; due to an earthquake; due to the effect of nuclear fuel during the transport of radioactive materials; due to military operations, military manoeuvres, riots or terrorist acts, if it has been

515. *See*: Article 27a, LMIT.
516. *See*: Article 27, LMIT.
517. *See*: Article 28, LMIT.
518. *See*: Article 29, LMIT.

proved that there is a causal connection between such effects and the damage incurred – will not be entitled to seek damages. It is evident that the LMIT uses two approaches to portray persons who will not be entitled to seek damages.[519] First, by directly describing the capacity of the person, as in the first three cases, and second, by describing the risks that are not covered by the motor insurance, as in the fifth case. The right of the lessee is again stipulated in this article of the LMIT, although this article relates to persons who are not entitled to seek damages. Also, the issue deliberated before the Montenegrin courts was: who could be considered a third person? The owner or co-owner of the vehicle whose use caused the damage does not have the right to compensation, regardless of who drove the vehicle, because the owner cannot be held responsible for damage that the insurance organisation assumes towards third parties. In the same court decision, it was emphasised that parents do not have the right to compensation for damages when use of their vehicle causes damage to their property.[520] By another court decision, the user of a vehicle to whom the owner has entrusted that vehicle, as an employer, is excluded from the circle of third parties and does not have the right to compensation for damages based on motor liability insurance.[521]

*485.* Damages to third parties will be covered by the insurer even in the case of a loss of entitlement from the insurance contract. So, the motor liability insurance shall also cover liability for damages caused to third parties by the use of a motor vehicle by a person who has: operated the motor vehicle without an appropriate driving licence; not used the vehicle for the intended purpose; been trained for operation of a motor vehicle in road traffic without being supervised by an authorised driver/instructor; used the motor vehicle without the knowledge or approval of the owner or authorised user of such a vehicle; operated the vehicle under the influence of alcohol above the set limit, narcotics, psychoactive medicines or other psychoactive substances, and who has avoided or refused to be subject to alcohol or other testing; caused damage intentionally; caused damage by a technically deficient vehicle and has been aware of such a circumstance; come into illegal possession of the motor vehicle; left the scene after a traffic accident, without providing personal and insurance information.[522] All these cases are presented by the insurer as those in which the insurance contract will not be valid, but the third person should not suffer because of this.[523] The LMIT insists on the obligation of the insurer, but it gives the insurer the right of recourse to claim the amount of damage that the insurer has compensated, the interest, and pertaining expenses from the party liable

519. *See*: Article 30, LMIT.
520. *See*: Supreme Court of Montenegro, Rev. No. 161/12.
521. *See*: Supreme Court of Montenegro, Rev. No. 933/18.
522. *See*: Article 30, para. 1, LMIT.
523. In one case before the Supreme Court of Montenegro, the right of recourse towards an owner of a motor vehicle who was solely responsible for the accident was in question, since the insurance contract was voided due to alcohol intoxication. The court decided that an insurer who has compensated damage against an injured party has the right of recourse from the driver of the motor vehicle insured against liability towards third parties who has exclusively caused the damage. In the event that the driver's alcohol level exceeds 0.5 parts per thousand, it is assumed that alcohol was the cause of the traffic accident that caused the damage, until the contrary is proven. *See*: Supreme Court of Montenegro, Rev. No. 132/11.

for the damage. But the LMIT also presents the limits of such compensation in cases where the liable party is a natural person so that the compensation may not be greater than the amount of twenty-four average net monthly earnings in Montenegro according to the latest official data of the administrative body responsible for statistics.[524] According to the Supreme Court's decision, the statute of limitations for the insurer's claim against its own insured on the basis of recourse in compulsory insurance begins to run from the day the compensation is paid to the injured party and not from the day when the settlement was concluded in that direction.[525]

*486.* Since the reason for motor insurance is the risk of inflicting damages by the use of the vehicle, the question is: are the rights of the owner of the insured vehicle transferred with the transfer of ownership of the vehicle? The LMIT contains a special provision stating that if the owner of a motor vehicle changes during the period of insurance coverage, the rights and responsibilities arising from the motor liability insurance contract shall be transferred to the new owner and shall be valid until the expiry of the current insurance period.[526]

## §5. Limits of the Insurance Sum

*487.* Limitation of the insurance sum is one of the characteristics of all motor insurances in all countries. In Montenegro, the limits are set as the lowest limit possible to be contracted by the parties, so it can be stipulated by the parties that the limit will be higher than the one set in the law.[527] It is interesting that the changes in the limits are recent, so up until 2021, the limits were set for material damage and for loss due to death, bodily injury or health impairment. The following limits were applied in respect of loss due to death, bodily injury and impaired health: EUR 750,000 for buses and cargo vehicles; EUR 550,000 for other motor and unknown vehicles; and EUR 800,000 for vehicles transporting hazardous substances. In respect of losses due to material damage or destruction: EUR 500,000 for buses and cargo vehicles; EUR 300,000 for other motor vehicles; and EUR 550,000 for vehicles transporting hazardous substances. Since the changes in 2021, the lowest insured sum is in cases of damage due to death, bodily injury or damage to health up to the amount of EUR 6,070,000 per harmful event, regardless of the number of injured persons, and in cases of destruction or damage to things – up to the amount of EUR 1,220,000 per harmful event, regardless of the number of injured persons.[528] The decision regarding the increase of the sum insured may be passed by the government at the proposal of the regulatory authority. In an earlier decision of the Supreme Court of Montenegro, it was elaborated that the insurer, within the limits of the insurance sum, is liable for all damage suffered by third parties as a result of an accident caused by the insured. Thus, the court clarified that there is liability

524. *See*: Article 30, paras 2 and 3, LMIT.
525. *See*: Supreme Court of Montenegro, Rev. No. 865/09.
526. *See*: Article 32, LMIT.
527. *See*: Article 33, para. 1, LMIT.
528. *See*: Article 33, para. 2, LMIT.

on the part of the insurer for damages due to mental pain due to the death of a close relative and compensation for material damages for the construction of a tombstone, costs of funeral equipment, flowers and wreaths.[529]

*488.* Since the insurance sum is the maximum limit of the insurer's liability in cases where there are several claimants and the total compensation of damages exceeds the amount of the insurer's liability, the rights of the claimants in relation to the insurance company shall be proportionately reduced up to the specified sum insured. So, the total amount of the insurer's obligation will not be increased, but in the opposite case, the claimants will receive proportionally reduced compensation so that all of them receive the same percent of the damages.[530] If the insurer has paid a claim in an amount higher than the claimant is due to receive, since the insurer was not or could not have been aware that there are other claimants, the insurer will reduce the compensation to other claimants proportionately in accordance with the described rules and will remain liable to such other claimants only up to the amount of the remaining insured sum.[531] In this case, a claimant who has received the full amount of compensation will not be obliged to return the higher amount, and the limit and the rule on lowering the payments will only affect the other claimants.

## §6. Compensation of Damage Caused Abroad

*489.* In the event that the owner of an insured vehicle in Montenegro wants to drive outside the territory of Montenegro, they must obtain an international motor liability insurance document (green card), which will be checked by the competent authorities on the occasion of leaving the territory of Montenegro. The insurer who has issued a green card will have the obligation to compensate the claimant for damage caused by the use of such a vehicle abroad up to the amount stipulated by the motor liability insurance regulations of the state in which the damage occurred, or in accordance with an international agreement, if the international document is valid

529. *See*: Supreme Court of Montenegro, Rev. No. 332/13.
530. This was the subject of one of the earlier principle legal positions of the Federal Court of Yugoslavia, No. 8/88 from 1988, which was later reiterated by the Supreme Court of Montenegro in Rev. No. 642/11. The limit of the insurer's liability is determined according to the total damage in one harmful event, regardless of the number of injured persons. At the same time, the amount of damage, according to which the scope of liability of the insurer is determined, is calculated by taking the monetary damage in the amount in which it occurred, and the non-monetary material damage and non-material damage are determined according to the prices or the criteria at the time of the harmful event. If the amount of damage does not exceed the amount of the insured sum, the insurance association is obliged to fully compensate for the damage even when the amount of damage according to the prices or the criteria at the time of the court decision exceeds the amount of the insured sum. If the amount of damage is determined in this way, the insurance company is obliged to compensate for part of the damage according to the ratio between the insured sum and the amount of damage determined in this way.
531. *See*: Article 33, paras 4 and 5, LMIT.

in the state in which the damage occurred.[532] After receipt of the compensation request, according to the procedure established by international agreements to which the Insurers Association is a signatory in its capacity as the national green card bureau, the insurer has to compensate the damage within ninety days. If the insurance company fails to pay the damage within the deadline, the claim may then be presented to the Insurers' Association, which will have a right of recourse against the company that had liability to cover the damage for the amount of the damages paid.[533]

## §7. Compensation of Damage from Motor Vehicles with Foreign Registration Plates

*490.* If a vehicle registered in a foreign country enters the territory of Montenegro, the owner or user of that vehicle must present a valid international document, green card or other evidence recognised by the Insurers' Association on motor liability insurance that is valid in Montenegro, that covers damage at least up to the amount specified in the LMIT. The Insurers' Association guarantees the liabilities that arise from the use of that vehicle.[534] The validity of an international insurance document or border insurance will be verified by the administrative authority competent for interior affairs at a border crossing on the occasion of a motor vehicle entering the territory of Montenegro.[535] If the vehicle entering Montenegro does not have a valid international document, the owner or user of the vehicle will be obliged to sign a motor liability insurance contract at the border with the national insurance company, which is valid only for the territory of Montenegro and will be concluded for the period of stay of that vehicle, but no shorter than fifteen days. This insurance will be valid for the territories of the European Economic Area too, after Montenegro's accession to the EU, since the implementation of this provision has been postponed until that moment.[536] There are many paragraphs in Montenegrin laws whose implementation has been postponed until the accession of Montenegro to the EU. These types of norms are introduced in the amendments to the existing laws in the process of harmonising the national legislation in the implementation of EU law. The majority of EU-law-influenced norms are applicable right away, but some require postponement of the application. In recent years, many amendments to the existing legislation have been made in order to implement EU legislation, and usually, the major influences in the method of harmonisation are found in those EU Member States that were members of the former Yugoslavia, since we share the same legal history.

532. This was the opinion of the Supreme Court of Montenegro, Rev. No. 417/09, stating that the damage caused by the use of a vehicle abroad must be compensated by the insurance organisation with which the vehicle is insured up to the limit determined by the regulations on compulsory insurance of the country in which the damage occurred.
533. *See*: Article 34, LMIT.
534. *See*: Article 35, LMIT.
535. *See*: Article 37, para. 1, LMIT.
536. *See*: Article 36, LMIT.

*491*. The procedure for compensation for damage caused by a vehicle with foreign registration plates also underwent changes in 2021. The procedure is simplified by the new rules, and all possible debtors of the obligation of payment have the same deadline for the fulfilment of the obligation. By the old rules, there was a difference in deadlines if the claim was submitted to the Insurers' Association, which had sixty days to compensate the claim or pass a reasoned decision on denial of the request. The deadline of thirty days was established for the insurance companies or the person whom the association has authorised to perform operations arising from an international agreement on liability insurance for owners of motor vehicles against damages caused by the use of motor vehicles in the country or abroad. If the claim was submitted to the insurance company first and it failed to meet the deadline, the Insurers' Association had an additional thirty days to make the decision. So, the claim could not be presented to the court in either case prior to the sixty-day expiration. Now the procedure is simplified, and the deadline for all actors is the same: ninety days, which is also the time limit within which the claimant may not initiate court proceedings, before the Insurers' Association has had an opportunity to resolve the issue.[537] The compensation for the claim may be determined at the maximum amount specified by the LMIT.

*492*. If the damage was caused on the territory of Montenegro by the use of a motor vehicle with foreign registration plates, whose owner has had motor liability insurance concluded with a national insurance company/border insurance, this company is liable for the damages, and it will compensate the damages according to the national rules, as in the case of a vehicle with Montenegrin national plates.[538]

*493*. In event that the damage was caused by an uninsured motor vehicle with foreign registration plates, the claim may be presented to the Insurers' Association, which will be paid out from the Guarantee Fund. The right of recourse of the Insurers' Association against the competent organisation of the state where the vehicle is registered is established by the LMIT for all the amounts of damages paid, as well as interest and expenses.[539]

## §8. Appointment of a Claims Representative

*494*. In the process of approximating the laws with the EU acquis, Montenegro has implemented some rules but has postponed their application until after Montenegro's accession to the EU. One of these provisions is the provision on the appointment of claims representatives.

537. *See*: Article 38, LMIT.
538. *See*: Article 39, LMIT.
539. *See*: Article 40, LMIT.

*495.* By the articles of the LMIT, a motor liability insurance company must appoint its representative for settlement of claims in respect of such types of insurance contracts in all the EU Member States, which shall not influence the substantive law applied in the processing of compensation claims nor shall it alter the court's jurisdiction. This authorised representative may be either a natural person with residence or a legal entity with a registered office, in such a country, qualified to resolve any issues that may arise with regard to the compensation claim in the language officially used in the country for which the authorised representative has been appointed and will be responsible for processing, settling and payment of compensation claims in respect of damage incurred by the persons insured by the company that appointed the authorised representative to persons with residence in the Member State for which the authorised representative is appointed. There is no limitation on the number of insurers that this person may represent. The responsibility of the authorised representative in the claim procedure is to collect all the required information in order to establish the cause of the insured event, the amount of the loss incurred, and undertake other actions aimed at settlement of the compensation claim and fulfilment of obligations arising from such a request.[540]

*496.* The same rules apply to the appointment of authorised representatives of the insurance company with registered offices in EU Member States when a representative is appointed in Montenegro. Also, the activities of this representative in Montenegro are the same as those of the representatives of Montenegrin insurance companies appointed in other EU countries.[541]

*497.* These rules are meant to simplify and ease the procedure of claim settlement, since there will be a representative of each insurer in every national system in the EU, so it is expected that citizens will opt to present their claims through the authorised representative in the language officially used in that Member State. But the right of the claimant to directly submit the compensation claim to the liable company at its registered office or the office of its branch is not affected by these rules. The appointment of authorised persons is meant to be a simplification of the procedure since there will be a representative of the liable insurance company with whom they can communicate in the official language of their own country.

540. *See*: Article 41, paras 1 to 4, LMIT.
541. *See*: Article 41, para. 6, LMIT.

# Part V. Insurance of Persons

## Chapter 1. Workers' Compensation and Occupational Diseases

*498.* Insurance for workers against accidents at work and occupational diseases is regulated within the domain of public social health insurance,[542] voluntary health insurance and accident insurance. It is significant to notice that Montenegro has signed a number of conventions of the International Labour Organisation which deal with the issues of workers' compensations and occupational diseases, such as: the Workers' Compensation Convention (Agriculture), 1921 (No. 12); the Workers' Compensation Convention (Accidents), 1925 (No. 17); the Workers' Compensation Convention (Occupational Diseases), 1925 (No. 18); Sickness Insurance Convention (Industry), 1927 (No. 24); Sickness Insurance Convention (Agriculture), 1927 (No. 25); Employment Injury Benefits Convention, 1964 [Schedule I amended in 1980] (No. 121); Occupational Cancer Convention, 1974 (No. 139); Occupational Safety and Health Convention (Dock Work), 1979 (No. 152); Occupational Safety and Health Convention, 1981 (No. 155); Occupational Health Services Convention, 1985 (No. 161); Safety and Health in Construction Convention, 1988 (No. 167); and Promotional Framework for Occupational Safety and Health Convention, 2006 (No. 187).

*499.* Compulsory health insurance is part of the social insurance system, which, based on the principles of compulsoriness, reciprocity and solidarity, provides rights to all insured persons' illnesses or injuries sustained either during work or outside of the workplace. Rights from compulsory health insurance are: the right to health care, the right to salary compensation during temporary incapacity for work, and the right to reimbursement of travel expenses related to the use of health care. The right to salary compensation may be exercised after two months of being insured without interruption or after four months with interruptions in the last twelve months, except in the case of emergency medical assistance and an injury at work.[543]

*500.* The funds for the work of compulsory health insurance are provided by the state budget, according to the provisions of the last changes in the field. Before 2021, obligatory compensation payments by employees and employers were used

542. *See*: Law on Compulsory Health Insurance, OJM, No. 145/21.
543. *See*: Article 12, Law on Compulsory Health Insurance.

to create funds for the functioning of the social healthcare system. The status of the insured is obtained according to the statutory provisions of the Law on Compulsory Health Insurance.[544]

544. *See*: Article 6, Law on Compulsory Health Insurance.

## Chapter 2. Bodily Injuries

*501.* Bodily injury is a risk covered by a voluntary insurance contract. In an accident insurance contract, the contractor undertakes to pay the insurer a premium, and the insurer undertakes to, if the insured event occurs, pay the insured or the beneficiary the insured amount, or part of it. An accident is considered any sudden event independent of the will of the insured that, acting mostly externally and abruptly on the body of the insured, results in their death, complete or partial disability, temporary inability to work, or health impairment that requires medical assistance. The insurer, according to the contracted insurance, has the obligations for the following events: death due to an accident; permanent loss of general working ability (disability); temporary incapacity for work (daily allowance); health impairments that require medical assistance (treatment costs and days in hospital); and other contracted cases that are regulated by supplementary conditions. In the general terms of insurance against accidents, the possible accidents are listed, as are the cases in which there will be no obligation of the insurance company.

*502.* According to the general terms of insurance against accidents, persons from the age of 14 to the age of 75 may be insured. Persons younger than 14 and older than 75 may be insured only if this is stipulated in special or supplementary conditions. Persons with partial disabilities caused by some serious illness, serious physical defects or deficiencies are insured with the payment of an increased premium. Also, persons completely deprived of business capacity are, in any case, excluded from insurance, unless otherwise stipulated by law. These limitations are not applicable in the case of compulsory insurance of passengers on public transport, since in that insurance only the capacity of the person as a passenger is relevant, so the age of the passengers is irrelevant.

*503.* When an accident occurs, the insurer pays the amounts agreed in the insurance contract, namely: the sum insured in the event of death, if the death of the insured occurred as a result of an accident; or the sum insured in the case of disability, if 100% of the disability of the insured occurred as a result of the accident. The insurer will pay a percentage of the insured amount in the case of disability, which corresponds to the percentage of partial disability, if the insured party has been partially disabled as a result of the accident. The insurer will have the obligation to pay a daily allowance if the insured is temporarily unable to work, that is, to perform their regular occupation, and to reimburse the treatment costs if the insured, due to the accident, needed medical help and had medical expenses as a result. If the insured is hospitalised, the insurer will be obliged to pay the compensation for a day in hospital if the insured is being treated in an in-patient institution. The insurer's obligations are limited by the contractual term of the insurance and the upper limit of the insurer's liability set by the contract. Accident insurance may be contracted for the performance of the regular occupation of the person or for a special role of the insured person, such as in the case of athletes, hunters, drivers or passengers in a motor vehicle, excursionists, firemen, dismantlers of mines, grenades and other explosive objects, stuntmen, etc.

*504.* The obligation of the insurer regarding the temporary incapacitation of the insured for work is limited to the duration of such incapacity per a medical report, for reasons strictly related to the insured event, and by a maximum of 200 days. If the temporary incapacity for work is extended for any health reasons, the insurer is obliged to pay a daily allowance only for the duration of the leave caused solely by the accident. This right of the insured is strictly related to their employment, so in cases where the insured is incapacitated for work but was unemployed at the time of the accident, the insured would not be entitled to a daily allowance. Obligation of the insurer towards reimbursement of treatment costs is limited to real and necessary costs that have been incurred, within no more than one year from the date of the accident, and the contracted amount of compensation per day in the hospital for a maximum of thirty days, again incurred within no more than one year from the date of the accident. Costs of transportation for treatment purposes are not considered a treatment cost. Both obligations of the insurer may amount only to the maximum of the contracted sum insured for treatment costs. If the death of the insured occurs after the insurer has already made payments for the medical expenses of the insured and his incapacitation for work, the insurer will be liable to pay the beneficiary the amount of the insured sum provided for such cases, regardless of these previous payments.

*505.* A number of risks are excluded from the contract. They can relate to contractual exclusions, per the terms of the insurance, such as risk from earthquakes, terrorist acts, participation in armed actions (unless this is the regular occupation of the insured), a committed crime, and a causal link between the effects of alcohol or narcotics on the insured and the occurrence of an accident. But, some of the risks are excluded by the LO itself, such as the risk of wilfully causing an accident by the insured,[545] the risk of suicide[546] and the risk of war manoeuvres.[547]

*506.* One of the obligations of the insurance contractor is to report to the insurer circumstances relevant for the risk assessment and any changes to them during the contract. In that regard, a change in the occupation of the insured is an especially relevant fact that the insured should report to the insurer. In cases where such a change represents an increase in risk, the insurer will offer an increase in the premium, and in the opposite case, according to the terms of the insurance, the insurer will offer a reduction of the premium or an increase in the insured sum. Failure to carry out the obligation to inform the insurer about these changes in the event of an insured event occurrence is equated to the consequences of non-acceptance of the increase or a decrease in the premium within fourteen days in the event of the occurrence of the insured event. In these two cases, the insured sum will be reduced or increased in line with the proportion of the premium that was paid and the premium which should be paid.

545. *See*: Article 1048, LO.
546. *See*: Article 1046, LO.
547. *See*: Article 1049, LO.

*507.* Unlike the bodily injury risk covered by voluntary insurance contracts, there are cases in which there is an obligation to conclude a compulsory insurance contract, such as in the case of passenger insurance against accidents on public transport. The person operating a means of transport is obliged to sign and renew on a regular basis a compulsory insurance contract with an insurance company for as long as the means of transport remains in use in traffic. This insurance contract is one of the compulsory insurance contracts in Montenegro regulated by the LMIT. The provisions of the LMIT are a separate law with regard to the LI and LO. The concept of public transport, passengers and the minimum amount of the insurance sum is stipulated by the LMIT. The lowest sums insured applicable to accident insurance of passengers on public transport per passenger are: EUR 8,000 in the event of death of a passenger; EUR 16,000 in the event of permanent loss of general working ability (disability) of a passenger; and EUR 4,000 in the event of temporary incapacity to work, on account of the compensation for loss of income and the actual and required costs of the passenger's treatment. But an increase in the insured sum may be adopted by the Government of Montenegro at the proposal of the Regulatory Authority.[548] In the event of the insured event occurring, the passenger affected by the accident, or their beneficiary in the case of a passenger's death, has the right to directly claim the payment under the insurance contract from the insurance company that provided for the insurance in a specific case. If the contract on insurance against accidents was concluded with an insurance company which is now undergoing bankruptcy proceedings or whose licence was revoked by the Regulatory Authority, the entitled person has the right to make a claim directly to the Guarantee Fund. In cases where no contract has been concluded, the entitled person has the same right to present their claim to the Guarantee Fund.[549]

548. *See*: Article 23, LMIT.
549. *See*: Article 24, LMIT.

## Chapter 3. Private Health Insurance

*508.* Health insurance in Montenegro is provided via a public system of health insurance. Private health insurance is a voluntary insurance contract treated by the LI as a non-life insurance activity.[550] Even though the LI provides a strict division between life insurance and non-life insurance activities, in prescribing the types of insurance activities that these companies may perform, an exception is made with regard to private health insurance. So, an insurance company engaged in life insurance activities may also perform activities related to associated accident insurance and voluntary health insurance with respect to healthcare expenses, provided that these classes of insurance refer to the person who concluded the life insurance contract.[551]

*509.* Private health insurance in Montenegro is regulated by the terms and conditions of private health insurance. Most insurance companies in Montenegro offer health insurance. The status of public health insurance does not influence the status of the insured under the contract for private health insurance. Regardless of the existing coverage by the public system, any person may obtain private health insurance.

*510.* Life insurance companies that offer health insurance as an ancillary to their life insurance contracts offer several types of health insurance that must be contracted separately, such as additional personal insurance against severe illnesses, surgical interventions or malignant diseases. Non-life insurance companies, however, offer basic health insurance (with limited coverage) and additional health insurance (with coverage for serious illnesses and surgical interventions). Also, non-life insurance companies offer health insurance to foreign citizens residing in Montenegro and travel insurance for Montenegrin citizens travelling abroad. This travel insurance includes providing certain services to the insured during their travel abroad, such as assistance during their stay and reimbursement of expenses.

*511.* Insurance companies in non-life insurance usually offer individual health insurance, but there are some that offer collective insurance, usually concluded by an employer for the benefit of the employees in their company, regardless of whether this insurance is covered by the insured's salary or by the employer as the insurance contractor. In fact, one of the insurance companies does not offer individual health insurance, retaining this product only for contracting this insurance as collective insurance intended for the entire family or for all employees of the insurance contractor. One of the benefits of this collective health insurance is the possibility of negotiating a lower premium per insured person rather than in the case of an individual contract, since it is negotiated for a group of employees, so some circumstances that usually influence the amount of the premium paid by the individual are less burdensome for the insurance contractor and will influence to a lesser extent the decision of the insurance company on the amount of the premium.

550. *See*: Article 9, para. 1, item 2, LI.
551. *See*: Article 20, LI.

*512.* Since the public health sector is under a large amount of strain due to insufficient funds, low investments in recent years and the large number of insured, private health insurance has found its place in the insurance market since there is a demand for the services provided by private health institutions in Montenegro, which are members of the networks of healthcare providers included in the offer of health insurance contracts.

*513.* Some insurers even provide medical contact centres, where on-call medical staff will provide the insured with all the necessary professional help in the form of advice, information about the health facilities available in the medical network of a certain insurer, and organising and scheduling a visit to an appropriate doctor. Medical expenses for the insured events stipulated by the insurance policy are then covered directly by the insurer. All insurers require that the insured contact the insurer prior to setting up an appointment at the medical facility, even if this facility is part of the insurer's network of medical facilities. This obligation is contained in the terms and conditions of the health insurance, and the insurance policy in particular, and this is usually repeated on the health insurance card provided to the insured, pointing to the contact telephone line of the insurer and this obligation to report the need for the use of the medical services under the health insurance contract.

*514.* The overall offer of health insurance coverage differs too much to permit the presentation of the usual differences between the providers, and it is very hard for the average citizen to make an informed decision, since there are so many insurance products on the market. Each insurer usually offers several health insurance products intended for individual or collective contracting, with different services and risks covered by a specific contract, some presented as basic, others as additional, with different sums of insurance in the contracting period and, accordingly, a different amount of premium in each case. It is expected that the insurance contractors will make the decision on contracting an individual product, in most cases, based on the amount of the premium.

*515.* The common characteristics are that the insurance contractor must be a fully legally capable person, older than 18, in the case of natural persons. The insured may be younger than 18, and the offer to this category of insured person usually differs from the one offered to the insured above this age limit. It must be noted that some insurance companies limit the upper age limit of those insured, in some cases to the age of 67 and in other cases to the age of 75.

## Chapter 4. Life Insurance

*516.* Life insurance contracts in Montenegro are contracts of insurance for persons, life insurance and accident insurance, in which the amount of insurance to be paid by the insurer upon the occurrence of the insured event is determined in the insurance policy by agreement between the contracting parties.[552] The basic risks covered in a life insurance contract are the death of the insured or their survivorship. In legal theory, a differentiation is made on the basis of the number of persons protected by the insurance contract. In cases where an individual insurance contract is concluded for each insured person, these cases are considered to be individual insurance. Only in cases where the insurance contract covers more than one individual person is it considered to be a group life insurance contract.[553]

### §1. Individual Life Insurance

*517.* Individual life insurance is based on an insurance contract that covers the life of the individual. In some cases, we can include in this group a contract on insuring the lives of spouses as mutual beneficiaries, which is offered by some insurance companies in Montenegro, since membership of a specific group is not relevant for the conclusion of this type of contract. The basic risks covered by the insurers are: the risk of death, the risk of survivorship, or a combination of both in one contract – the risk of death and of survivorship.

*518.* Life insurance covering only the risk of death can be divided into: classical risk insurance and credit insurance, since some of the insurers in Montenegro offer more than one product related to the risk of death, but intended for different purposes. The offer of insurance for the risk of death as the sole risk usually excludes the possibility of the additional contracting of accident insurance or insurance of serious illnesses, since this insurance is usually contracted as credit insurance. If the insured event occurs, the insurer is obliged to pay the insured sum to the insurance beneficiary, which is equal to the remainder of the principal amount of the loan according to the annuity plan that is an integral part of the insurance contract. The obligation of the insured is to pay the premiums on time, and the terms and conditions of this insurance contain the provisions for a breach of this obligation. The insurer has the obligation to notify the insured of a breach of obligation and must provide for additional time for the payment of the obligation by the insured or by an interested third party. Only in the event of the expiration of that additional time may he terminate the insurance contract, retaining all previously paid premiums without the obligation to return them. If the insured lives until the expiration of the contracted insurance period, the insurance contract ceases to be valid, and the insurer has no obligations towards the insured person or to the beneficiary of the insurance. The insurance beneficiary in this case is the commercial bank that has

552. *See*: Article 1039, LO.

553. Predrag Šulejić, *supra,* p. 77; Zdravko Petrović & Dragan Mrkšić, *Životna osiguranja (Life Insurance),* Beograd, 2005, p. 102.

granted the loan to the insured, which will be the beneficiary up until the moment of the repayment of the debt. In the event that the insured continues to pay the insurance premiums, the beneficiary will be determined either by the insurance contract or by the rules of inheritance. In the event that the insurer has concluded a life insurance contract not for the purpose of insuring credit, there are additional rules regarding the death of the insured due to illness in the first six months of the contract. In this case, the insurance will pay to the beneficiary specified in the insurance policy 50% of the contracted insured sum in the case of death, if the insurance was concluded without a medical examination and the full contracted insured sum in the case of death, if the contract was concluded with a medical examination, with a previously submitted electronic health record, or if the death occurred as a result of pregnancy or childbirth, or if the death occurred during a contract concluded within thirty days of the expiration of the previous contract.[554] In all these cases of insurance against the risk of death, the general terms regarding life insurance are applicable, which explain all the necessary conditions for the conclusion of a life insurance contract. Under the general conditions of life insurance, the insurer makes a decision on the need and type of medical examination in the risk assessment procedure. The age limits are set at an entry age of 14 years, with the condition that the entry age of the insured at the time of the expiry of the insurance contract may be a maximum of 75 years. Only healthy persons are accepted for life insurance, and persons who are not completely healthy and/or whose working ability is reduced due to illness, severe physical defects or deficiencies, or for any other reason that represents an increased risk may be insured in accordance with the conditions of the insurer who insures them. All other relevant questions, such as the issuance of the insurance policy, the beginning and end of the insurance obligation of the insured, payment of premiums, the exclusions and limitations of the insurer's liability, the termination and reduction of the insurance contract, etc., are covered by the general terms of life insurance. At the policyholder's request, the insurer is obliged to pay the repurchase value of the policy in accordance with the Table of Repurchase and Reduced Values if at least three annual premiums have been paid by then and if at least three years have passed since the beginning of the insurance. If the request for repurchase of the insurance contract is submitted after its reduction, the insurer will pay the redemption value of the reduced amount of the sum insured. The repurchase value does not correspond to the amount of premiums paid up until then. It is calculated based on valid regulations and on mathematical and technical bases. At the request of the life insurance policyholder, the insurer may pay part of the insured sum in advance, up to 90% of the purchase value of the policy. Advance payments may not be made with insurance in case of death, if this risk was the sole risk in the insurance contract. The terms and amount of the advance payment are determined in the annex to the life insurance contract concluded by the insurer and the policyholder. The annex of the insurance contract must contain: the amount of the

554. The issue of accessing the health records of the insured was raised, since the Personal Data Protection Act (OJM, Nos 79/08 & 70/09) has strict rules governing this. This was the cause of the Opinion of the Agency for Personal Data Protection and Free Access to Information, Nos 261/12–397/12 of 28 Feb. 2012. According to this opinion, it was clarified in general terms that if there is consent from the insured person, there is no violation of the Personal Data Protection Act, so insurance companies may access the health records of their clients.

advance; the interest rate; the amount and due dates of the interest; the possibility of returning the advance; and the consequences of non-payment of the due interest.[555]

*519.* Life insurance covering only the risk of survivorship limits the entry age of the insured to the age of 14 up to a maximum age of 75 at the time of the insurance expiry. Some insurance companies extend the eligible age of the insured up to the age of 85. With this insurance contract, the policyholder undertakes to pay the premium and the insurer undertakes, if the insured lives to the end of the premium payment period, to pay to the beneficiary the contracted personal annuity or to pay to the insurance beneficiary the paid insurance premium in the event that the insured dies during the period of payment of the premiums. The medical examination in this contract is not that relevant for the risk assessment, since the insurer is not covering the risk of death. The specificities of this contract are in the areas of the premium payment, misrepresentation of the insured's age, repurchase of the insurance, and the right of participation in the profit on the premiums already paid. If the policyholder does not pay the premium when it is due, the insurer does not have the right to demand its collection in court proceedings but is obliged to notify the policyholder in writing to pay the premium due. Again, the additional period may not be shorter than one month from the date of the notification. In the event of failure to pay after the expiration of the additional time, the insured may terminate the insurance contract in the event that the premium has been paid for less than two years, with the provision that the premium paid until then shall not be returned to the policyholder; or declare to the policyholder that he is reducing the contracted personal annuity to its capitalised value, if the premium was paid for at least two years. In this case, the insurance is valid with a reduced personal annuity without further payment of the premium. If personal annuity insurance is contracted with a refund of the premium in the event of the insured's death during the delay period and the insured dies within the waiting period, the insurer will have to return the premiums paid up to that time to the insurance beneficiary. Repurchase of the insurance policy in the case of this type of insurance is not possible. The insured participates in part of the profit realised on the basis of the placement of personal annuity insurance funds. Profit sharing serves to increase the contracted personal rent. The amount and method of dividing the realised profit that belongs to the insured or the beneficiary of the policy is determined by the decision of the competent body of the insurer, information about which is delivered to the policyholder in writing.[556]

*520.* Life insurance covering both the risk of death and the risk of survivorship is the most beneficial type of life insurance for the insured and their beneficiaries. The beneficiaries will receive the insured sum in the event of the insured's death within the contracting period, and in the event that the insured survives a particular

---

555. *See*: Opšti uslovi za osiguranje života, Wiener Stadtische, of 5 Dec. 2019. Available at: https://www.wiener.co.me/files/Uslovi%20PDF/Op%C5%A1ti%20uslovi%20za%20osiguranje%20%C5%BEivota.pdf.

556. *See*: Opšti uslovi za osiguranje lične rente, Wiener Stadtische, of 3 Sep. 2016. Available at: https://wiener.co.me/files/Uslovi%20PDF/Opsti%20uslovi%20za%20osiguranje%20licne%20rente.pdf.

moment, they will be entitled to the agreed sum and the profit realised during the duration of the insurance that will be paid to them or, in the case of their subsequent death, to their heirs or beneficiaries. So, there is a difference in the obligation of the insurer in the event of the death and in the event of the survivorship of the insured. The obligation to pay the sum specified in the policy exists in the event of the insured's death. The obligation to pay the specified sum in the case of survivorship and the additional payment of the profit realised during the duration of the insurance exists only in the event of survivorship of the insured at a certain moment. In the event of the death of the insured during the contracted duration of the insurance, the insurance beneficiary specified in the policy shall be paid, if the insured's death is due to an accident, one sum assured for the event of death at the time of occurrence of the insured case and, after the expiry of the insurance, another sum insured in the event of death and realised profit during the duration of the insurance. If the natural death of the insured occurred during the insurance period, upon expiry of the contracted insurance period, the beneficiary shall pay out: 50% of the contracted insured sum in the event of death, if the death occurred within the first six months of the insurance period and if the insurance was concluded without a medical examination; and the contracted insured sum in the case of death, if the death occurred in the first six months of the insurance period and if the insurance was concluded with a medical examination; and the same sum, if the death occurred after six months and up to two years into the insurance period. If the death occurred after two years into the insurance period, in addition to the insured sum, the accrued profit calculated until the occurrence of the insured event is paid.[557]

## §2. Group Life Insurance

*521.* Group life insurance is usually used in cases where an employer insures the lives of their employees or in the case of insurance of the members of a certain association, cultural arts society, sport or similar association.[558] Although the insurance contractor is an organisation, the insured has direct rights and obligations under the insurance contract, and there are no additional contracts between the insurer and the member of the group. In legal theory, there are differences of opinion about whether a contract for a group is the only one needed for the creation of the obligation of an insurer or whether there is an obligation to conclude additional individual contracts with the members of the group. Regardless of these differences, the obligation of premium payment is on the insurance contractor, regardless of whether the insurance contractor uses their own funds or the funds of their employees, by deducting the premium from their salaries. The payments from the insurer are made directly to the beneficiaries.[559]

557. *See*: Dopunski uslovi za mješovito osiguranje života sa utvrdjenim rokom isplate osigurane sume, Wiener Stadtische, of 11 Feb. 2011. Available at: https://www.wiener.co.me/files/Uslovi%20PDF/Dopunski%20usl.za%20mjes.os.ziv.sa%20utvr.rokom%20isp.osig.sume%20-%20E%20tarifa.pdf.
558. Zdravko Petrović & Dragan Mrkšić, *Životna osiguranja (Life Insurance)*, Beograd, 2005, p. 102.
559. Predrag Šulejić, *supra*, p. 79.

*522.* Insurers in Montenegro offer group life insurance. But their initial approaches are somewhat different. The difference is whether the insurers require the members of the group to conclude individual life insurance contracts with them or not. At least two insurers in Montenegro offer this type of insurance, but one of them distinctly requires that the members of the group be accepted into the insurance. The other insurer offers the possibility of individually concluding this type of insurance as a member of the group or by the employer for all the employees and offers the possibility that if the insured person leaves the collective, upon agreement with the employer, they can transfer the policy into their own name. Also, it is possible to change the insured person where the collective does not transfer the life insurance policy to a member of the collective who leaves the collective and to insure a new member of the collective under the same policy. Regardless of this, if the employer insures the lives of their employees, he will have to have his written consent in order for this contract to be valid under the terms of the LO.

*523.* The advantage of this insurance is advertised in comparison with individual mixed life insurance, in that the higher insured sums for the same amount of premium, both for the basic and supplementary insurances, are offered by this type of insurance. In legal theory, this is recognised as an advantage of group life insurance, as is the profitability of these contracts for the insurers and the economic advantages for the insured.[560] Also, one of the advantages was pointed out by a judgment of the Supreme Court of Montenegro. The amount paid out on the basis of collective insurance may only be deducted from non-material damage based on the reduction of general life activity, while it is not deducted from other types.[561]

560. *Ibid.*
561. *See*: Supreme Court of Montenegro, Rev. No. 6/12.

## Chapter 5. Pension Funds

*524.* Reform of the Montenegrin pension system began at the end of 2006 with the adoption of the LVPF.[562] This law, evident from the name itself, introduced the possibility of establishing a third pillar of pension reform in the form of voluntary pension savings. Montenegro, in cooperation with the World Bank, decided to introduce the concept of a three-pillar pension system. After this reform, the first and third pillars exist in the Montenegrin pension system. The first pillar, which is based on the collective principle, includes payments from currently employed employees that are used for pension payments, i.e., the pay-as-you-go system. The third pillar, as already mentioned, represents the system of voluntary pension savings. Therefore, in this reform, introduction of the second pillar, which is the key to the reform in the World Bank system, was missing because this would shift the focus of pension financing from the public intergenerational system to an individual, capitalised and, if possible, privately managed insurance system.[563] By opting for this approach, Montenegro started implementing a reform that was 'painless' because it introduced only the third pillar of voluntary pension insurance and thus avoided the issue of the high transition costs of switching to a multi-pillar pension insurance system.

*525.* At the very beginning of the reform, it was expected that it would contribute to an increase in freedom of the use of capital and savings, reduce the role of the state in the pension system and reduce spending.[564] In addition to this effect on the personal plan for the members of the future pension funds, great benefits are expected for society as a whole, considering the possibility of using the accumulated capital for profitable investments through the capital market. So, much was expected from the reform, but were those expectations justified?

*526.* Voluntary pension funds are regulated as funds of a special type, which represent only assets and are not legal entities. The law provided for a number of mechanisms to protect the interests of members of a voluntary pension fund from the membership rules themselves: equal treatment of all members; the right to choose the fund; the right to change the fund; financial control measures; conditions for withdrawing from the fund; and other rules necessary for the successful functioning of voluntary pension funds in Montenegro. The establishment of voluntary pension funds in Montenegro was followed by significant activity by the Montenegrin Securities Commission (today the Capital Market Authority), which was chosen to be the regulator that will monitor and control the operation of these funds in the Montenegrin market, and by the ISA of Montenegro, which will monitor the insurance market in Montenegro. Three management companies have been licensed

562. Law on Voluntary Pension Funds, OJM, Nos 78/06 & 14/07.

563. Predrag Bejaković, Robert Holzmann & Richard Hinz (eds.). *Old-Age Income Support in the 21st Century: An International Perspective on Pension Systems and Reform*, Revija za socijalnu politiku, god. 14, br. 2, Zagreb, 2007, p. 281.

564. Godišnji izvještaj o stanju na tržištu kapitala radu Komisije za hartije od vrijednostiu u 2006.godini. p. 15. Available at: https://www.scmn.me/images/files/Izvjestaji-o-radu-Komisije/Godisnji-izvjestaj-o-radu-Komisije-za-2006.pdf. Date of access: 15 Apr. 2022.

by the Capital Market Commission to operate in the Montenegrin market. However, only two funds were established, while the third management company lost its licence soon after its establishment. Two voluntary pension funds were created.

*527.* Thus, the management of these funds in Montenegro is entrusted to a specialised joint-stock company. A system of direct control by the competent regulatory body is established by the LVPF in order to ensure that the actions of the management companies are in accordance with the law and the best interests of the members themselves. In Montenegro, there is no so-called 'threshold of entry', i.e., minimum investment amount in the voluntary pension fund, but pension fund members have a legally established obligation to pay management fees,[565] which is a logical consequence of the fact that management companies are primarily of a lucrative nature. This fee represents a percentage of the value of the fund's assets, which further encourages the interest of management companies to achieve positive returns with the funds invested in the fund. The rules on investment can be characterised as the strong promotion and imposition on management companies of a restrictive investment policy whose primary goal is not profit maximisation but the liquidity of the fund's assets and the safe return of invested funds.[566]

*528.* The money paid into the fund is collected on a separate individual account of the fund member, which represents the grounds for the future payments of the fund, so these funds are not based on the concept of guaranteed, i.e., predetermined amounts of compensation to investors.[567] The monetary funds are converted into a fraction of the accounting units determined by the daily value of the fund's unit on the day of the investment. Each accounting unit represents, for valuation purposes, a proportionate share of the total net assets of the fund. The daily fund value is closely monitored by the custodian bank and the Capital Market Authority, which monitor and make parallel calculations of the total net asset of the fund each day, which must match in all three calculations. A pension fund management company is obliged to annually deliver to each member of a pension fund written information on the assets in their account, and the dates and amounts of payment of contributions that they had during a particular period. But a member may ask for this information at any time, and it must be delivered immediately upon receipt of the request.[568]

*529.* One person may be a member of more than one voluntary pension fund, and their membership in the fund is not related to their employment relationship, as is the case with open pension funds. The employment status of the member is a point of interest in the case of established closed funds for the needs of employers, trade unions and other organisations.[569] The transfer of funds from one voluntary pension fund to another is a right of the investor that the investor may claim at any

565. *See*: Article 36, LVPF.
566. *See*: Articles 38 and 39, LVPF.
567. *See*: Article 34, LVPF.
568. *See*: Article 52, LVPF.
569. *See*: Article 26, para. 6, LVPF.

time,[570] but they cannot request the payment of funds until they reach the age of 50.[571] After the member of the pension fund reaches the age of 50, they may, at any time, request the withdrawal of the funds in one of two ways. They may request no more than 30% to be paid in cash on the date of fulfilment of the requirements determined by the Rules on Managing the Pension Fund and Membership Contract and the remainder in monthly or periodical annuities within a period no longer than three years as of the date of withdrawing from the Pension Fund. The other way to receive the funds is to transfer the total amount to the business company performing the pension payments in compliance with the regulations.[572]

*530.* In 2019, the Capital Market Authority revoked the operating licences of both voluntary pension fund management companies operating in the territory of Montenegro. Given that there were no other pension fund management companies in Montenegro, the Capital Market Authority could not use the option given by the LVPF to choose a new management company. For the same reasons, it was not possible for the Commission to inform the members of the fund that they themselves are obliged to transfer to another fund in the event that no management company responded to the public call and for it to reassign the persons who did not act on the Commission's instructions in time. The only option left under the LVPF was to start the fund's liquidation procedure. Since the liquidation of these funds, there have been no attempts to establish pension fund management companies, and thus no possibility of establishing new pension funds in the Montenegrin market.

*531.* The first signs of problems in the voluntary pension fund market were noticed at the very start of the implementation of the LVPF. The major problem was not that this law was lacking in the regulatory framework or that there was a lack of provision on the rules of investment. The absence of legally guaranteed financial incentives was identified as the primary cause of the failure of voluntary pension funds in Montenegro.[573]

---

570. *See*: Article 32, LVPF.
571. *See*: Article 33, para. 1, LVPF.
572. *See*: Article 33, para. 2, LVPF.
573. Vladimir Savković & Nikola Dožić, *Destimulativan zakonski okvir kao uzrok neuspjeha sustava dobrovoljnog mirovinskog osiguranja: studija crnogorskog slučaja kao pokazatelj važnosti financijskih poticaja*, Revija za socijalnu politiku, Zagreb 2018, god. 25, No. 3, p. 280.

# Part VI. Private Insurance – Social Security

*532.* The Montenegrin system of social security is primarily a public (state-owned) system of compulsory insurance, regulated by the Law on Contributions for the Mandatory Social Insurance (LCMSI), which has been amended many times since its introduction in 2007.[574] This law determines the contributions for mandatory social insurance, the payers, bases and rates of contributions, the person responsible for calculation and payment, deadlines for payment, and other issues related to the payment of contributions for mandatory social insurance. According to the initial provisions of this law, contributions for mandatory social insurance were: contributions for mandatory pension and disability insurance, contributions for mandatory health insurance, and contributions for unemployment. Each of these contributions formed the income of the appropriate institutions that were established: the Pension and Disability Insurance Fund of Montenegro, the Montenegrin Health Insurance Fund, and the Montenegrin Employment Agency. The mandatory contributions from the insured were the main source of income for these funds, which were supplemented by the allocations of the missing funds from the state budget. Since the last amendments to this law, the contribution for mandatory health insurance has been removed from the law, so there is no obligation for the insured to pay a health insurance contribution. This social insurance is now entirely financed from the state budget by the allocation of the funds necessary for its functioning. The contributions for unemployment, pensions and disability are still mandatory for all insured citizens.

*533.* The basis for the calculation and payment of contributions is the employee's gross salary, which includes: salary for work performed and time spent at work; increased salary; salary compensation; and other income determined by law, the collective agreement and the employment contract, on which tax is paid as income by a natural person. The gross salary of an employee also includes fees that are directly related to work and work performance, on which personal income tax is paid.[575] The insurance is related to the employment of the person, so the employer is the one who must calculate and pay the contribution in the name of the employee, since the employer is the one who is paying the income to the employee. In some cases, there

574. OJM, Nos 13/07, 79/08, 86/09, 78/10, 40/11, 14/12, 62/13, 08/15, 22/17, 42/19, 59/21, 145/21 & 152/22.
575. *See*: Article 3a, LCMSI.

is an obligation of the Montenegrin Employment Agency to pay a pension contribution to a person who is earning income per the rules of the unemployment regulation and the obligation of religious communities in relation to the persons employed by these organisations.[576]

*534.* Mandatory pension and disability insurance in Montenegro is based on current financing, which provides the insurance based on their work, depending on the length of investment and the amount of the base on which the contribution for pension and disability insurance is paid. With the application of the principles of reciprocity and solidarity, it provides rights in the event of old age, disability and physical impairment and, for their family members, the right in the event of the death of the insured or the beneficiary of the rights. Under the provisions of the law governing this area of social insurance, the Pension and Disability Fund is established, which is competent for the materialisation of the rights of the insured.[577] Although this law states that pension and disability insurance in Montenegro includes: mandatory pension and disability insurance based on current funding; mandatory pension insurance based on individual capitalised savings; and voluntary pension insurance based on individual capitalised savings, this law regulates only the rights regarding the first type of insurance. The third option is regulated by the LVPF and was described in the previous chapters. Mandatory pension insurance, based on individual capitalised savings – or the second pillar – is only mentioned in this law, but this option has not been regulated in the Montenegrin legal system so far. According to the Pension and Disability Insurance Act (PDIA), three categories of compulsory insurance are set: insurance for employees, insurance for entrepreneurs, and insurance for agriculturalists. The person may be insured at the age of 15. Rights from pension and disability insurance are in the following cases: old age – the right to a retirement pension and early retirement pension; disability – the right to a disability pension; death – the right to a family pension and the right to compensation for funeral expenses; and bodily injury caused by injury at work or occupational disease – the right to monetary compensation for bodily injury.[578]

*535.* The retirement pension is attainable after meeting several conditions. The conditions are related to the length of service and age of the person. The full length of service, forty years, will lead to a maximum pension per contribution paid, but the retiree must be at least 61 years old. The other option for fulfilling the criteria for retirement is for a male of 66 or a woman of 64 to have at least fifteen years of service. In this case, there is positive discrimination towards women. The exception is the case of workers in the metal processing and mining industries, with thirty years of service, of which at least twenty must be in these sectors, where insurance is calculated with increased duration. Early retirement is possible at the age of 63

576. *See*: Articles 5 and 7, LCMSI.
577. Pension and Disability Insurance Act (PDIA), OJM, Nos 54/03, 39/04, 61/04, 79/04, 81/04, 29/05, 14/07 & 47/07 and OJM, Nos 12/07, 13/07, 79/08, 14/10, 78/10, 34/11, 39/11, 40/11, 66/12, 36/13, 38/13, 61/13, 06/14, 60/14, 60/14, 10/15, 44/15, 42/16, 55/16, 80/20, 145/21, 145/21 & 86/22.
578. *See*: Article 16, PDIA.

with at least fifteen years of service.[579] Since the general trend in Europe is the ageing of the population, the upper limits for retirement have been increased several times over the years, so the PDIA has applicable transitional provisions for retirement up until 2032.[580] The amount of the pension at the moment of retirement depends on the length of service and the amount of contributions paid by the individual retiree. Since there is a need to protect the existential level of employees who had the lowest incomes or were unemployed for a long period of time, the state guarantees a minimum pension. Periodically, pensions are adjusted to the cost of life and wages.[581]

*536.* Disability pensions are payable to persons with a permanent (full or partial) disability for work which cannot be remedied by treatment or medical rehabilitation and has occurred due to an injury at work, an occupational disease, an injury outside of work, or illness. The disability pension, in the case of a full disability which is caused by an injury at work or occupational disease, is determined in the amount of the old-age pension that would belong to an insured person with forty years of pensionable service and in the amount of 75% of this in the case of partial disability of the insured. So, these pensions are not conditioned by the length of service or the age of the retiree. In cases of disability caused by injuries occurring outside of work or due to illness, they are treated by somewhat different rules, which consequently means a lower amount of pension.[582]

*537.* A family pension is intended for the spouses or children of the deceased insured person who has completed at least five years of service, has met the requirements for an old-age or disability pension, or was a beneficiary of an old-age or disability pension. If the death was caused by an injury at work or an occupational disease, family members are entitled to a family pension, regardless of the length of insurance of the insured person. Spouses must have been married at the time of the insured person's death, except in the case of a divorced spouse who has been awarded the right to support by a final judgment. Children of the insured (biological, adopted or stepchildren) supported by the beneficiary have the right to a family pension until the age of 19 or 25 if they are studying. The right to a family pension is granted to the extramarital spouse and to the life partner of the deceased insured in the case of a life partnership of persons of the same sex.[583] The amount of the family pension is determined on the grounds of the old-age or disability pension that would have belonged to the insured person at the time of death, or of the pension that belonged to the beneficiary at the time of death, in a percentage that is determined according to the number of family members who are entitled to that pension. This percentage varies from 70% for one member to 100% for four or more members who have the right to a family pension.

579. *See*: Article 17 and 17a, PDIA.
580. *See*: Articles 197–200, PDIA.
581. *See*: Article 58, PDIA.
582. *See*: Article 39, PDIA.
583. *See*: Article 43a and 43b, PDIA.

*538.* The right to monetary compensation for bodily injury exists in the case of the loss of, significant damage to, or significant disability of certain organs or parts of the body that hinders the normal activity of the body and requires greater efforts to meet their living needs, regardless of whether it causes disability or not. Physical impairment must amount to at least 50% of the granting of this compensation. There are six degrees of physical impairment set in the law according to the severity of the impairment.[584]

*539.* Compulsory health insurance provides for: the right to health care, the right to salary compensation during temporary incapacity for work, and the right to reimbursement of travel expenses related to the use of health care. The right to salary compensation may be exercised after two months of being insured without interruption or four months with interruptions in the last twelve months, except in the case of emergency medical assistance and an injury at work.[585] The status of the insured is obtained according to the statutory provisions of the Law on Compulsory Health Insurance,[586] and it is usually related to the employment of the person, but the status of insured may be gained on the basis of family ties to the insured, in the case of immediate family members supported by the insured under the law, and by extended family members of the insured if these family members are permanently and completely unable to work in terms of special regulations and if the insured is supporting them.[587] The Law on Compulsory Health Insurance prescribes the conditions and duration of the insurance of children, spouses, ex-spouses and extramarital spouses. Private health insurance is possible, but it is not regulated by law, so the general provisions on insurance apply in these cases.

*540.* Unemployment insurance is part of the mandatory social insurance system, which, on the principles of reciprocity and solidarity, provides rights to all insured persons. The domain of unemployment is regulated by the Law on Employment Intermediation and Rights During Unemployment,[588] which regulates, among others, the areas of rights and obligations of the unemployed person and the procedure for exercising rights during unemployment. This law promotes an active employment policy. Unemployment insurance is compulsory for all employed and self-employed persons in Montenegro, so they must pay unemployment contributions. This will entitle the insured to exercise rights to: monetary compensation during unemployment; financial assistance and compensation for transportation costs during education and training; inclusion in other measures aimed at increasing employment or reducing unemployment; and one-time financial aid and compensation for travel and moving expenses if the employment relationship is based on an indefinite period outside the place of residence.[589]

584. *See*: Articles 52–56, PDIA.
585. *See*: Article 12, Law on Compulsory Health Insurance.
586. *See*: Article 6, Law on Compulsory Health Insurance.
587. *See*: Article 8, Law on Compulsory Health Insurance.
588. OJM, No. 24/19.
589. *See*: Article 9, Law on Employment Intermediation and Rights During Unemployment.

*541.* Unemployment insurance entitles an unemployed person to monetary compensation, and during this period, they will be provided with a pension, disability and health insurance. One of the conditions for exercising the right to monetary compensation is that unemployment must not be the consequence of the consent or the fault of the insured. The other condition is related to the duration of the status of the insured, which must not be shorter than nine months continuously or, with interruptions, in the last eighteen months. The same rights are guaranteed to the entrepreneur, under the same conditions, and to the part-time employed, if they meet the criteria upon the redistribution of their working time to full-time.[590] The entitled must file a request with the employment agency thirty days after the termination of insurance or sixty days if they miss the registration deadline for a valid reason. The right to monetary compensation will be acknowledged on the day of the termination of the insurance. The duration of the monetary compensation is in correlation with the duration of the insurance duration, varying from three months to twelve months or, in the case of an insured with more than thirty-five years of insurance, until they are re-employed or until they fulfil the conditions regarding the age limit or insurance experience for exercising the right to an old-age pension.[591] The monetary compensation amounts to 120% of the calculation value of the coefficient established by the law and other regulations, with the addition of contributions for pension and disability insurance and health insurance calculated on this amount.[592] An unemployed person referred by the Employment Agency to education, training or other measures aimed at increasing employment or reducing unemployment, has the right to financial assistance in the amount of up to 15% of the average monthly gross salary of employees in Montenegro, and if they are referred outside the place of residence, has the right to reimbursement of transportation costs for the time for which they are referred.[593]

590. *See*: Articles 47 and 48, Law on Employment Intermediation and Rights During Unemployment.
591. *See*: Article 52, Law on Employment Intermediation and Rights During Unemployment.
592. *See*: Article 57, Law on Employment Intermediation and Rights During Unemployment.
593. *See*: Article 58, Law on Employment Intermediation and Rights During Unemployment.

# Part VII. Insurance Intermediaries

## Chapter 1. Law of Establishment and Supervision

*542.* Insurance intermediation may be carried out by intermediation companies and insurance agencies, and some tasks in the insurance business may be entrusted to ancillary insurance service providers. The law that regulates the establishment, licensing and supervision of these companies is the same as in the case of insurance companies – the LI. By the very provisions of the LI, the law governing the legal status of business organisations also applies to insurance companies, parts of insurance companies without a head office in Montenegro, insurance intermediaries and agents, and insurance ancillary service providers, unless otherwise prescribed by this law.[594]

### §1. Intermediation Companies

*543.* Insurance brokerage activities are: activities related to managing temporary activities pertaining to entering into an insurance contract, as well as the provision of assistance when exercising rights under the insurance contract. These types of activities may be carried out only by an insurance intermediation company licensed by the regulatory authority for the pursuit of such activities. A company that has received a licence for intermediation in insurance must, in its legal name, have an indication of this type of business.

*544.* The LI presents several limitations in conducting business in insurance intermediation. The mandatory form for the establishment of this type of company is set in law, so the founders may choose between two forms of companies: a joint-stock company or a limited liability company.[595] The other major limitation is that the intermediation company is prohibited from engaging in insurance agency activities.[596]

*545.* The process for obtaining a licence for intermediation in insurance starts with an application to the Insurance Supervision Authority, which must be accompanied by:

594. *See*: Article 8, para. 1, LI.
595. *See*: Article 55, LI.
596. *See*: Article 52, LI.

- a memorandum of association;
- proposed articles of association;
- a list of the shareholders or owners of holdings;
- evidence that the natural persons nominated as members of the board of directors and the executive director meet the conditions;
- evidence of at least two persons who are to be employed in the company, having authorisation for the pursuit of insurance brokerage activities, with a precontract on employment, and with the personal data of the persons to be responsible for insurance brokerage activities;
- a statement on relations with respect to holdings in capital or voting rights of insurance companies, reinsurance companies, insurance brokerage companies or insurance agency companies;
- evidence on liability insurance for damages that may result from the pursuit of business in the amount of at least EUR 200,000 for each damage or EUR 250,000 on an aggregate basis for one year;
- a business plan for the following three years, including data and evidence on the personnel and the technical capacity of the company; and
- any other evidence and data as may be requested by the regulatory authority.[597]

*546.* The deadlines for rendering the decision are the same as in the case of the insurance company – ninety days from the submission of the application. The decision is final and may be challenged in an administrative dispute.[598] The registration of the company in the Central Registry of Commercial Entities is the same as in the case of an insurance company, with the same deadlines for the application for registration and submission of the decision on registration to the regulatory authority.[599]

*547.* Once obtained, the licence of the insurance intermediation company may be revoked if: the company is no longer meeting one of the conditions for obtaining the licence; the operation of the company threatens the interests of the insured persons, or a violation of the law and other regulations was established; the company acts for an insurance company that is not licensed for the pursuit of insurance activities; the licence was obtained by stating false data; or the company is in breach of timely reporting to the regulatory authority or fails to act in accordance with the imposed measures.[600]

*548.* Since one of the requirements for the licensing of an insurance intermediation company is to have two authorised brokers employed, it is important to present the rules on obtaining a licence for the natural persons who will conduct the business within the company. The LI presents a list of the conditions for natural persons who may obtain the licence. The list is short, so the natural person must have: full legal capacity evidence of passing the insurance brokerage exam; evidence that a

597. *See*: Article 56, LI.
598. *See*: Article 57, LI.
599. *See*: Article 58, LI.
600. *See*: Article 59, LI.

safety measure or measure of prohibition of business conduct has not been imposed on them by a final and non-appealable court ruling; evidence that they have not been unconditionally sentenced by a final and non-appealable decision for criminal offences against property or economy to imprisonment exceeding three months. The content of and procedure for the examination on insurance brokerage are prescribed by the Ministry of Finance and the exam is conducted by the commission of the regulatory authority. If a foreign natural person meets the same conditions described above and has been authorised for insurance brokerage by a competent foreign authority, the Montenegrin ISA will issue an authorisation to this person as well.[601] The authorisation of the broker will be revoked: if it was obtained based on false and incorrect information; in a case when the natural person no longer fulfils the conditions for issuing the licence; or in the case that this person has breached the provisions of the LI governing the pursuit of insurance brokerage.[602]

## §2. Insurance Agency

*549.* Insurance agency activities are: activities of initiating, proposing, preparing and concluding insurance contracts on behalf of and for the account of insurance companies.

*550.* The LI presents several limitations in conducting business in insurance agency operations. The mandatory form for establishment of this type of company is set in the law, so the founders may choose between two forms of companies: a joint-stock company or a limited liability company,[603] which is the same as in the case of insurance intermediary companies, but the activity of an insurance agency may also be carried out by a natural person who acts as an entrepreneur. Both the insurance agency company and the entrepreneur must conduct the activity of the insurance agency as their sole business activity, be licensed by the ISA, and contain the designation of their business in the name of the company or the agent.[604] They may also provide intellectual and technical services related to the insurance business in accordance with the regulations of the regulatory authority.

*551.* The LI has granted the banks the option of engaging in an insurance agency with the approval of the Central Bank of Montenegro and with the consent of the ISA. Insurance activities within the bank must be conducted separately from other banking operations and may be performed only by persons employed by the bank with an authorisation of the regulatory authority to carry out insurance agency activities.

*552.* One of the major restrictions in the area of insurance agency is, in accordance with the type of contract, that operators in insurance agency, as a rule, may

601. *See*: Article 60, LI.
602. *See*: Article 61, LI.
603. *See*: Article 68, LI.
604. *See*: Article 67, LI.

act on behalf of only one insurance company. Exceptions to this rule are possible, so the first exception is where the operators conduct agency for several companies for products that are not in direct competition with one another; and the second exception is in the case of direct competition, if the operators have the written consent of all insurance companies for products that are in direct competition with one another.[605]

*553.* The process for obtaining a licence for an agency company in insurance starts with an application to the Insurance Supervision Authority, which must be accompanied by:

- a memorandum of association;
- proposed Articles of Association;
- a list of the shareholders or owners of holdings;
- evidence that the persons proposed as members of the bodies of the company meet the conditions prescribed by the law;
- personal data on at least two persons to be employed in the company who have been authorised for the pursuit of insurance agency activities, and personal data on the persons to be responsible for insurance agency activities;
- a statement on relations with respect to holdings in capital or voting rights of the insurance companies, reinsurance companies, insurance brokerage companies, or insurance agency companies;
- a pre-agreement or agreement between insurance agency and the insurance company, which contains provisions on the right of the insurance company to supervise the performance of such an agreement;
- a business plan for the following three years, with data and evidence on the personnel and the technical capacity of the company; and
- any other evidence and data as may be requested by the regulatory authority.[606]

*554.* The procedure for granting, revoking and terminating the validity of a licence for insurance brokerage companies accordingly applies to granting, revoking and terminating the validity of the licence of the insurance agency company or revoking and terminating the validity of consent.

*555.* The licensing of the entrepreneur (insurance agent) is mandatory and starts with the application of the natural person, which must be accompanied by:

- an authenticated copy of the identity document, with a photograph;
- evidence of permanent residence;
- evidence of education level;
- evidence that the applicant, for the last three years, has not been a member of a management body or an individual endowed with special authority in a legal entity that has undergone liquidation or bankruptcy proceedings;

605. *See*: Article 66, LI.
606. *See*: Article 69, LI.

- evidence that the applicant has not been unconditionally sentenced for crimes against payment operations, economic operations, and property and official duty to imprisonment exceeding three months;
- evidence from a competent authority on the settled tax liabilities of the applicant; the authorisation for insurance agency pursuant;
- a business plan for a three-year period, with data and evidence on the personnel and technical capacity for pursuit of insurance agency activities;
- a pre-agreement or agreement on agency signed with an insurance company, which contains provisions on the right of the insurance company to supervise the performance of the agreement;
- a statement on relations with respect to holdings in capital or voting rights in insurance companies, reinsurance companies, insurance brokerage companies, or insurance agency companies; and
- any other evidence and data as may be requested by the regulatory authority.[607]

*556.* The procedure for granting, revoking and terminating the validity of a licence for insurance agency companies accordingly applies to granting, revoking and terminating the validity of the licence of the entrepreneur and registration with the Central Registry of Commercial Companies. Since one of the requirements for licensing an entrepreneur is that they are authorised by the regulatory authority, it is important to present the rules for obtaining authorisation for natural persons. An authorisation may be issued to a person who: has full business capacity; has passed the professional examination for the pursuit of insurance agency activities; has not had a safety measure or measure of prohibition of business conduct imposed on them by a final and non-appealable court ruling; has not been unconditionally sentenced, by a final and non-appealable verdict, for criminal offences against property, official duty or payment operations, and economic operations, to imprisonment exceeding three months.

*557.* The content of and procedure for the insurance agency examination are prescribed by the Ministry of Finance and conducted by the commission of the regulatory authority. If a foreign natural meets the same conditions described above and has been authorised for insurance brokerage by a competent foreign authority, the Montenegrin ISA will issue an authorisation to this person as well.[608]

## §3. Ancillary Insurance Service Provider

*558.* An ancillary insurance service provider is a legal person engaged in activities of determining and assessing risks and claims, intermediation in the sale and sales of the remains of insured damaged items, and provision of other intellectual and technical services related to insurance activities.[609]

607. *See*: Article 71, LI.
608. *See*: Article 72, LI.
609. *See*: Article 76, LI.

*559.* One of the major limitations of this company is that it may not engage in insurance activities, insurance brokerage and insurance agency activities.[610] The other limitation is the mandatory formation of a joint-stock company or limited liability company, if this activity is the sole business activity of the company. Any other commercial entity may provide ancillary insurance services if it has a separately organised unit for performing these activities and if it has the staff and technical capacity to provide these types of services. As with all other companies in the insurance business, the ancillary insurance service provider company must be licensed by the Insurance Supervision Authority.

*560.* The application for licensing must be accompanied by: a memorandum of association; proposed articles of association; a business plan for a three-year period; a list of the shareholders, or owners of holdings, with data as in the case of an insurance company; evidence that the natural persons nominated as members of management bodies meet the conditions set within the law; evidence of the staffing and technical capacities; evidence of not being a related party of insurance companies, insurance agency companies, or insurance brokerage companies, according to the provisions of the LI and the law governing the legal status of business organisations; any other evidence and data as may be requested by the regulatory authority.

*561.* The procedure for granting and revoking a licence for insurance brokerage companies accordingly applies to the granting and revoking of the licence for ancillary insurance services companies and to their registration with the Central Registry of Commercial Companies.[611]

610. *See*: Article 77, LI.
611. *See*: Article 81, LI.

## Chapter 2. Insurance Intermediaries and Insurance Contracts

*562.* Subsidiary application of the LO is envisaged by the very provisions of the LI, as in the case of the establishment of these companies. The LO and other laws governing contracts in certain classes of insurance shall apply to insurance contracts, insurance brokerage contracts and insurance agency contracts.[612] Some aspects of the obligations of the insurance intermediaries are set by the LI. These obligations refer to the precontractual obligations of the intermediary company and to the payment of a fee for intermediation. In other aspects not regulated by the LI, the LO will be applied as a subsidiary. The new legal provisions on the precontractual obligations of insurance intermediaries have found their place in the LI in the process of harmonising Montenegrin insurance law with EU law in the area of insurance. Although these types of provisions are more appropriate to the law regulating insurance contracts, in the case of Montenegro's harmonisation of its legislation, these norms have ended up in the LI. One of the reasons is that, in the process of harmonisation of the laws, the competence for the harmonisation of the insurance law is in the Ministry of Finance, but the LO is in the competence of the Ministry of Justice. Recently, it has become clear that sometimes the ministries do not cooperate enough, so this lack of cooperation is the motive for these unusual changes. In all similar cases, one of the ministries is the leading one for the necessary changes and is the one that is responsible for meeting the deadlines, but the other ministry is usually not so interested in cooperation.

*563.* Precontractual obligations of the insurance intermediaries and insurance agents are prescribed by the LI,[613] so insurance agents are obliged to provide the insurance policyholder with the following information before concluding an insurance contract, as well as when amending, supplementing, or renewing the contract:

- first name, surname and address;
- the register in which it is entered, with the registration number and address of the register;
- name of the insurance brokerage or insurance agency company where he/she is employed;
- the name and registered office of the insurance company with which the contract has been concluded;
- data on the own or holding of the insurance brokerage or insurance agency company in capital or voting rights of the insurance company for which he/she provides brokerage or agency services, if such holding is more than 10%;
- data on holding of the insurance company or parent insurance company in the capital or voting rights of the insurance brokerage or insurance agency company, if such holding exceeds 10%;
- information on rights to a complaint and manner of dispute resolution between user of services and provider of services.

612. *See*: Article 8, para. 2, LI.
613. *See*: Article 81c, LI.

*564.* The same manner of information delivery is envisaged as in the case of the obligation of the insurance companies to deliver information to the insurance contractor. The information must be delivered in written form, in a clear and comprehensible manner, in the language of official use in Montenegro, unless otherwise agreed by the parties. But here is where the rules differ. The data may be given orally, at the request of the insurance contracting party, or in cases where risk coverage needs to be provided without delay, in which case there is an obligation to provide those data in the manner described before, immediately after the conclusion of the insurance contract.

*565.* Payment of any commission or other charge may not be requested by the insurance intermediation company unless otherwise explicitly stipulated by the contract entered into with the insurance contractor. An insurance brokerage company is entitled to a commission as of the day of commencement of the validity of the insurance contract. If the right to a commission or to another charge has been explicitly stipulated in the contract with the insurance contractor, the insurance intermediation company will not have the right to request a commission or other charge from the insurer under that insurance contract. It is strictly forbidden for an insurance intermediation company to subsequently agree to a change in the manner of calculation or level of commission for concluded insurance contracts that have been brokered. In the case of an insurance agency company, the request for payment of commission or any other charge may be brought only to the insurer. There is no option to stipulate this obligation in the contract with the insurance contractor.[614]

*566.* In the pursuit of insurance business or insurance activities, an insurance brokerage company or authorised insurance broker must protect the interests of the insurance contractor or the insured person. The LI defines some of these obligations explicitly, whereby the insurance brokerage company or authorised insurance broker must:

- prepare an adequate risk analysis and propose adequate coverage;
- prepare an evaluation of the solvency of the insurance company based on the information on the business operations of the company;
- mediate, for the purpose of negotiating on the conclusion of an insurance contract with the insurance company, in line with the request of future policyholders in terms of adequate coverage;
- inform the insurance company about the intention of the insured person to conclude the insurance contract, offer the terms and conditions of an insurance policy to the insured person, and inform them about the rules for calculating the premium;
- check the contents of the insurance policy;
- help the insured person during the insurance contract validity, before and after the occurrence of an insurable event, and especially take care that the insured person performs actions important for maintaining or exercising the rights from the insurance contract within the specified time schedule;

614. *See*: Article 81b, LI.

- follow the execution of the insurance contract that the insured person has concluded through their mediation; and
- permanently check the insurance contracts and prepare a proposal for the amendment of the concluded insurance contract for the purpose of ensuring the safety of the insured person.[615]

*567.* Some of the obligations specified by the LI are elaborated further. So, the obligation of preparing an adequate risk analysis and a proposal of adequate coverage must be prepared in writing by comparing several adequate insurance contracts available on the market in order to provide adequate recommendations for concluding the insurance contracts that the policyholder would use to meet their needs and requirements.[616] Also, the insurance brokerage company or authorised insurance broker must protect the interests of the insurance company in the pursuit of the insurance activities that the insurance contractor has to protect before or after the insurance contract is concluded.[617] This means that they, as an intermediary, have all the obligations as the insurance contractor for which they are intermediating and that they must notify the insurance company of all the risks that were known to them or must have been known to them.

*568.* The payment of funds to the insurance brokerage company by the insured or by the insurance company is also regulated. Any payment by the insured to the insurance brokerage company will be deemed to be paid to the insurance company. In the case of a payment made by the insurance company to the insurance brokerage company, it will be deemed to have been paid to the insured person, but in this case, there is an addendum specifying that the day of the payment will be the day when the insured person receives the funds.[618] Obviously, it was the intention of the legislator to protect the insured person in the payment of the funds, so his obligation will be fulfilled on the day of his payment to the insurance brokerage company and, in other cases, when he receives the funds. Intermediation by the brokerage company may not be the reason for later fulfilment of the obligation by the insured person, but in the case of the payment of the obligation by the insurance company, it may be. These rules create the situation as intermediation does not exist.

*569.* In the case of a conflict of interest, an insurance brokerage company is obliged to notify the insured person of all their legal and economic relations with the insurance company that might affect the impartiality of the insurance brokerage company in meeting its obligations towards the insured person. The source of the conflict of interest may be in the contract that the insured signed with the insurance company, by which he is obliged to act exclusively towards concluding the

615. *See*: Article 62, paras 1 and 2, LI.
616. *See*: Article 62, para. 3, LI.
617. *See*: Article 62, para. 4, LI.
618. *See*: Article 62, para. 5, LI.

insurance contract with the particular insurance company, or that he has contracted the right to an increased commission in relation to the usual brokerage commission for certain classes of insurance.[619]

619. *See*: Article 63, LI.

# Part VIII. Reinsurance, Co-insurance, Pooling

## Chapter 1. Reinsurance

*570.* Contractual relations in reinsurance are not regulated by the LO or by any other legal text in Montenegro. As has been stated on several occasions, according to the LO, the provisions of this law do not pertain to reinsurance.[620] This is the only time the LO mentions reinsurance. Since the provisions of the LO were intended to regulate relations between the insurer and the insured, always keeping in mind the specificity of this relation, it is clear why the legislators have opted to exclude application of these provisions to reinsurance contracts between two professionals, such as an insurer and a reinsurer. The contractual relations in reinsurance are left to the contractual stipulations of the terms for the contracting parties in this contract. The argument for not regulating reinsurance contracts could be that in Montenegro, bearing in mind its size and the number of potential cases of insurance and the number and ownership structure of insurance companies, it is to be expected that reinsurance contracts will be concluded with reinsurance companies abroad. But there is a regulatory framework for the establishment of reinsurance companies and the possibility of their establishment in Montenegro. Up until the day of the preparation of this text, there were no registered reinsurance companies in Montenegro, nor were there any pending cases for licensing such a company before the ISA.

*571.* Since reinsurance is one type of insurance activity, the rules on the establishment of these companies are set by the LI. The LI defines reinsurance as the acceptance of an obligation by a reinsurer, in the event of the occurrence of an insured event reinsured, to assume part of the risk or the entire risk reinsured, while the insurer cedes to the reinsurer part of the premium proportionate to the part of the risk assumed.[621] In the definition of the term 'reinsurance', the legislator foresees two options in a reinsurance contract on the side of the insurer. The first option would be for the insurer to reinsure part of the risk, and the second would be for the insurer to reinsure the entire risk. For the obligation of the insured, the only option in the definition is to cede to the reinsurer part of the premium proportionate to the part of the risk assumed. These options in the definition in the LI are not the only options available in the reinsurance contract in theory and in practice, and we must

620. *See*: Article 996, para. 2, LO.
621. *See*: Article 2, para. 1, item 2, LI.

emphasise that this paragraph in the LI is only the definition in regard to the LI and further use of this term in the LI, which regulates the establishment and licensing of a reinsurance company in Montenegro.

*572*. In the LI, there is another definition of reinsurance pertaining to the activities of a reinsurance company. By this definition, reinsurance activities are activities in concluding and executing contracts on reinsurance of the insured surplus risks exceeding the self-insured retention amount of an insurance company with a reinsurance undertaking.[622] The LI adopts the territorial principle in the regulation of reinsurance activities, so an insurance company that operates in Montenegro may be reinsured by a domestic or foreign reinsurance company.[623] The LI prescribes the obligation of the insurance company to reinsure the obligations under an insurance contract exceeding the self-insured retention limit with a reinsurance company. The self-insured retention limit is the amount of risk undertaken by insurance contracts that an insurance company retains as its own coverage.[624]

*573*. Reinsurance activity may be undertaken by a company with its head offices in Montenegro or by a branch of a foreign company that has been licensed by the regulatory authority for reinsurance activities.[625] A company that has applied for a licence for reinsurance activities may not conduct insurance activities.[626] So, if a company opts for this type of activity, it may not engage in life or non-life insurance nor in voluntary pension insurance activities.[627] One of the most important requirements for the establishment of a reinsurance company is that the amount of share capital may not be below EUR 3 million, and this may be raised in accordance with the LI.[628] The same amount of capital is required for the establishment of a non-life insurance company, so there is no difference in the amount of capital that is required for the establishment of insurance and reinsurance companies in Montenegro. Cross-ownership of capital or voting rights in insurance companies, reinsurance companies, insurance brokerage companies and insurance agency companies is strictly prohibited by the LI.[629]

*574*. The documentation needed for licensing is listed according to the documentation presented by the insurance company, with appropriate exceptions in the business plan of the reinsurance company.[630] A licence may be awarded to a

622. *See*: Article 3, para. 4, LI.
623. *See*: Article 4, para. 4, LI.
624. *See*: Article 12, LI.
625. *See*: Article 3, paras 1 and 2, LI.
626. *See*: Article 19, para. 1, LI.
627. *See*: Article 19, LI.
628. *See*: Article 21, para. 1, LI.
629. *See*: Article 22, LI.
630. *See*: Article 32, LI.

company that has its head office in Montenegro or to a foreign company with a registered branch in Montenegro. In the case of branch, it is the foreign company that is applying for the licence.[631] This company must submit an application accompanied by the following:

- operating licence, articles of association and financial reports with reports of the audits conducted for the last three years;
- data on qualifying holders (first name, surname and permanent residence for natural persons, or the name and head office for legal persons, data on the level of holding in the capital or voting rights in the insurance company, and a list of related parties);
- the decision on the establishment of the branch;
- a business plan of the branch for the following three years, with a detailed description of the intended insurance or reinsurance activities, the expected premium income, expected expenses for insurable events, and a foundation and start-up cost estimate;
- approval of the supervisory authority of the country of the head office for establishment of the branch in Montenegro; evidence on the capital adequacy of the branch;
- data on at least two persons who will be responsible for the pursuit of insurance activities or reinsurance activities in the branch and who meet the requirements referred to in the LI;
- evidence on the organisational, personnel and technical capacity of the branch to carry out activities; and other evidence and data as may be requested by the regulatory authority.[632]

The original documents or authenticated photocopies are accepted, with certified translations of these documents in the language officially used in Montenegro.

*575.* In the part where the expenses of the companies are elaborated, the LI regulates the expenses of reinsurance companies that, besides the expenses for indemnities and contracted sums insured, for insurance companies, in the case of the reinsurance companies, are: expenses for indemnities under inward reinsurance operations; expenses for premiums related to outward reinsurance operations; other expenses from insurance activities; expenses for the pursuit of insurance and reinsurance business (costs of implementing insurance and reinsurance); as well as costs of financing, non-operating expenses, and extraordinary expenses.[633]

*576.* Other provisions of the LI governing insurance companies apply accordingly, not only in the case of the licensing of the reinsurance company but also for the pursuit of reinsurance activities and the operation of reinsurance companies.[634]

631. *See*: Article 42, paras 1 and 2, LI.
632. *See*: Article 42, para. 3, LI.
633. *See*: Article 103, LI.
634. *See*: Article 38, LI.

*577.* The LOBORAT contains some special rules on insurance in air transport and consequently one provision on reinsurance. The provisions of the LOBORAT relating to insurance are also applied to reinsurance of the object of insurance under this law if it is concluded under the conditions usual for air transport insurance.[635]

*578.* The LMIN also contains one provision on reinsurance. In the part of the law dedicated to contracts on marine insurance, it is stated that the provisions of that chapter of the law will also apply to the insurance of ships under construction and items intended for their construction, to the insurance of items that are in warehouses, warehouses, or other places before or after being transported by ship or are transported by other means of transport, to the reinsurance of the items listed in this member, as well as other insurances and reinsurances if they were concluded according to the policies or conditions usual for navigation insurances.[636]

*579.* There are no other provisions in Montenegro that regulate reinsurance business or contracts on reinsurance. The absence of reinsurance companies in the Montenegrin insurance market can be justified by the country's small population and relatively underdeveloped insurance market. The majority of the companies in the Montenegrin insurance market are owned by foreign insurance companies, which conclude reinsurance contracts on foreign reinsurance markets. The fact that there are no rules in the LO that would regulate reinsurance contracts can be justified by the fact that these contracts are very specific types of contracts that are usually regulated by autonomous regulation and not by the acts of the state. However, the existence of the regulation of reinsurance in air and marine transport is expected, and it always points to the corresponding application of the rules on insurance contracts regulated by these laws if the reinsurance contract was concluded under conditions that are usual for the type of insurance in question.

635. *See*: Article 124, LOBORAT.
636. *See*: Article 728, para. 2, LMIN.

## Chapter 2. Co-insurance and Pooling

*580*. Co-insurance is the horizontal diversion of risk between more than one insurer but by means of one contract. This contract contains the rules on collective exposure and division of risks between the insurers who are the signatories to such a contract. For the purpose of insuring high risk without putting a burden on the individual insurer, this contract provides the chance for several insurers to take and divide the risks among themselves.[637] This contract has the same purpose as a reinsurance contract, but the differences between these contracts are evident since reinsurance is a case of vertical risk division and there is no direct relationship between the reinsurer and the insurance contractor or insured.

*581*. The LI states that licensed companies may carry out insurance, co-insurance and reinsurance activities. There is a limitation in conducting insurance and co-insurance activities for insurance companies, since these activities may be undertaken only for those classes of insurance for which these companies were licensed by the regulatory authority.[638]

*582*. This contract must be differentiated from the case of multiple insurance. In the case of multiple insurance, there is more than one insurer, which is insuring the interest on a specific object of insurance. In multiple insurance, the insurers do not need to know about the existence of multiple insurance, and in the case of insurance of an object whose insurance exceeds its value, the rules on double insurance will apply. In the case of co-insurance, the insurers know about the other insurers, since they bear and share the risks jointly, as indicated in the same contract. In the event that the insurance sum of the insured object exceeds the value of the object, the rules on over-insurance will be applied. So, a contract on co-insurance may not be treated as a special type of multiple insurance.

*583*. According to the provisions of the LI, co-insurance is defined as a contract by which several insurance companies have agreed to bear and share the risks jointly so that each of the insurers indicated in the insurance policy is liable to the insured person for complete indemnity in case of the occurrence of an insured event.[639] This would mean that in the case of the realisation of the risk, the insured would have the right to seek complete indemnity from any insurer that is the signatory of the co-insurance contract. The same object of insurance is insured against the same risks by at least two insurers under a single contract.

*584*. The LO contains provisions that create the same obligation for the individual insurer towards the insured in the case of co-insurance. So, in the event that an insurance contract is concluded with several insurers who agree on the joint bearing and distribution of risk, each insurer designated in the insurance policy is liable

637. *See*: Article 3, para. 3, LI.
638. *See*: Article 4, para. 3, LI.
639. *See*: Article 2, para. 1, item 3, LI.

to the insured person for the entire compensation.[640] This rule creates a more favourable position for the insured than the general rules on divisible obligations in civil and commercial law contracts. If there are several debtors in a divisible obligation, such an obligation will be divided between them in equal shares, unless a different kind of division is determined, and each shall be liable for their share of the obligation.[641] Since the obligation of the insurer is a pecuniary obligation, it is divisible, and in the case of a civil law contract, this would apply as the general rule. In commercial law contracts, if several debtors exist in a divisible obligation, they shall be jointly and severally liable to the creditor, unless the contracting parties have explicitly eliminated joint and several liability. This general rule in commercial contracts is less favourable to the insured since it would give the co-insurers the option to limit their liability to part of the obligation. So, the special rule that creates the liability of all insurers for the entire compensation is more favourable to the insured. A more favourable position to the insured is most evident in the case of insolvency proceedings against one of the insurers, in which case he will have the right to full compensation for the claim from the other insurers.

*585.* This special rule is applicable in all areas of insurance, with the exception of marine insurance, since the LMIN has a special rule on the divisible obligations of insurers. According to this rule, if an insurance contract is concluded with several insurers indicating their separate shares, each insurer is obliged to compensate the damage only in proportion to their own share.[642] Since the LO has declared that the provisions of the LO do not pertain to marine insurance, there is no conflict of laws, and the different rules will be applied accordingly to the area of insurance in which the contract on co-insurance was concluded by the insurers. The general provision of insurance pertains to the regulation of inequality among the contracting parties in insurance contracts, which is less pronounced in marine insurance contracts, but perhaps it is more important that marine insurance is related to the international insurance market, in which the principle of contracting party autonomy is more pronounced. This may be the main reason why the norms in the laws pertaining to this area of insurance are of a dispositive nature and may be changed by the will of the contracting parties.[643]

640. *See*: Article 1032, LO.
641. *See*: Article 421, para. 2, LO.
642. *See*: Article 765, LMIN.
643. Borislav Ivošević, *supra*, p. 54.

# Part IX. Taxation of Insurance

*586.* Taxation of insurance can refer either to taxation of the payments made by an insurance contractor (insurance premiums) or to taxation of the payments made by an insurance company in the case of the insured event occurring (insurance sum). In that regard, we will present these cases and have special regard for the differences in the taxation of natural and legal persons since they are regulated by different laws.

## §1. Taxation of Insurance Premiums

*587.* One of the precontractual obligations of an insurance company is to provide information to the insurance contractor on the amount of the insurance premium, the method of payment of the insurance premium, the amount of contributions, taxes and other costs that are charged in addition to the insurance premium, and the total amount of the payments.[644] So, in the precontractual phase, the insurance contractor will be informed of the obligation to pay appropriate taxes on the premium.

*588.* The obligation to pay tax on the insurance premium is regulated by the Law on Insurance Premium Tax.[645] According to the original provisions of this law, from 2004 to 2014, the obligation of an insurance premium tax was established only for the insurance of users or owners of motor vehicles and trailers against liability for damage caused to third parties by the use of a motor vehicle, as in the case of Casco motor vehicle insurance. In 2014, this provision was changed, so now tax on insurance premiums is paid on all types of non-life insurance, except in the case of: accident insurance, voluntary health insurance, and agricultural insurance. Life insurance is exempt from the obligation of tax payment, as are these three aforementioned categories of insurance.[646] The exemption was made in areas where there is a relation between the exempted cases and the life insurance contracts, as in the case of accidents and health insurance, which may be concluded as ancillary risks in life insurance contracts. The exemption in the case of agricultural insurance was made in order to promote the significance of this type of insurance, which is almost

644. *See*: Article 81d, para. 1, item 4, LI.

645. Law on Insurance Premium Tax, OJRM, Nos 27/04 & 37/04 and OJM, Nos 73/10, 40/11, 61/13 & 06/14.

646. *See*: Article 3, Law on Insurance Premium Tax.

non-existent in Montenegrin insurance practice, even though the Government of Montenegro has promoted this type of insurance by subsidising a percentage of the premiums. In all other cases, the insurance premium tax is set by the amendments made to the law in 2014. So, insurance tax premiums in Montenegro started very modestly with the introduction of a tax on only two types of insurance but ended up with a model in which almost all types of non-life insurance are subject to an insurance premium tax.

*589.* The payers of this tax are insurance companies that conclude contracts with legal and natural persons and collect insurance premiums.[647] But, as in the case of other similar taxes, this tax will, in the end, be paid by the insurance contractor in the form of an increase in the premium, since the insurance company will transfer the cost of the tax to the insurance contractor. The tax base for the insurance premium tax is the collected gross insurance premium.[648] The tax rate was established at 6% until 2014 but was changed to 9% after amendments were made to the law.[649] Bearing in mind the changes in the tax rate, the question was raised: were the already concluded contracts still valid after the amendments, or did the insurance contracts need to be amended in order to calculate the tax at the new rate? The Insurance Supervisory Agency issued the opinion that the tax on insurance premiums is calculated and paid at the rate valid at the time of conclusion of the contract, even though the premium will be paid monthly, and there is no need for an amendment of already concluded contracts.[650] Diplomatic and consular missions and international organisations are exempt from the tax on motor vehicle liability insurance premiums if this is stipulated by an international agreement. The obligation to calculate the tax on insurance premiums arises at the moment of contract conclusion with legal or natural persons, and it must be paid by the fifteenth of the month for the previous month. The consequential application of the law governing the tax procedure is set by the law for all relationships that are not specifically regulated by this law. Failure to pay this tax is a misdemeanour, and a pecuniary fine is prescribed for the insurance company as a legal person and for the responsible person in the legal entity in cases described by the law.[651]

## §2. Taxation of the Insurance Sum

*590.* Taxation of the insurance sum is the second option for the possible tax obligation of the insured, but in the case of payments made by the insurance company to the insured, two laws are relevant, since the income of natural persons and legal persons is taxable under separate laws.

647. *See*: Article 4, Law on Insurance Premium Tax.
648. *See*: Article 5, Law on Insurance Premium Tax.
649. *See*: Article 6, Law on Insurance Premium Tax.
650. Opinion of the Insurance Supervisory Authority, No. 04-2075/1 of 11 Mar. 2014.
651. *See*: Articles 7–11, Law on Insurance Premium Tax.

*591.* The Law on Personal Income Tax regulates the obligations in the case of insurance payments to the natural person as the insured.[652] By the provision of this law, the income of a natural person which is not considered taxable income may be earned, among others, on the basis of basic rights in the field of social protection, benefits from health insurance (except salary benefits), and on the basis of insurance of objects, life and property.[653] So, by the provisions of this law, the incomes of natural persons based on payments made by insurance companies are exempted from income taxation.

*592.* The Law on Corporate Income Tax regulates the obligations in the case of insurance payments to a legal person as the insured.[654] By the provision of this law, the sources of profit of the legal person in Montenegro are, among other things, income generated on the basis of insurance and reinsurance against risks realised in Montenegro.[655] In this case, the payment of an insurance company to an insured legal person represents an income which is taxable. Even the payment of the reinsurer to the insurer is taxable under the same rule. But these payments will be considered income only for risks that were realised in Montenegro. If the risk is realised elsewhere, the payment from the insurer or reinsurer will not be taxable.

*593.* So, there is a significant difference in the tax treatment of natural and legal persons in Montenegro when it comes to the taxability of insurance payouts. Natural persons are exempt from taxation of the payments from insurers, and in the case of legal persons, the situation is the opposite. Legal persons are taxpayers in cases where they receive a payment from the insurer, or the taxpayer is an insurer for the payment they received from the reinsurer, if the risk was realised in Montenegro.

---

652. OJRM, Nos 65/01, 12/02, 37/04, 29/05, 78/06 & 04/07 and OJM, Nos 86/09, 73/10, 40/11, 14/12, 06/13, 62/13, 60/14, 79/15, 83/16, 67/19, 59/21, 146/21 & 152/22.
653. *See*: Article 5, para. 1, items 3, 5 & 11, Law on Personal Income Tax.
654. OJRM, Nos 65/01, 12/02 & 80/04 and OJM, Nos 40/08, 86/09, 40/11, 14/12, 061/13, 55/16, 146/21, 152/22 & 28/23.
655. *See*: Article 5, para. 1, item 10, Law on Corporate Income Tax.

# Selected Bibliography


Bejaković, Predrag, Holzmann Robert & Hinz Richard (eds). *Old-Age Income Support in the 21st Century: An International Perspective on Pension Systems and Reform*. Revija za socijalnu politiku, god. 14, br. 2, Zagreb, 2007.

Dožić, Nikola. *Bonus-malus sistem u osiguranju od autoodgovornosti u Crnoj Gori*. Bezbjednost saobraćaja, osiguranje i naknada štete – XVIII Međunarodni naučni skup – Udruženje za odštetno pravo, 2015.

Dožić, Nikola. *Dužnost prijavljivanja okolnosti značajnih za ocjenu rizika i prevare u osiguranju*. Osiguranje i nkanada štete, XVI Međunarodni naučni skup – Udruženje za odštetno pravo, 2013.

Dožić, Nikola. *Nesavjesnost obije ugovorne strane kod nadosiguranja imovine*. XXI Međunarodni naučni skup – Udruženje za odštetno pravo, 2018.

Dožić, Nikola. *Nasledivost prava i obaveza iz ugovora o osiguranju od autoodgovornosti u pravu Crne Gore*. XXII Međunarodni naučni skup – Udruženje za odštetno pravo, Beograd, 2019.

Ivošević, Borislav. *Transporno osiguranje (Transport Insurance)*. Pravni fakultet Univerziteta Union u Beogradu, 2009.

Jakša, Branko. *Pravo osiguranja (Insurance Law)*. Informator, Zagreb, 1972.

Kašćelan, Vladimir & Novović Milijana. *The Development of Insurance Market in Montenegro, Monograph 'Achieved Results and Prospects of Insurance Market Development in Modern World'*. Chapter 8, Faculty of Economics, University of Belgrade, Centar za izdavačku delatnost Ekonomskog fakulteta u Beogradu (CID), 2012.

Kašćelan, Vladimir & Novović Milijana. *Osiguranje i akturaska matematika, I izdanje, Univerzitet Crne*. Gore, Podgorica 2009, page 206.

Kostić-Mandić, Maja. *Međunarodno privatno pravo (Private International Law)*. Pravni fakultet Univerziteta Crne Gore, Podgorica, 2017.

Kostić-Mandić, Maja. *Private International Law in Montenegro*. Walters Kluwer, 2022.

Marijanski, Vladimir, *Ugovor o osiguranju (Insurance Contracts)*. Pravni fakultet u Novom Sadu, Novi Sad, 2007.

Pak, Jasna. *Pravo osiguranja (Insurance Law)*. Univerzitet Singidunum, Beograd, 2011.

Pavić, Drago. *Ugovorno pravo osiguranja – Komentar zakonskih odredbi*. Zagreb, 2009.

Perović, Slobodan & Stojanović Dragoljub. *Komentar Zakona o obligacionim odnosima*. Knjiga druga, Gornji Milanovac, 1980.

## Selected Bibliography

Petrović, Zdravko, Čolović Vladimir & Knežević Duško. *History of Insurance in Serbia, Montenegro and Yugoslavia until 1941.* Dosije studio, Belgrade, 2013.

Petrović, Zdravko, Mrkšić Dragan & Ivančević Katarina. *Neživotna osiguranja (Non-life Insurance).* Intermex, Beograd, 2007.

Petrović, Zdravko & Mrkšić Dragan. *Životna osiguranja (Life Insurance).* Beograd, 2005.

Radonjić, Dragan. *Pravo privrednih društava.* Pobjeda, Podgorica, 2008.

Rašović, Zoran. *Uvod u građansko pravo.* Pravni fakultet u Podgorici, 2009.

Savković, Vladimir. *Komentar zakona o privrednim društvima.* Pravni ekspert, Podgorica, 2022.

Savković, Vladimir & Dožić Nikola. *Destimulativan zakonski okvir kao uzrok neuspjeha sustava dobrovoljnog mirovinskog osiguranja: studija crnogorskog slučaja kao pokazatelj važnosti financijskih poticaja.* Revija za socijalnu politiku, Zagreb 2018.

Šulejić, Predrag. *Pravo osiguranja (Insurance Law).* Pravni fakultet Univerziteta u Beogradu, 2005.

Šturanović, Petar. *Zakonodavna nadležnost skupštine u savremenom parlamentarnom sistemu.* JU Službeni list Crne Gore, Podgorica, 2017.

# Index

*The numbers here refer to paragraph numbers.*

# Index